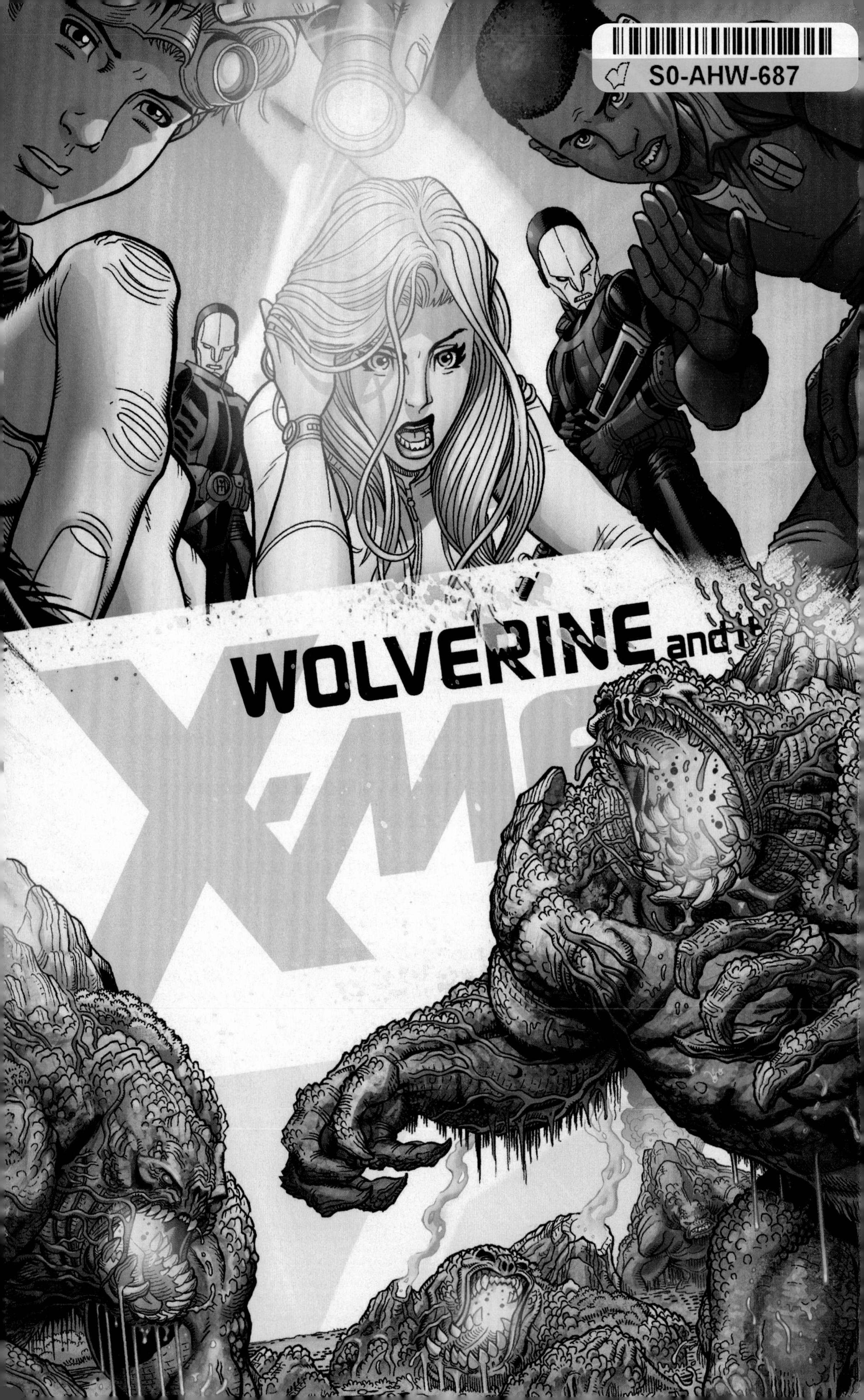
WOLVERINE and

WOLVERINE and the X-MEN

WRITER: **JASON AARON**

ISSUE #30
ARTIST: **PASQUAL FERRY** WITH **PEPE LARRAZ** & **SALVA ESPIN**
COLORIST: **JAMES CAMPBELL**

ISSUES #31-35
ARTIST: **NICK BRADSHAW** INKER: **WALDEN WONG** WITH **NICK BRADSHAW**
COLORIST: **LAURA MARTIN**
WITH **MATT MILLA, GURU-EFX, THOMAS MASON** & **SOTOCOLOR**

LETTERER: **VC'S JOE CARAMAGNA**
COVER ART: **NICK BRADSHAW** WITH **GURU-EFX** (#30),
MORRY HOLLOWELL (#31-34) & **MATT MILLA** (#35)

ASSOCIATE EDITOR: **JORDAN D. WHITE** • EDITOR: **NICK LOWE**

COLLECTION EDITOR:	SENIOR EDITOR, SPECIAL PROJECTS:	EDITOR IN CHIEF:
JENNIFER GRÜNWALD	**JEFF YOUNGQUIST**	**AXEL ALONSO**
ASSISTANT EDITORS:	SVP OF PRINT & DIGITAL	CHIEF CREATIVE OFFICER:
ALEX STARBUCK	PUBLISHING SALES:	**JOE QUESADA**
& **NELSON RIBEIRO**	**DAVID GABRIEL**	PUBLISHER:
EDITOR, SPECIAL PROJECTS:		**DAN BUCKLEY**
MARK D. BEAZLEY	BOOK DESIGNER:	EXECUTIVE PRODUCER:
	RODOLFO MURAGUCHI	**ALAN FINE**

WOLVERINE & THE X-MEN BY JASON AARON VOL. 7. Contains material originally published in magazine form as WOLVERINE & THE X-MEN #30-35. First printing 2013. ISBN# 978-0-7851-6600-9. Published by MARVEL WORLDWIDE, INC., a subsidiary of MARVEL ENTERTAINMENT, LLC. OFFICE OF PUBLICATION: 135 West 50th Street, New York, NY 10020. Copyright © 2013 Marvel Characters, Inc. All rights reserved. All characters featured in this issue and the distinctive names and likenesses thereof, and all related indicia are trademarks of Marvel Characters, Inc. No similarity between any of the names, characters, persons, and/or institutions in this magazine with those of any living or dead person or institution is intended, and any such similarity which may exist is purely coincidental. **Printed in Canada. ALAN FINE,** EVP - Office of the President, Marvel Worldwide, Inc. and EVP & CMO Marvel Characters B.V.; DAN BUCKLEY, Publisher & President - Print, Animation & Digital Divisions; JOE QUESADA, Chief Creative Officer; TOM BREVOORT, SVP of Publishing; DAVID BOGART, SVP of Operations & Procurement, Publishing; C.B. CEBULSKI, SVP of Creator & Content Development; DAVID GABRIEL, SVP of Print & Digital Publishing Sales; JIM O'KEEFE, VP of Operations & Logistics; DAN CARR, Executive Director of Publishing Technology; SUSAN CRESPI, Editorial Operations Manager; ALEX MORALES, Publishing Operations Manager; STAN LEE, Chairman Emeritus. For information regarding advertising in Marvel Comics or on Marvel.com, please contact Niza Disla, Director of Marvel Partnerships, at ndisla@marvel.com. For Marvel subscription inquiries, please call 800-217-9158. **Manufactured between 9/6/2013 and 10/14/2013 by SOLISCO PRINTERS, SCOTT, QC, CANADA.**

10 9 8 7 6 5 4 3 2 1

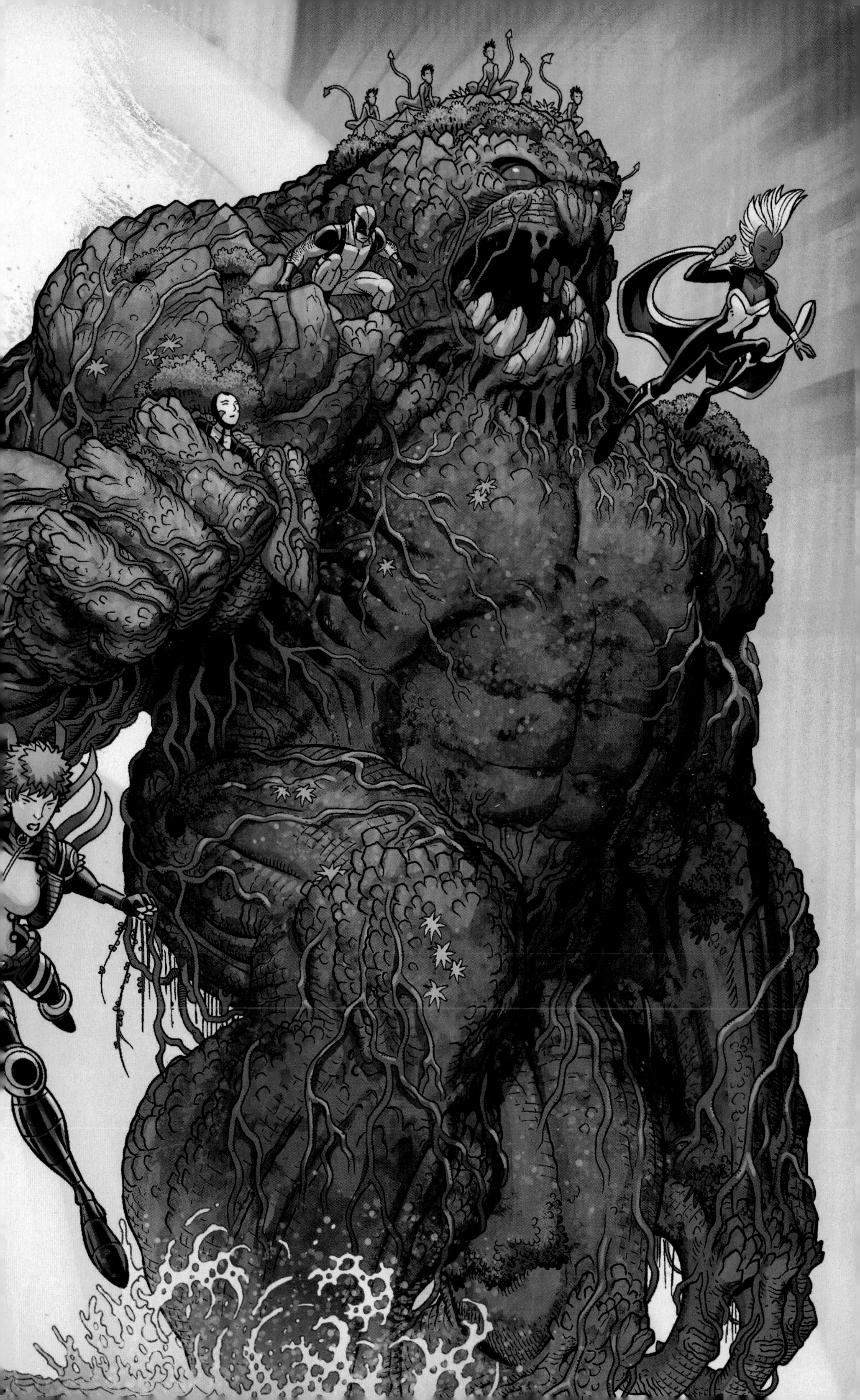

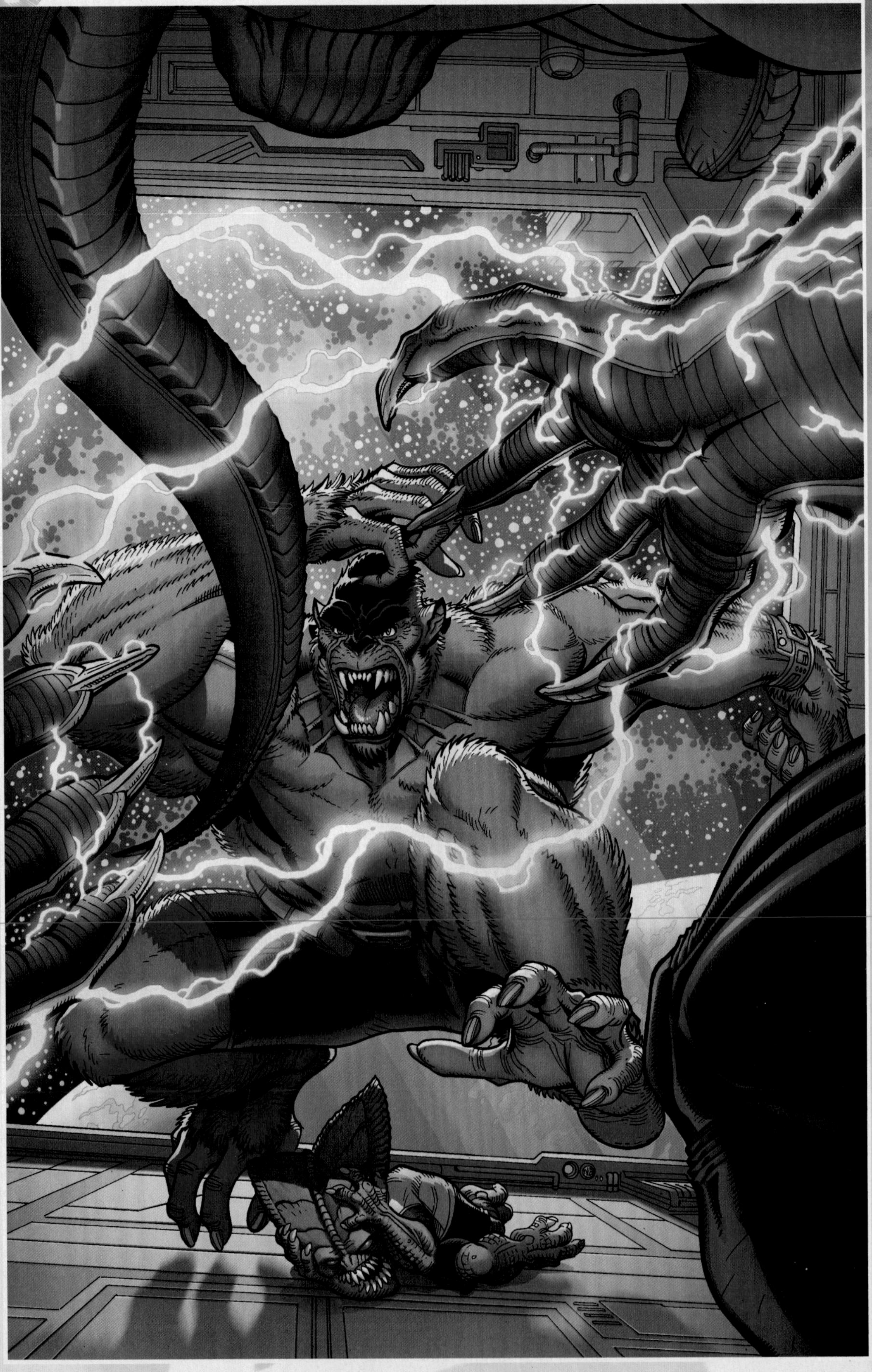

If you were born different with mutant super-powers, the Jean Grey School for Higher Learning is the school for you. Founded by Wolverine and staffed by experienced X-Men, you will learn everything you need to know to survive in a world that hates and fears you.

WOLVERINE and the X·MEN

WOLVERINE
Clawed Headmaster

BEAST
Animalistic, Intellectual Vice-Principal

KID OMEGA
Telepathic Student

OYA
Temperature Controlling Student

GENESIS
Flying, Eye-Blasting Student

GLOB HERMAN
Waxy, Blobbish Student

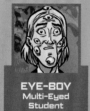

EYE-BOY
Multi-Eyed Student

SHARK-GIRL
Were-Shark Student

SPRITE
Rocky-Skinned, Winged Student

BROO
Feral Alien Student

PREVIOUSLY

AS SOON AS THE JEAN GREY SCHOOL PASSED ITS BOARD OF EDUCATION EVALUATION, KADE KILGORE AND HIS HELLFIRE CLUB BEGAN SUBJECTING IT TO THEIR OWN BRAND OF DEPRAVED TESTING. MOST OF THE TIME, THEY'VE ONLY OBSERVED FROM A DISTANCE, BUT KILGORE'S IMPOSITIONS HAVE BECOME IMPOSSIBLE TO IGNORE. HIS VILEST ASSAULT, SHOOTING BROO IN THE HEAD, TRANSFORMED THE STUDENT WHO WAS THE HEART AND BRAINS OF THE SCHOOL INTO A SNARLING ANIMAL. AND DESPITE DR. MCCOY'S BEST EFFORTS TO RESTORE BROO, AND HEADMASTER WOLVERINE'S OBSESSION WITH FINDING HIS ASSAILANT, BOTH QUESTS ARE BECOMING DESPERATE.

THIS ATMOSPHERE OF UNCERTAINTY HAS BEEN A CRUCIBLE FOR THE OTHER STUDENTS: SOME ARE BEGINNING TO ACT LIKE X-MEN, AND SOME HAVE GONE ASTRAY. WITHOUT BROO, HER FRIEND AND MORAL ANCHOR, IDIE'S AMBIVALENCE HAS BECOME FULL-BLOWN SELF-HATRED. ALONE IN THE NIGHT, SHE SAID GOODBYE TO AN UNCOMPREHENDING BROO, AND ASKED A HOODED FIGURE — SOMEONE SHE RECOGNIZED — TO TAKE HER TO HELLFIRE ACADEMY.

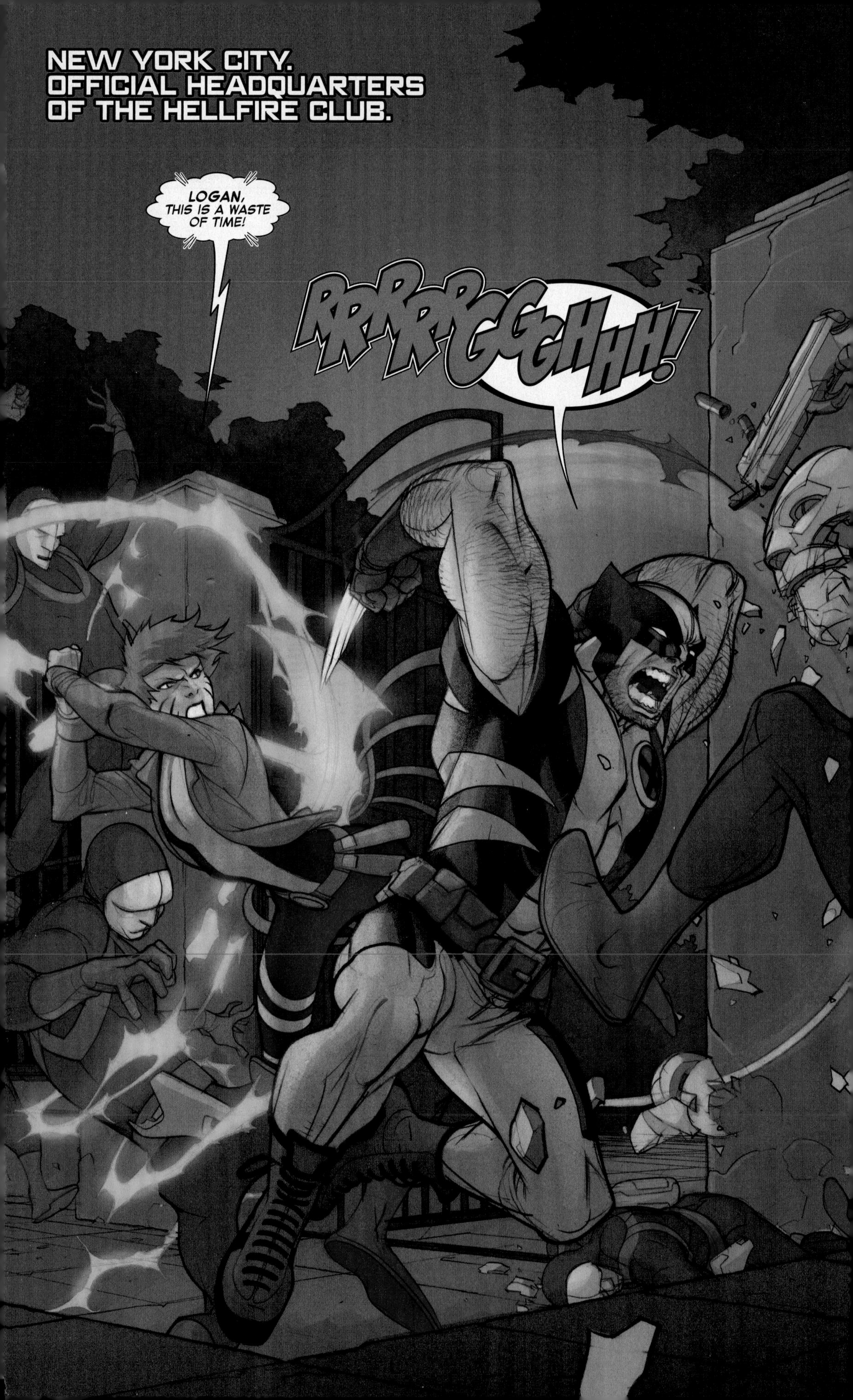
NEW YORK CITY.
OFFICIAL HEADQUARTERS
OF THE HELLFIRE CLUB.
LOGAN, THIS IS A WASTE OF TIME!
RRRRRGGGHHH!

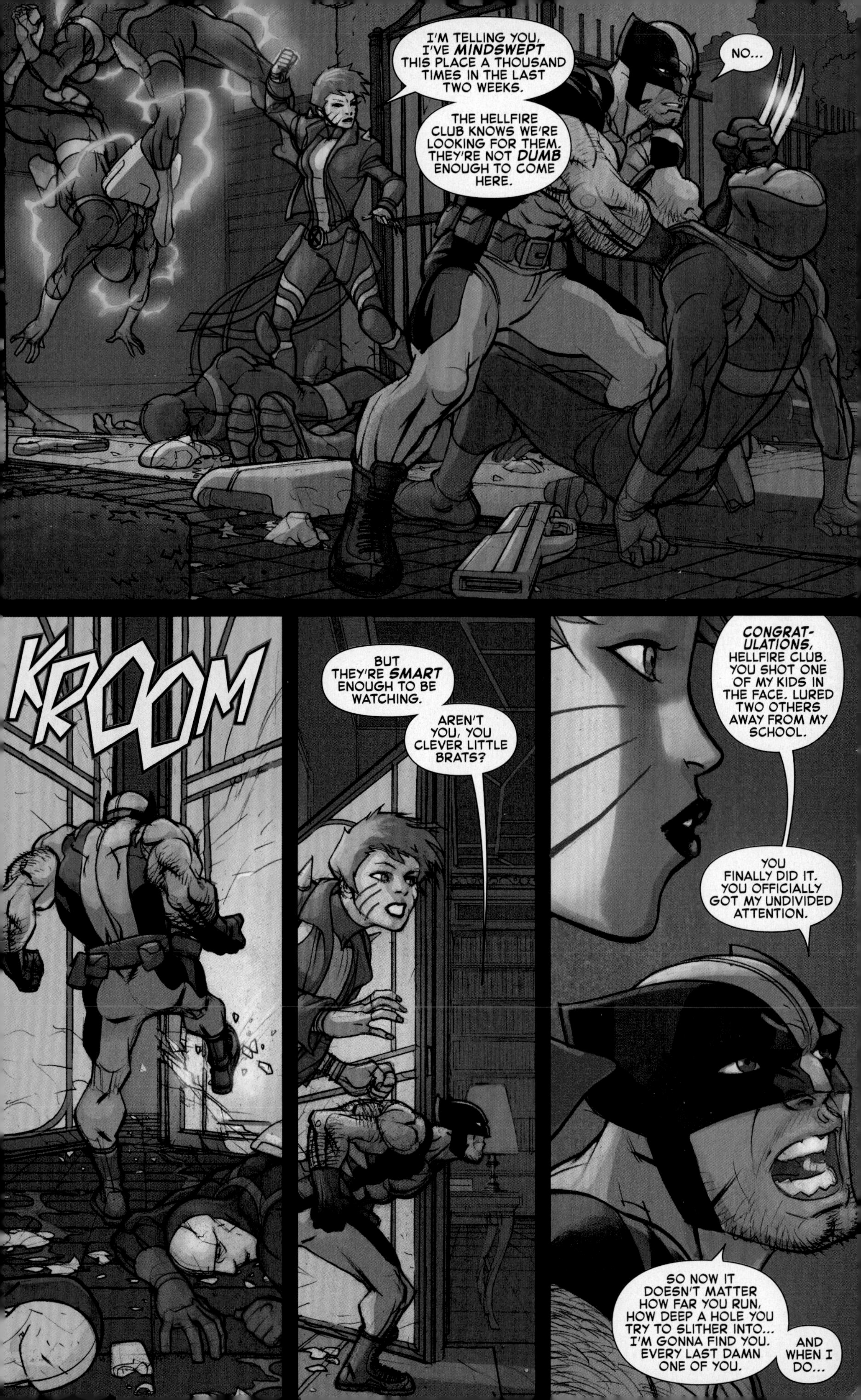

I'M TELLING YOU, I'VE *MINDSWEPT* THIS PLACE A THOUSAND TIMES IN THE LAST TWO WEEKS.
THE HELLFIRE CLUB KNOWS WE'RE LOOKING FOR THEM. THEY'RE NOT *DUMB* ENOUGH TO COME HERE.
NO...
KROOM
BUT THEY'RE *SMART* ENOUGH TO BE WATCHING.
AREN'T YOU, YOU CLEVER LITTLE BRATS?
CONGRAT-ULATIONS, HELLFIRE CLUB. YOU SHOT ONE OF MY KIDS IN THE FACE. LURED TWO OTHERS AWAY FROM MY SCHOOL.
YOU FINALLY DID IT. YOU OFFICIALLY GOT MY UNDIVIDED ATTENTION.
SO NOW IT DOESN'T MATTER HOW FAR YOU RUN, HOW DEEP A HOLE YOU TRY TO SLITHER INTO... I'M GONNA FIND YOU. EVERY LAST DAMN ONE OF YOU.
AND WHEN I DO...

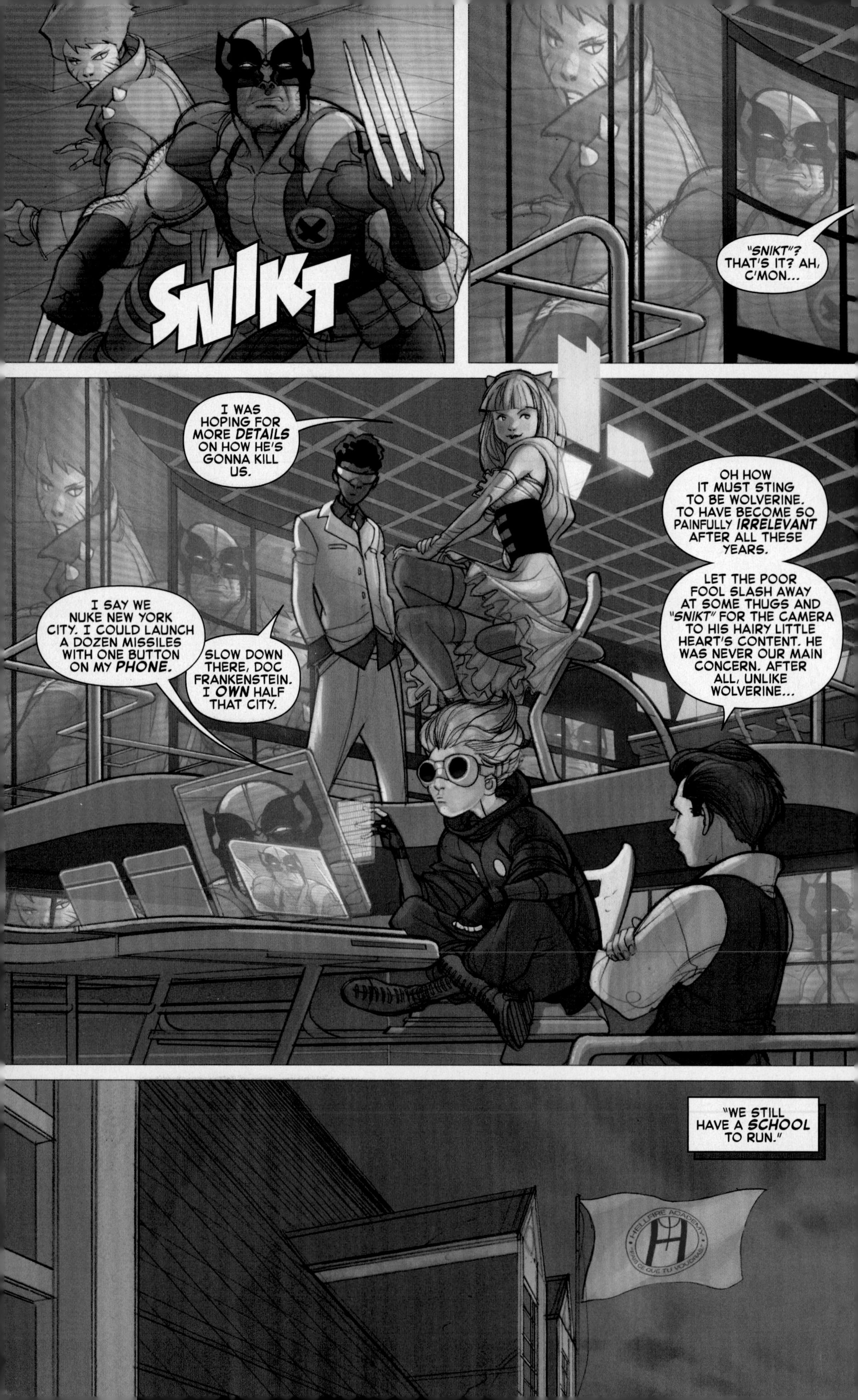
SNIKT
"SNIKT"? THAT'S IT? AH, C'MON...
I WAS HOPING FOR MORE DETAILS ON HOW HE'S GONNA KILL US.
OH HOW IT MUST STING TO BE WOLVERINE. TO HAVE BECOME SO PAINFULLY IRRELEVANT AFTER ALL THESE YEARS.
LET THE POOR FOOL SLASH AWAY AT SOME THUGS AND "SNIKT" FOR THE CAMERA TO HIS HAIRY LITTLE HEART'S CONTENT. HE WAS NEVER OUR MAIN CONCERN. AFTER ALL, UNLIKE WOLVERINE...
I SAY WE NUKE NEW YORK CITY. I COULD LAUNCH A DOZEN MISSILES WITH ONE BUTTON ON MY PHONE.
SLOW DOWN THERE, DOC FRANKENSTEIN. I OWN HALF THAT CITY.
"WE STILL HAVE A SCHOOL TO RUN."

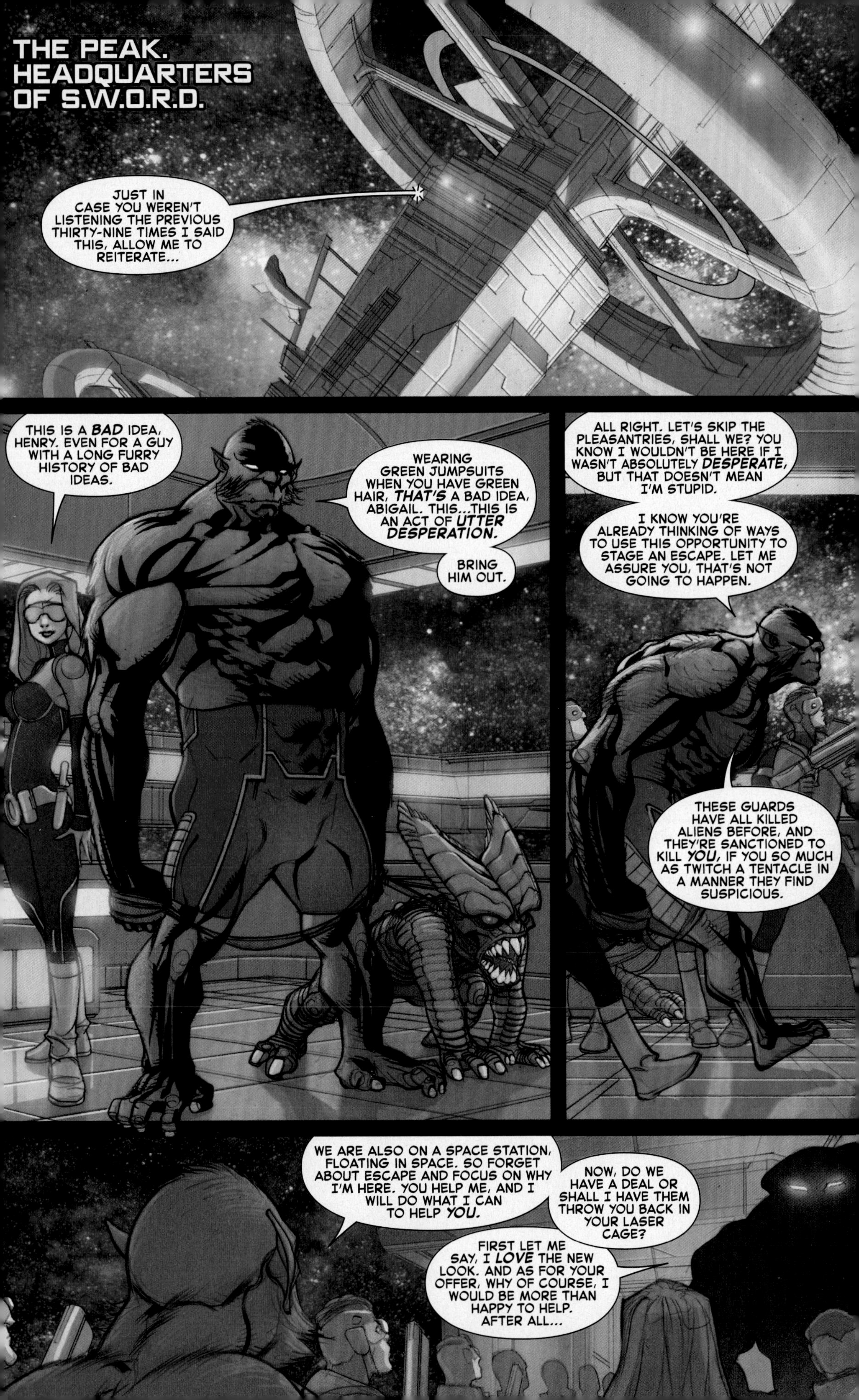
THE PEAK. HEADQUARTERS OF S.W.O.R.D.
JUST IN CASE YOU WEREN'T LISTENING THE PREVIOUS THIRTY-NINE TIMES I SAID THIS, ALLOW ME TO REITERATE...
THIS IS A BAD IDEA, HENRY. EVEN FOR A GUY WITH A LONG FURRY HISTORY OF BAD IDEAS.
WEARING GREEN JUMPSUITS WHEN YOU HAVE GREEN HAIR, THAT'S A BAD IDEA, ABIGAIL. THIS...THIS IS AN ACT OF UTTER DESPERATION.
BRING HIM OUT.
ALL RIGHT. LET'S SKIP THE PLEASANTRIES, SHALL WE? YOU KNOW I WOULDN'T BE HERE IF I WASN'T ABSOLUTELY DESPERATE, BUT THAT DOESN'T MEAN I'M STUPID.
I KNOW YOU'RE ALREADY THINKING OF WAYS TO USE THIS OPPORTUNITY TO STAGE AN ESCAPE. LET ME ASSURE YOU, THAT'S NOT GOING TO HAPPEN.
THESE GUARDS HAVE ALL KILLED ALIENS BEFORE, AND THEY'RE SANCTIONED TO KILL YOU, IF YOU SO MUCH AS TWITCH A TENTACLE IN A MANNER THEY FIND SUSPICIOUS.
WE ARE ALSO ON A SPACE STATION, FLOATING IN SPACE. SO FORGET ABOUT ESCAPE AND FOCUS ON WHY I'M HERE. YOU HELP ME, AND I WILL DO WHAT I CAN TO HELP YOU.
NOW, DO WE HAVE A DEAL OR SHALL I HAVE THEM THROW YOU BACK IN YOUR LASER CAGE?
FIRST LET ME SAY, I LOVE THE NEW LOOK. AND AS FOR YOUR OFFER, WHY OF COURSE, I WOULD BE MORE THAN HAPPY TO HELP. AFTER ALL...

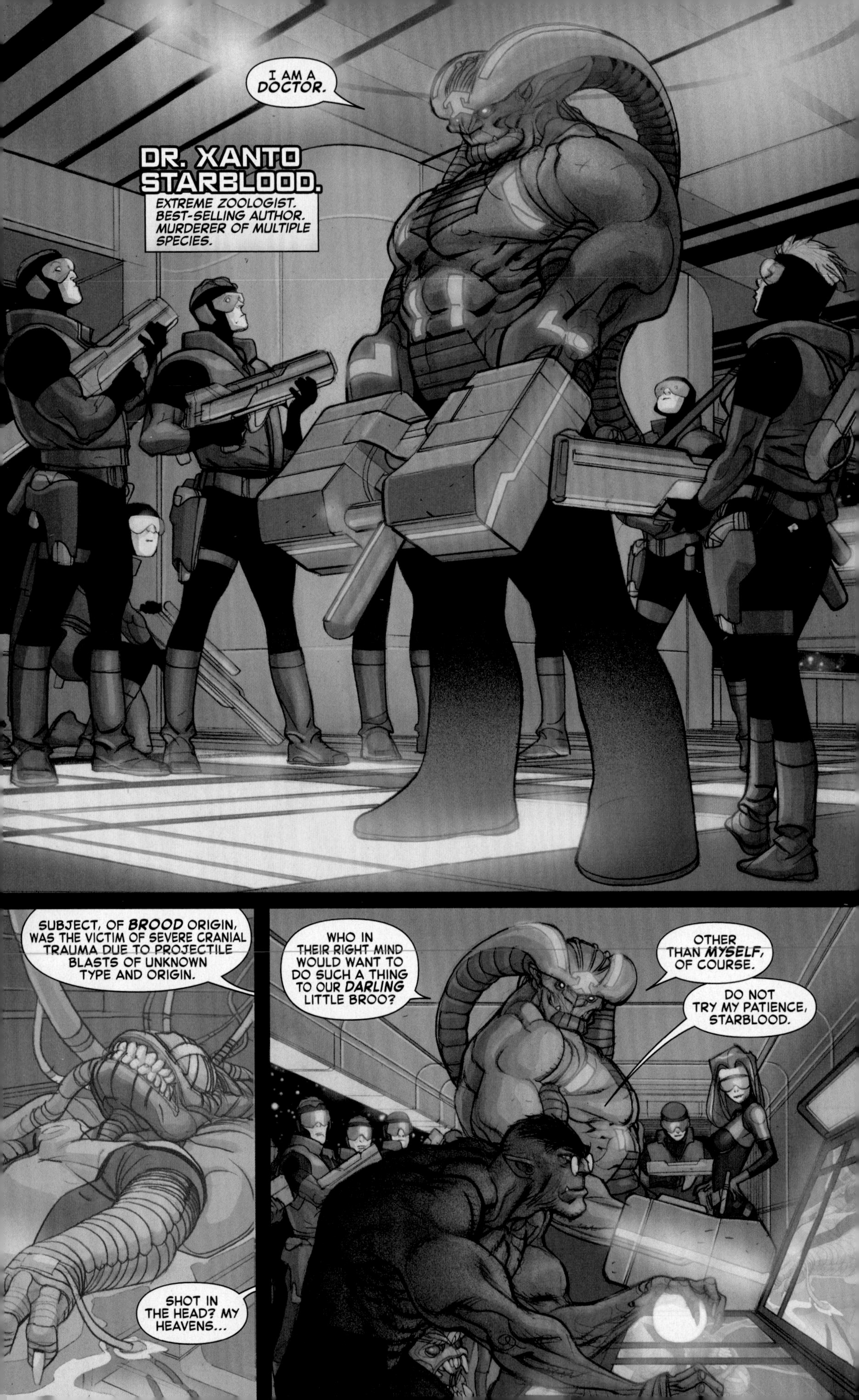
I AM A DOCTOR.
DR. XANTO STARBLOOD.
EXTREME ZOOLOGIST. BEST-SELLING AUTHOR. MURDERER OF MULTIPLE SPECIES.
SUBJECT, OF BROOD ORIGIN, WAS THE VICTIM OF SEVERE CRANIAL TRAUMA DUE TO PROJECTILE BLASTS OF UNKNOWN TYPE AND ORIGIN.
SHOT IN THE HEAD? MY HEAVENS...
WHO IN THEIR RIGHT MIND WOULD WANT TO DO SUCH A THING TO OUR DARLING LITTLE BROO?
OTHER THAN MYSELF, OF COURSE.
DO NOT TRY MY PATIENCE, STARBLOOD.

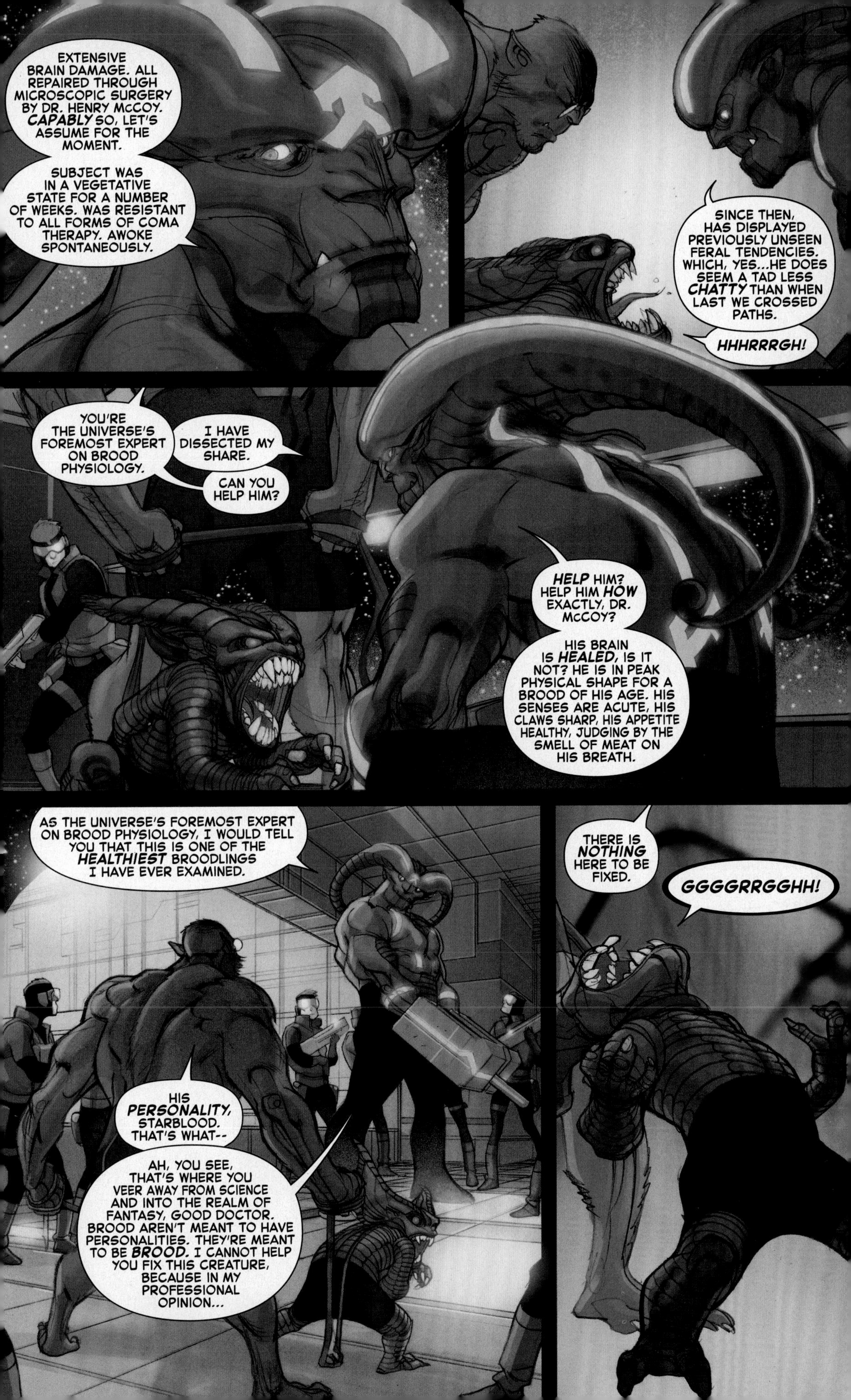
EXTENSIVE BRAIN DAMAGE. ALL REPAIRED THROUGH MICROSCOPIC SURGERY BY DR. HENRY McCOY. CAPABLY SO, LET'S ASSUME FOR THE MOMENT.
SUBJECT WAS IN A VEGETATIVE STATE FOR A NUMBER OF WEEKS. WAS RESISTANT TO ALL FORMS OF COMA THERAPY. AWOKE SPONTANEOUSLY.
SINCE THEN, HAS DISPLAYED PREVIOUSLY UNSEEN FERAL TENDENCIES. WHICH, YES...HE DOES SEEM A TAD LESS CHATTY THAN WHEN LAST WE CROSSED PATHS.
HHHRRRGH!
YOU'RE THE UNIVERSE'S FOREMOST EXPERT ON BROOD PHYSIOLOGY.
I HAVE DISSECTED MY SHARE.
CAN YOU HELP HIM?
HELP HIM? HELP HIM HOW EXACTLY, DR. McCOY?
HIS BRAIN IS HEALED, IS IT NOT? HE IS IN PEAK PHYSICAL SHAPE FOR A BROOD OF HIS AGE. HIS SENSES ARE ACUTE, HIS CLAWS SHARP, HIS APPETITE HEALTHY, JUDGING BY THE SMELL OF MEAT ON HIS BREATH.
AS THE UNIVERSE'S FOREMOST EXPERT ON BROOD PHYSIOLOGY, I WOULD TELL YOU THAT THIS IS ONE OF THE HEALTHIEST BROODLINGS I HAVE EVER EXAMINED.
HIS PERSONALITY, STARBLOOD. THAT'S WHAT--
AH, YOU SEE, THAT'S WHERE YOU VEER AWAY FROM SCIENCE AND INTO THE REALM OF FANTASY, GOOD DOCTOR. BROOD AREN'T MEANT TO HAVE PERSONALITIES. THEY'RE MEANT TO BE BROOD. I CANNOT HELP YOU FIX THIS CREATURE, BECAUSE IN MY PROFESSIONAL OPINION...
THERE IS NOTHING HERE TO BE FIXED.
GGGGRRGGHH!

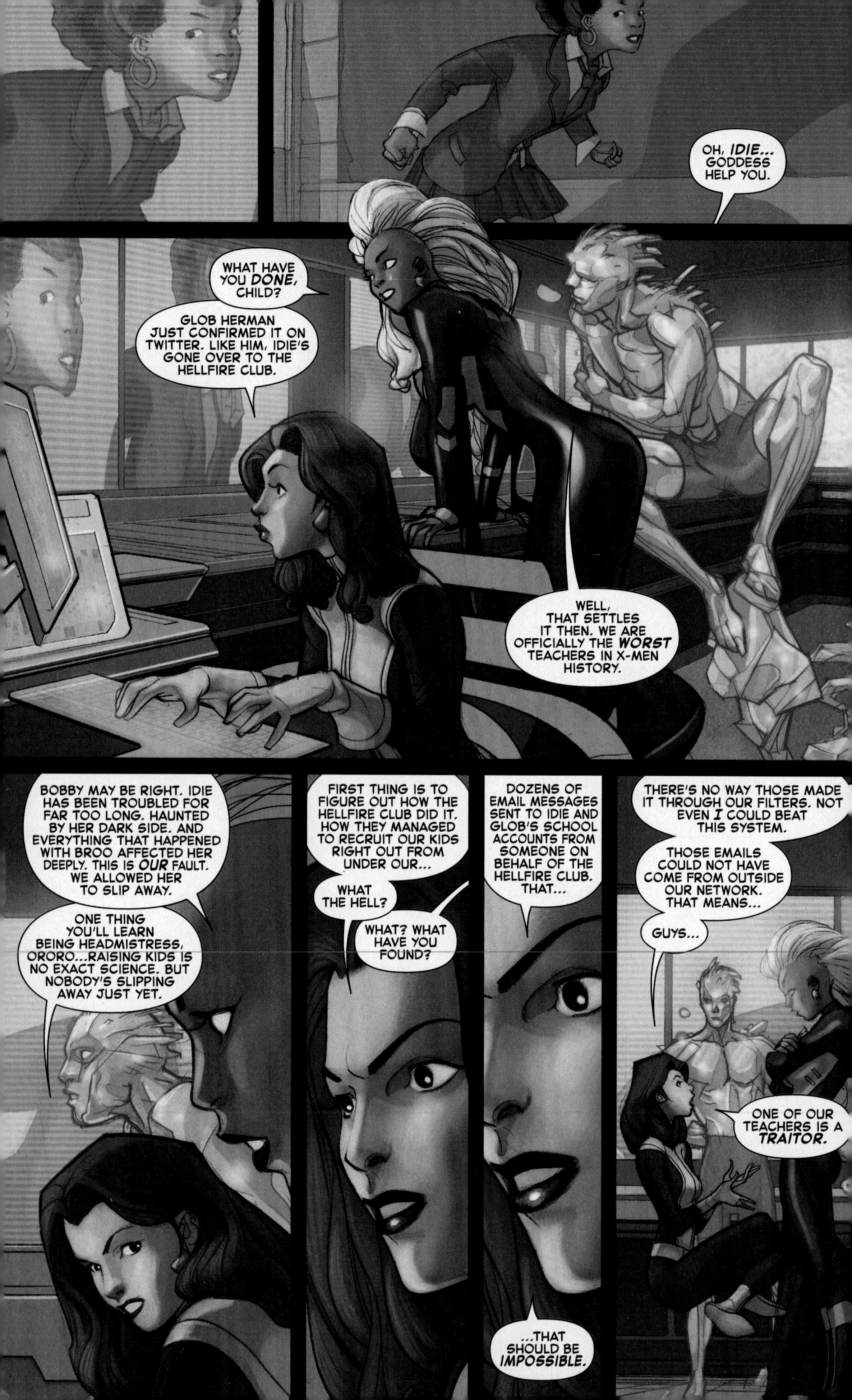

OH, IDIE... GODDESS HELP YOU.
WHAT HAVE YOU DONE, CHILD?
GLOB HERMAN JUST CONFIRMED IT ON TWITTER. LIKE HIM, IDIE'S GONE OVER TO THE HELLFIRE CLUB.
WELL, THAT SETTLES IT THEN. WE ARE OFFICIALLY THE WORST TEACHERS IN X-MEN HISTORY.
BOBBY MAY BE RIGHT. IDIE HAS BEEN TROUBLED FOR FAR TOO LONG. HAUNTED BY HER DARK SIDE. AND EVERYTHING THAT HAPPENED WITH BROO AFFECTED HER DEEPLY. THIS IS OUR FAULT. WE ALLOWED HER TO SLIP AWAY.
ONE THING YOU'LL LEARN BEING HEADMISTRESS, ORORO...RAISING KIDS IS NO EXACT SCIENCE. BUT NOBODY'S SLIPPING AWAY JUST YET.
FIRST THING IS TO FIGURE OUT HOW THE HELLFIRE CLUB DID IT. HOW THEY MANAGED TO RECRUIT OUR KIDS RIGHT OUT FROM UNDER OUR...
WHAT THE HELL?
WHAT? WHAT HAVE YOU FOUND?
DOZENS OF EMAIL MESSAGES SENT TO IDIE AND GLOB'S SCHOOL ACCOUNTS FROM SOMEONE ON BEHALF OF THE HELLFIRE CLUB. THAT...
...THAT SHOULD BE IMPOSSIBLE.
THERE'S NO WAY THOSE MADE IT THROUGH OUR FILTERS. NOT EVEN I COULD BEAT THIS SYSTEM.
THOSE EMAILS COULD NOT HAVE COME FROM OUTSIDE OUR NETWORK. THAT MEANS...
GUYS...
ONE OF OUR TEACHERS IS A TRAITOR.

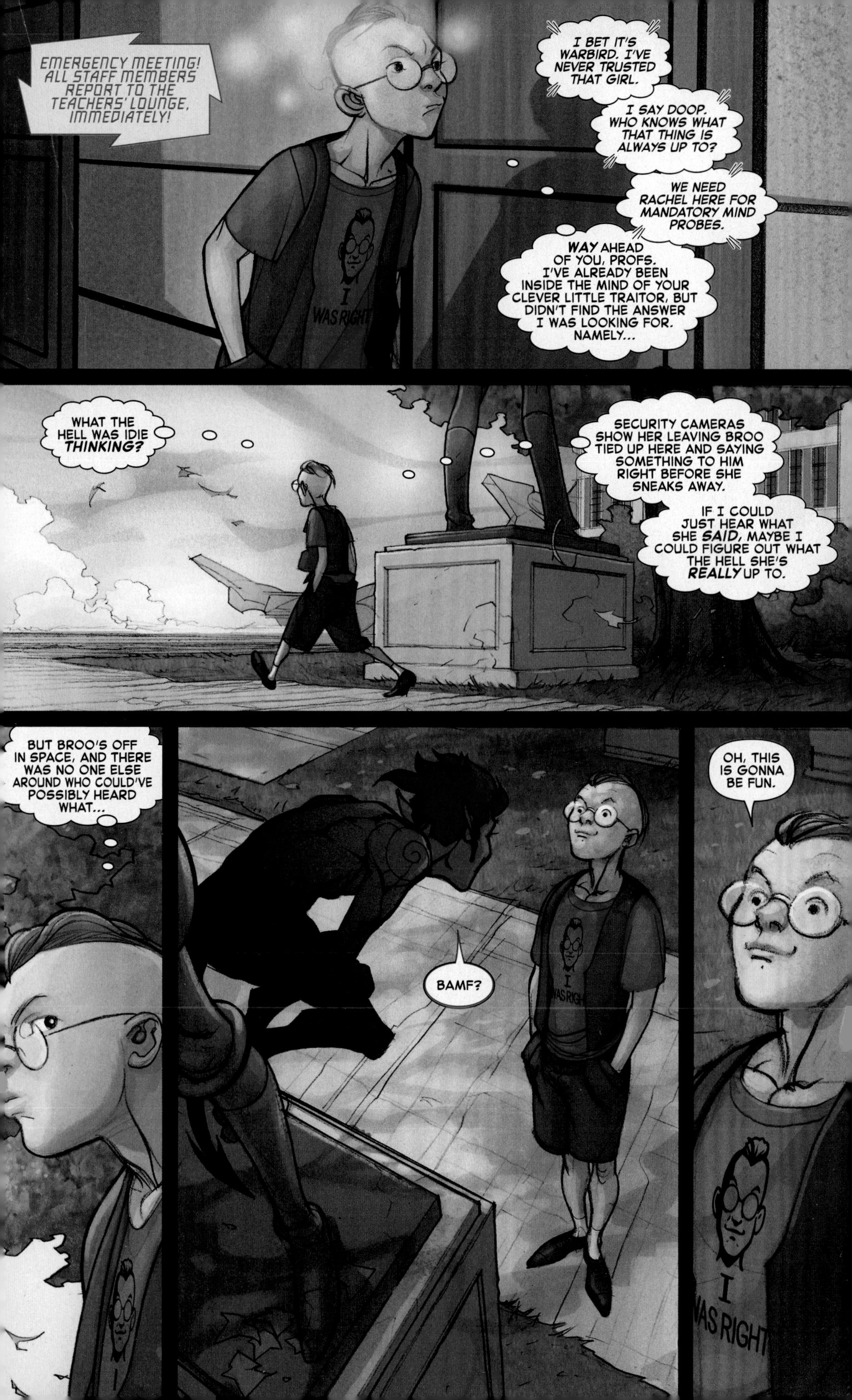
EMERGENCY MEETING! ALL STAFF MEMBERS REPORT TO THE TEACHERS' LOUNGE, IMMEDIATELY!
I BET IT'S WARBIRD. I'VE NEVER TRUSTED THAT GIRL.
I SAY DOOP. WHO KNOWS WHAT THAT THING IS ALWAYS UP TO?
WE NEED RACHEL HERE FOR MANDATORY MIND PROBES.
WAY AHEAD OF YOU, PROFS. I'VE ALREADY BEEN INSIDE THE MIND OF YOUR CLEVER LITTLE TRAITOR, BUT DIDN'T FIND THE ANSWER I WAS LOOKING FOR. NAMELY...
I WAS RIGHT
WHAT THE HELL WAS IDIE THINKING?
SECURITY CAMERAS SHOW HER LEAVING BROO TIED UP HERE AND SAYING SOMETHING TO HIM RIGHT BEFORE SHE SNEAKS AWAY.
IF I COULD JUST HEAR WHAT SHE SAID, MAYBE I COULD FIGURE OUT WHAT THE HELL SHE'S REALLY UP TO.
BUT BROO'S OFF IN SPACE, AND THERE WAS NO ONE ELSE AROUND WHO COULD'VE POSSIBLY HEARD WHAT...
BAMF?
OH, THIS IS GONNA BE FUN.

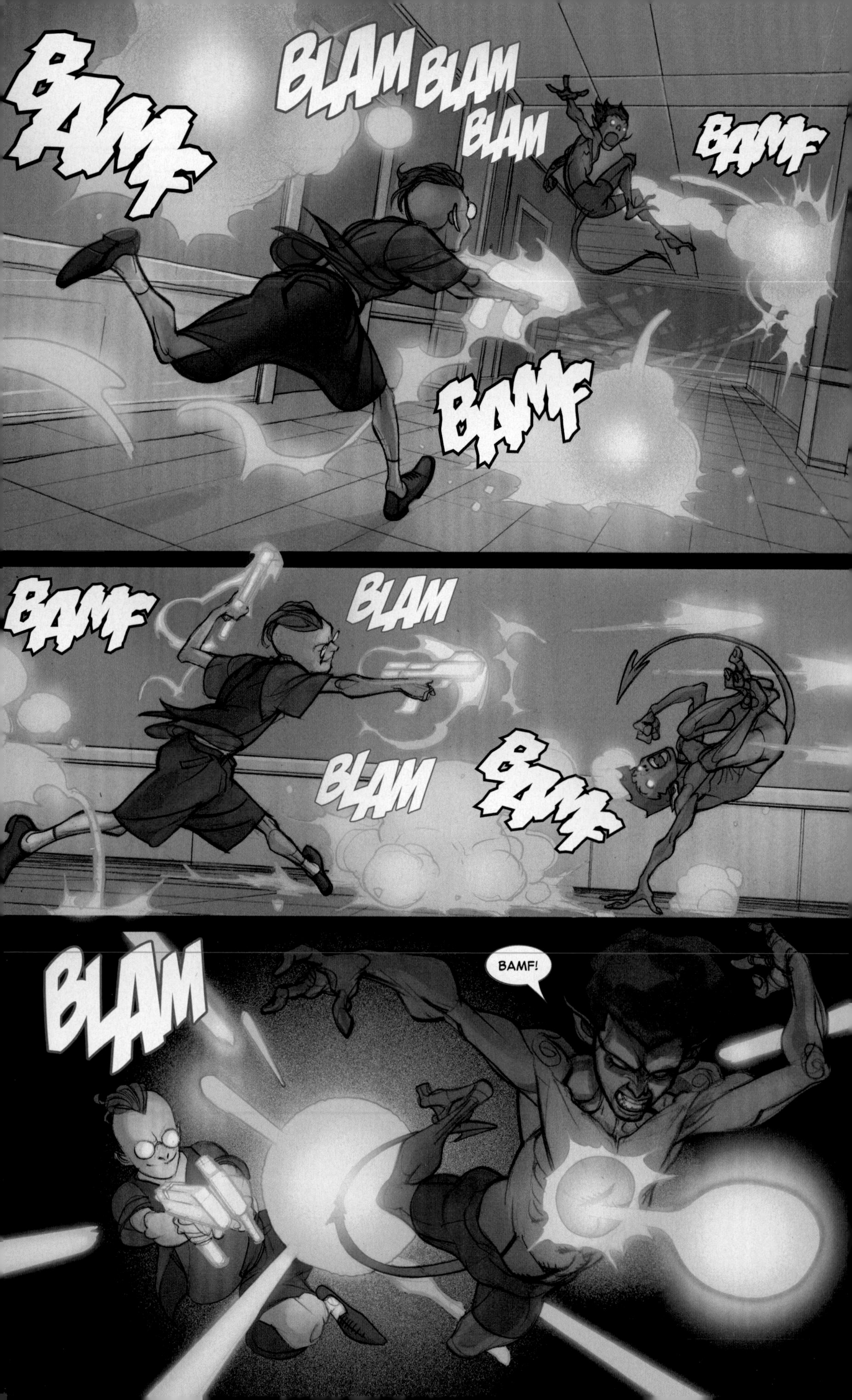
BAMF
BLAM BLAM
BLAM
BAMF
BAMF
BAMF
BLAM
BLAM
BAMF
BLAM
BAMF!

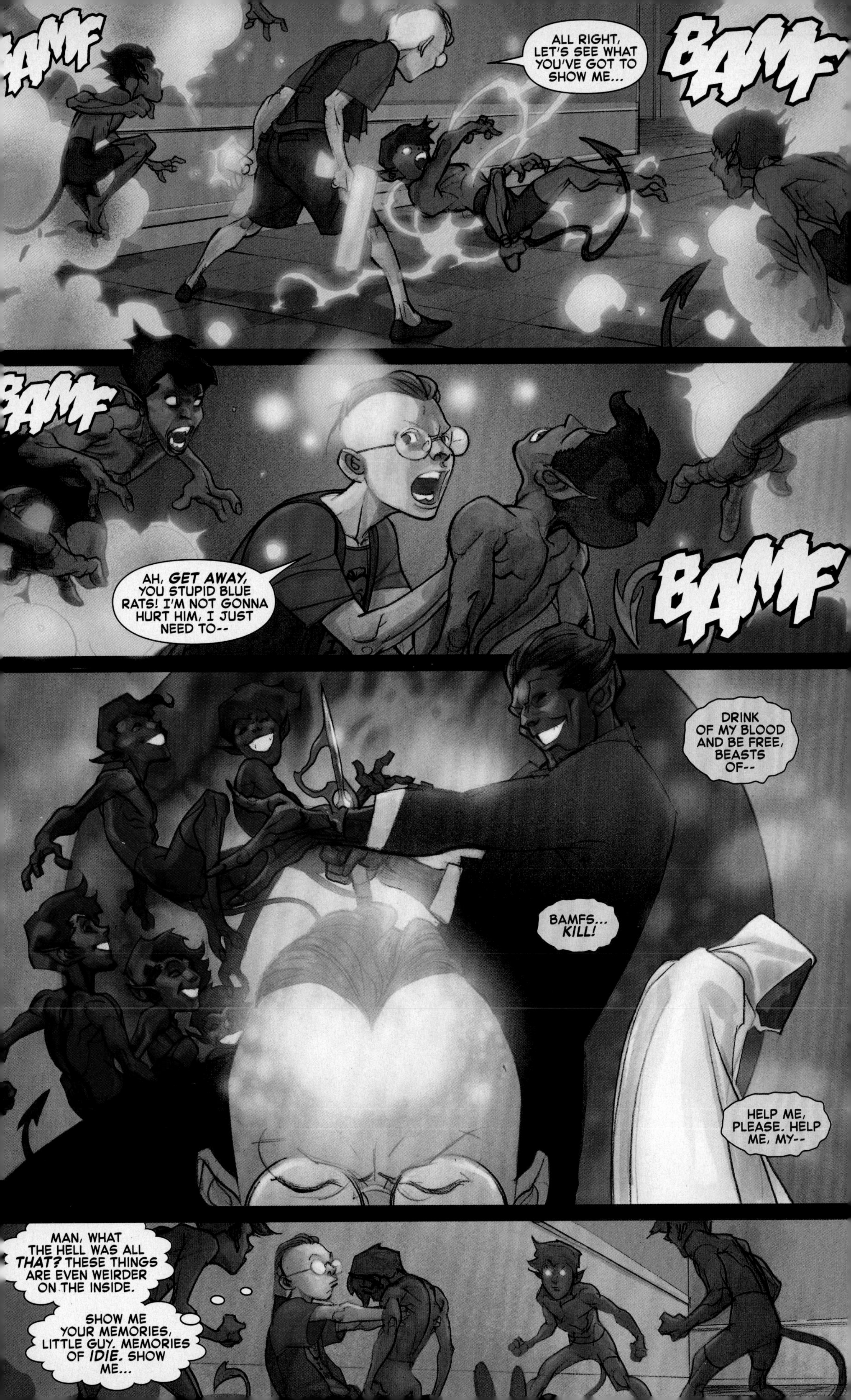
BAMF
ALL RIGHT, LET'S SEE WHAT YOU'VE GOT TO SHOW ME...
BAMF
BAMF
AH, GET AWAY, YOU STUPID BLUE RATS! I'M NOT GONNA HURT HIM, I JUST NEED TO--
BAMF
DRINK OF MY BLOOD AND BE FREE, BEASTS OF--
BAMFS... KILL!
HELP ME, PLEASE. HELP ME, MY--
MAN, WHAT THE HELL WAS ALL THAT? THESE THINGS ARE EVEN WEIRDER ON THE INSIDE.
SHOW ME YOUR MEMORIES, LITTLE GUY. MEMORIES OF IDIE. SHOW ME...

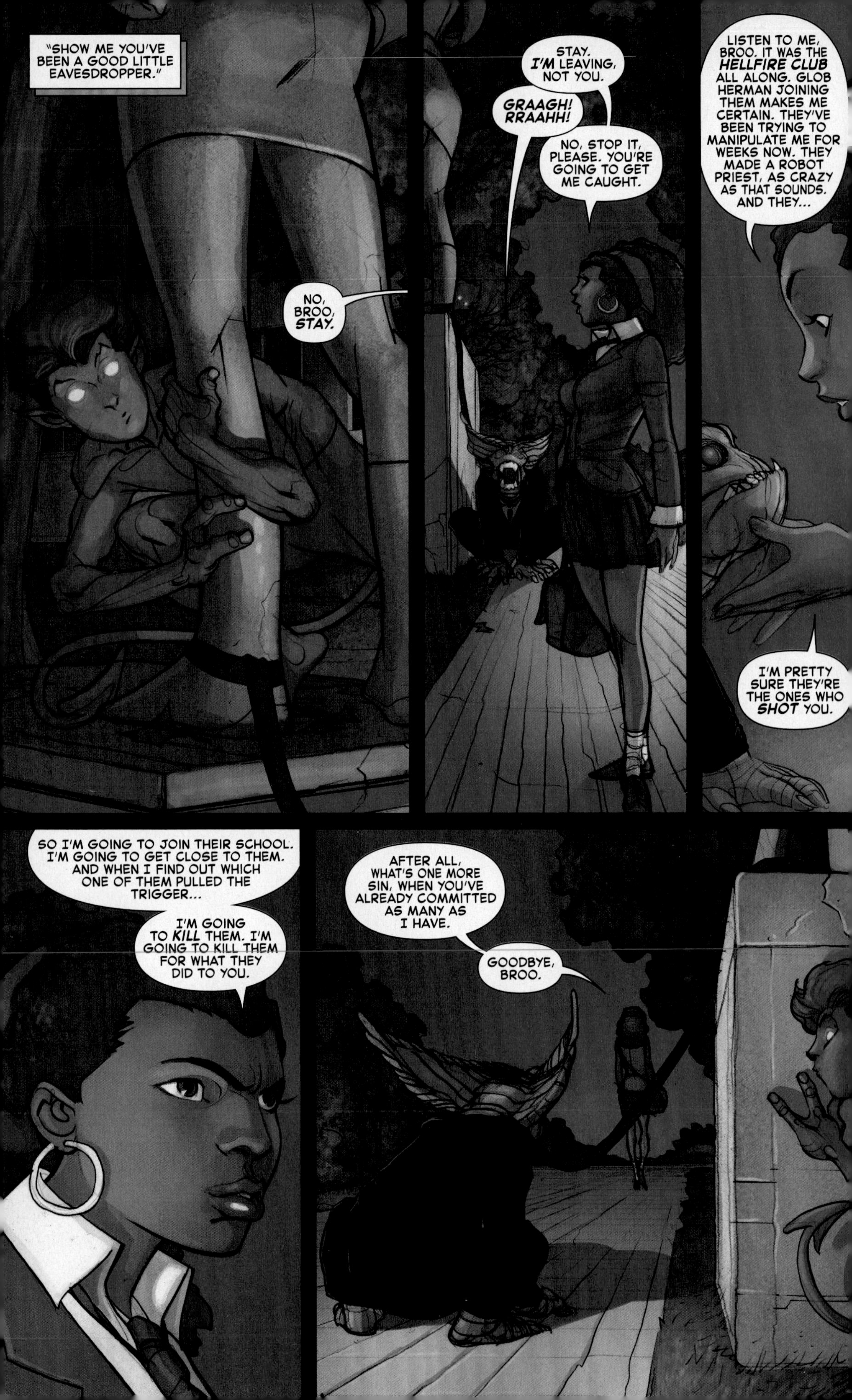
"SHOW ME YOU'VE BEEN A GOOD LITTLE EAVESDROPPER."
NO, BROO, STAY.
STAY. I'M LEAVING, NOT YOU.
GRAAGH! RRAAHH!
NO, STOP IT, PLEASE. YOU'RE GOING TO GET ME CAUGHT.
LISTEN TO ME, BROO. IT WAS THE HELLFIRE CLUB ALL ALONG. GLOB HERMAN JOINING THEM MAKES ME CERTAIN. THEY'VE BEEN TRYING TO MANIPULATE ME FOR WEEKS NOW. THEY MADE A ROBOT PRIEST, AS CRAZY AS THAT SOUNDS. AND THEY...
I'M PRETTY SURE THEY'RE THE ONES WHO SHOT YOU.
SO I'M GOING TO JOIN THEIR SCHOOL. I'M GOING TO GET CLOSE TO THEM. AND WHEN I FIND OUT WHICH ONE OF THEM PULLED THE TRIGGER...
I'M GOING TO KILL THEM. I'M GOING TO KILL THEM FOR WHAT THEY DID TO YOU.
AFTER ALL, WHAT'S ONE MORE SIN, WHEN YOU'VE ALREADY COMMITTED AS MANY AS I HAVE.
GOODBYE, BROO.

GOODBYE, FOREVER.

WELL, I SUPPOSE THAT SETTLES IT. HELLFIRE ACADEMY, HERE I COME.

I HEARD THAT.

LOCALIZED THOUGHT AMPLIFIER. DUG IT OUT OF BEAST'S CLOSET. SET TO FLAG ALL BRAIN CHATTER RELATED TO THE HELLFIRE CLUB, AND IT'S BUZZING LIKE A NEST OF HORNETS AROUND YOU.

WELL THAT'S RATHER INVASIVE, ISN'T IT? I'D LIKE TO FORMALLY LODGE A COMPLAINT WITH THE--

QUENTIN QUIRE...TRAITOR. HOW PREDICTABLY... PREDICTABLE.

NOW HOLD ON JUST A--

YOU'RE GOING TO TELL US EVERYTHING YOU KNOW OR EVEN THINK YOU KNOW ABOUT THE HELLFIRE CLUB, YOUNG MAN, OR YOU WILL BE SPENDING THE REST OF ETERNITY IN DETENTION. INSIDE A TORNADO.

IDIE'S IN TROUBLE.

THIS WE KNOW, PINK WHELP. TELL US SOMETHING USEFUL OR I CUT USEFUL THINGS OFF OF YOU.

THERE'S ONLY ONE PERSON WHO CAN SAVE HER.

ᔑ'ᒲᒷ ᔑ╎リ ᒷᔑ ⊣ᔑ⊣ᔑ╎ ᔑ'リᔑ ᔑ⊣リ ᔑ ᔑᓭᔑ ᔑ⍊ ⊣ᔑᔑ ᔑⱷᒲᒷᔑᔑᔑ ⊣リᔑᔑᔑ⊣ ⊣ᒲᒷᒷ

YOU WANNA KNOW WHY SHE LEFT? C'MON, ISN'T IT OBVIOUS?

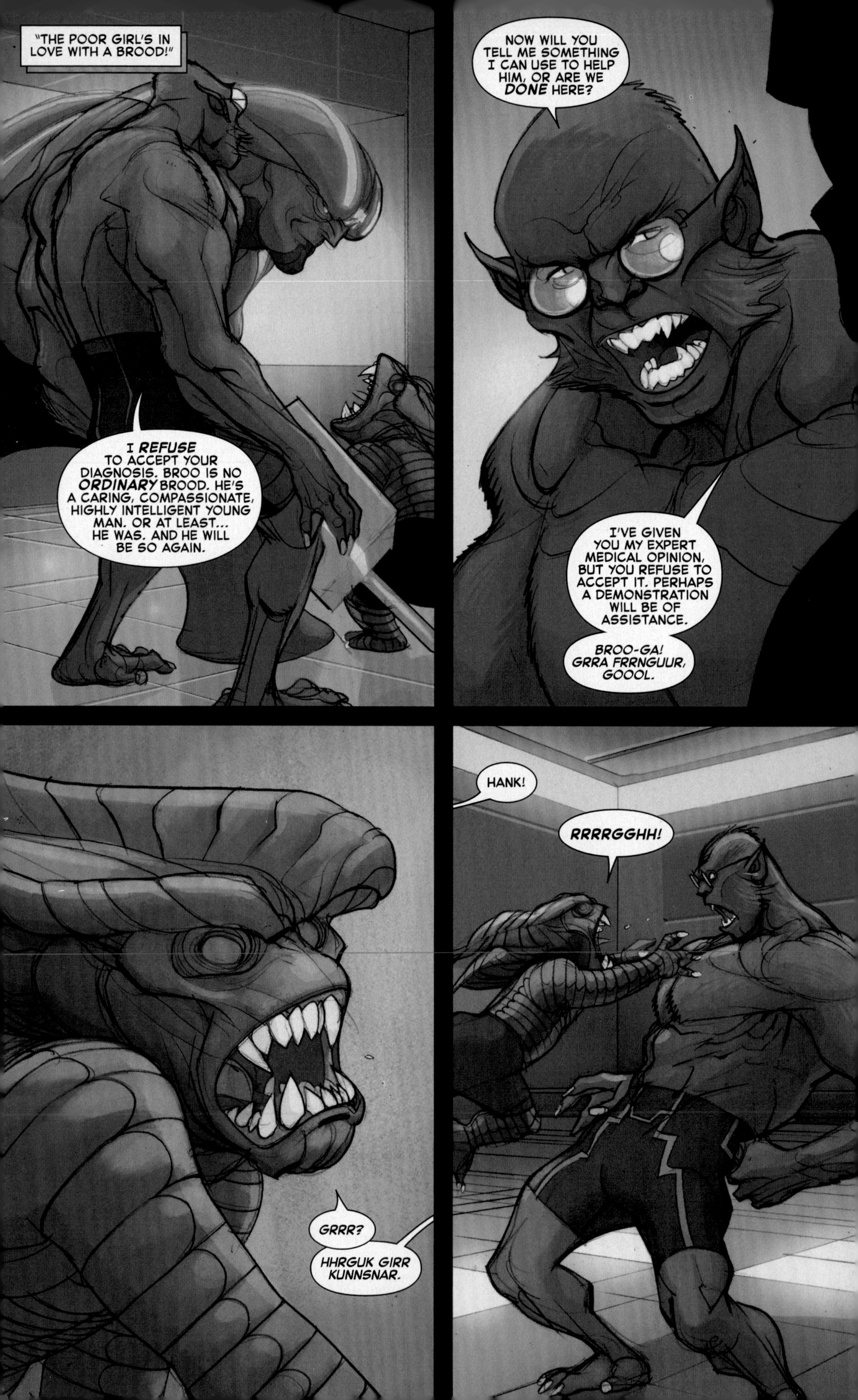
"THE POOR GIRL'S IN LOVE WITH A BROOD!"
I REFUSE TO ACCEPT YOUR DIAGNOSIS. BROO IS NO ORDINARY BROOD. HE'S A CARING, COMPASSIONATE, HIGHLY INTELLIGENT YOUNG MAN. OR AT LEAST... HE WAS. AND HE WILL BE SO AGAIN.
NOW WILL YOU TELL ME SOMETHING I CAN USE TO HELP HIM, OR ARE WE DONE HERE?
I'VE GIVEN YOU MY EXPERT MEDICAL OPINION, BUT YOU REFUSE TO ACCEPT IT. PERHAPS A DEMONSTRATION WILL BE OF ASSISTANCE.
BROO-GA! GRRA FRRNGUUR, GOOOL.
GRRR?
HHRGUK GIRR KUNNSNAR.
HANK!
RRRRGGHH!

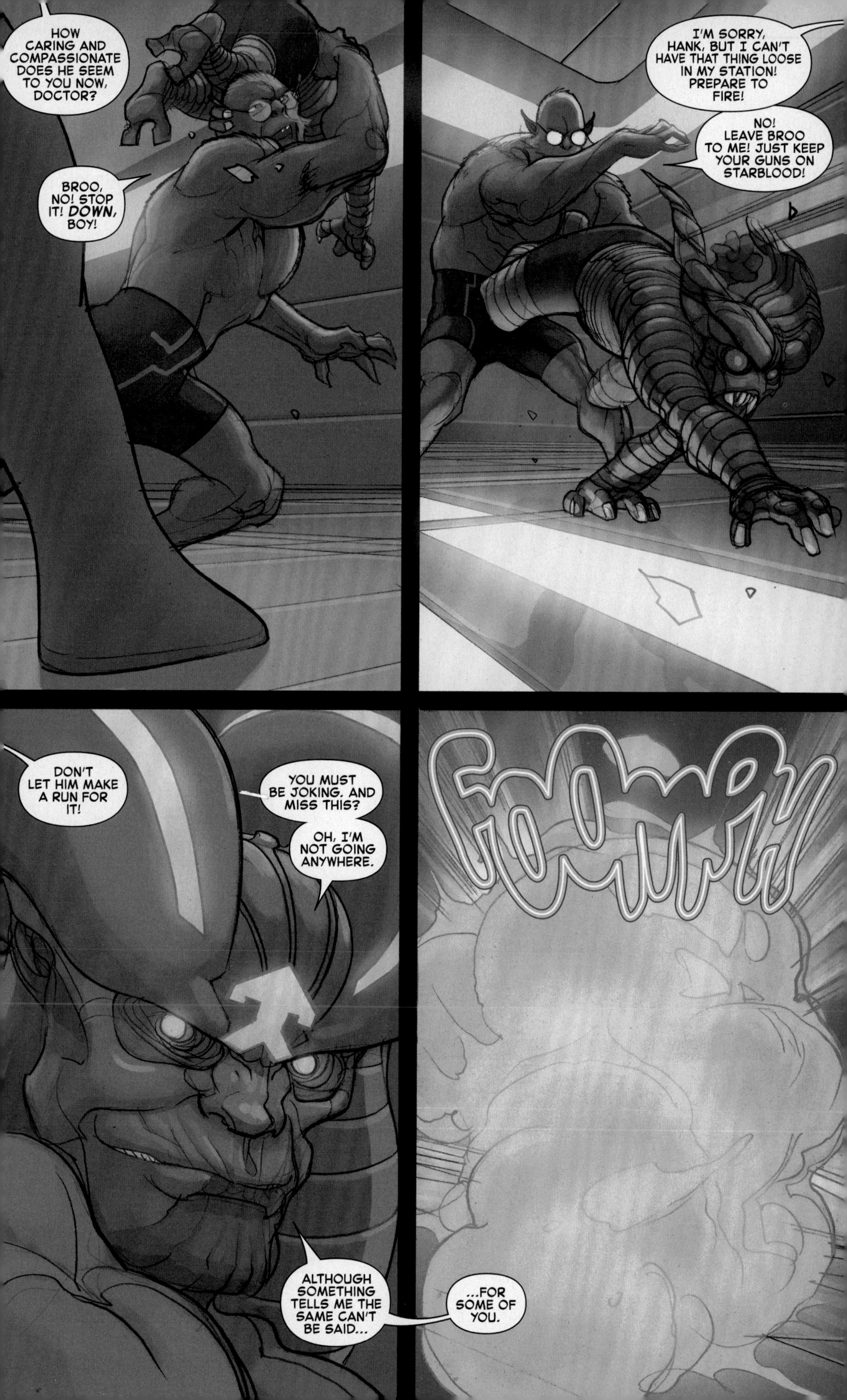
HOW CARING AND COMPASSIONATE DOES HE SEEM TO YOU NOW, DOCTOR?
BROO, NO! STOP IT! DOWN, BOY!
I'M SORRY, HANK, BUT I CAN'T HAVE THAT THING LOOSE IN MY STATION! PREPARE TO FIRE!
NO! LEAVE BROO TO ME! JUST KEEP YOUR GUNS ON STARBLOOD!
DON'T LET HIM MAKE A RUN FOR IT!
YOU MUST BE JOKING. AND MISS THIS?
OH, I'M NOT GOING ANYWHERE.
ALTHOUGH SOMETHING TELLS ME THE SAME CAN'T BE SAID...
...FOR SOME OF YOU.
FOOMP

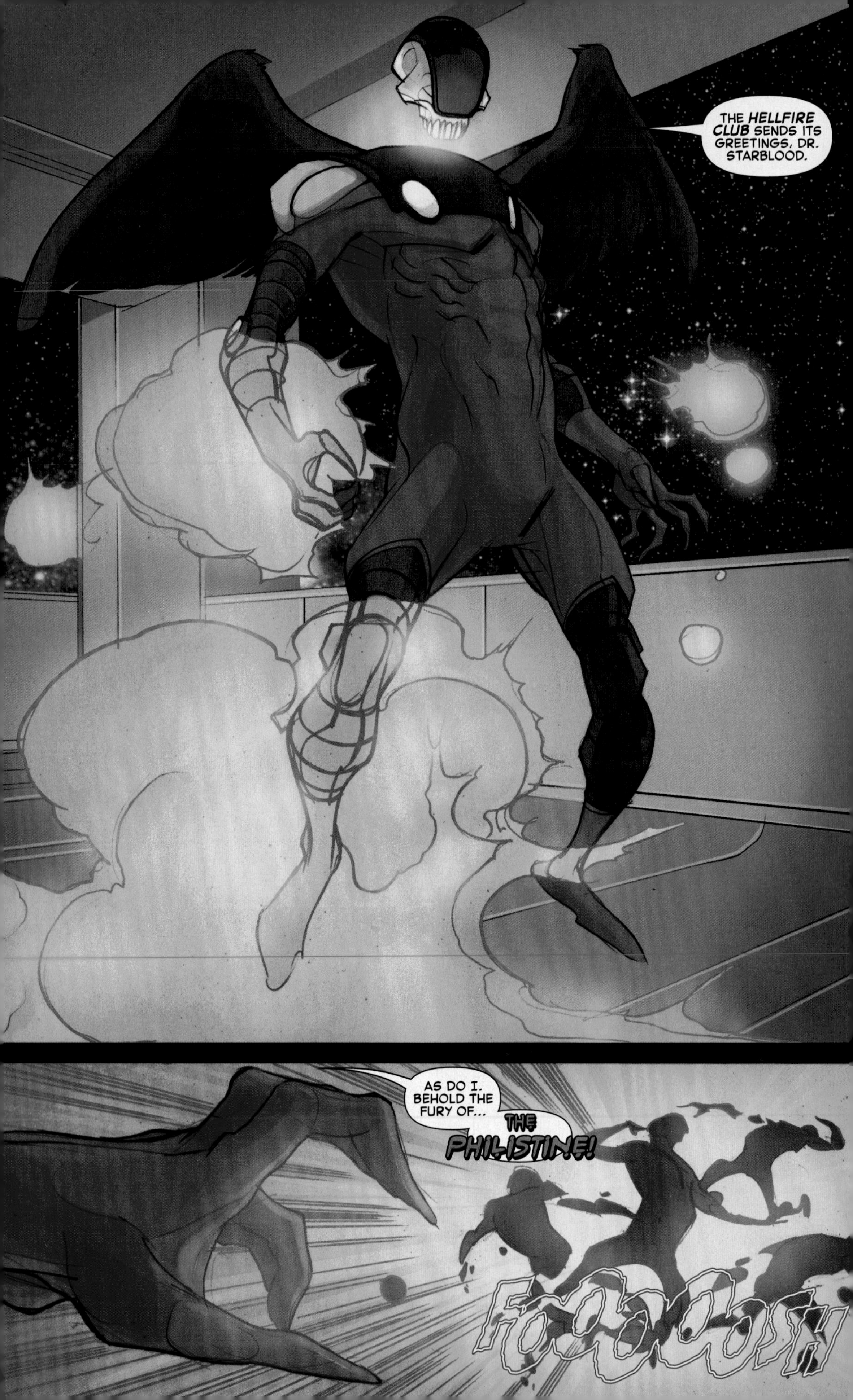
THE HELLFIRE CLUB SENDS ITS GREETINGS, DR. STARBLOOD.
AS DO I. BEHOLD THE FURY OF...
THE PHILISTINE!
FOOOOOSH

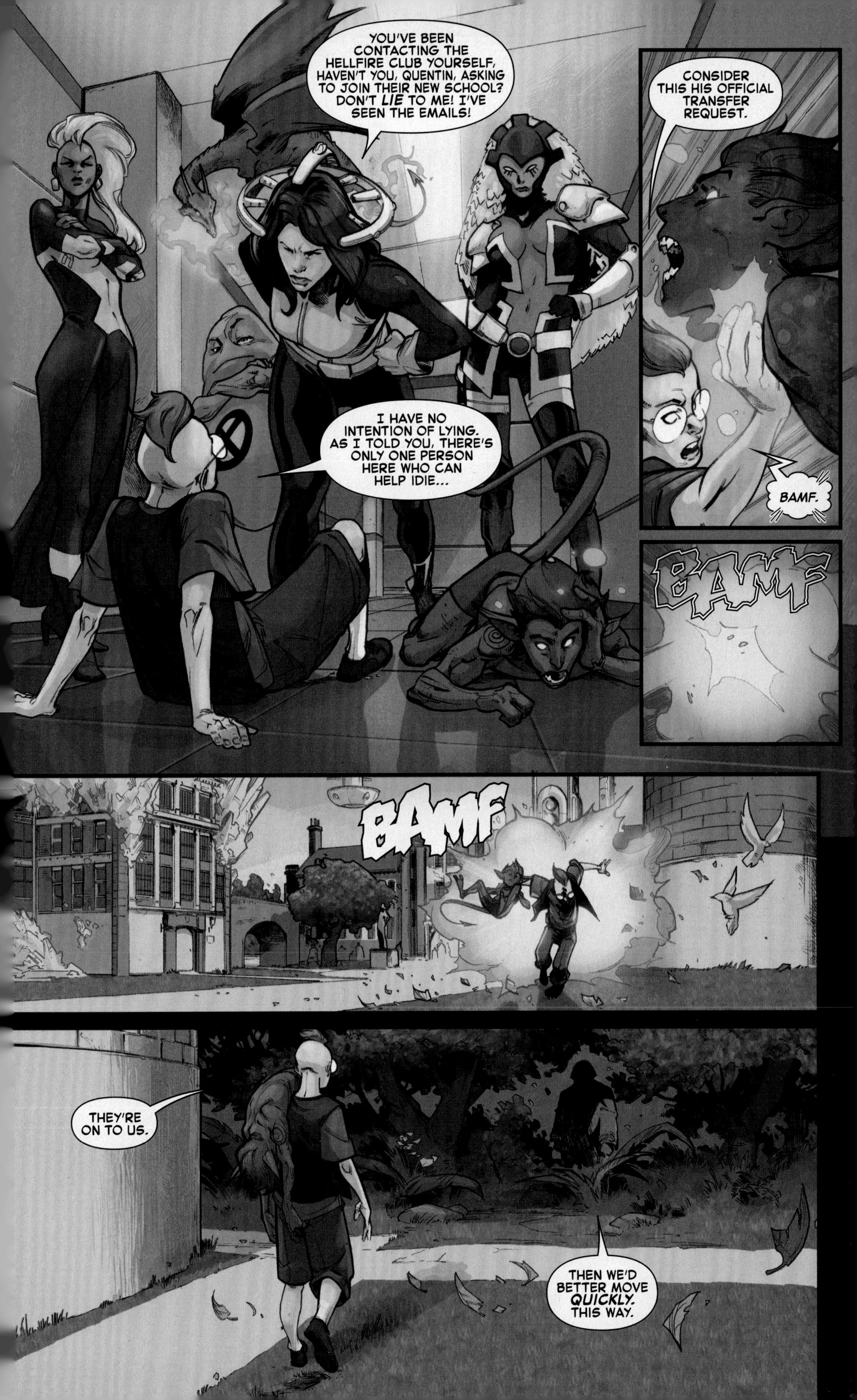

YOU'VE BEEN CONTACTING THE HELLFIRE CLUB YOURSELF, HAVEN'T YOU, QUENTIN, ASKING TO JOIN THEIR NEW SCHOOL? DON'T LIE TO ME! I'VE SEEN THE EMAILS!
I HAVE NO INTENTION OF LYING. AS I TOLD YOU, THERE'S ONLY ONE PERSON HERE WHO CAN HELP IDIE...
CONSIDER THIS HIS OFFICIAL TRANSFER REQUEST.
BAMF.
BAMF
BAMF
THEY'RE ON TO US.
THEN WE'D BETTER MOVE QUICKLY. THIS WAY.

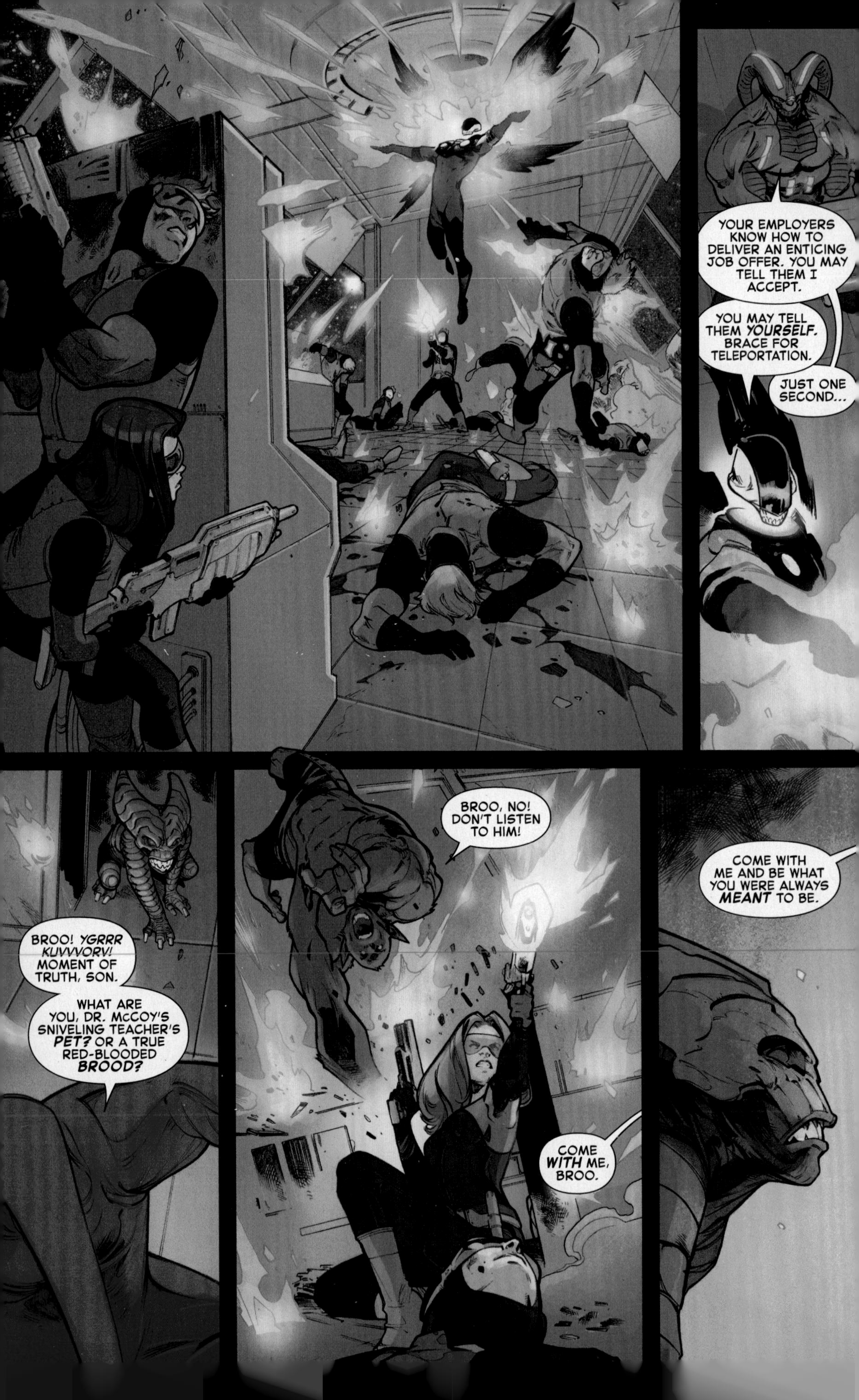
YOUR EMPLOYERS KNOW HOW TO DELIVER AN ENTICING JOB OFFER. YOU MAY TELL THEM I ACCEPT.
YOU MAY TELL THEM *YOURSELF.* BRACE FOR TELEPORTATION.
JUST ONE SECOND...
BROO! *YGRRR KUVVVORV!* MOMENT OF TRUTH, SON.
WHAT ARE YOU, DR. McCOY'S SNIVELING TEACHER'S *PET?* OR A TRUE RED-BLOODED *BROOD?*
BROO, NO! DON'T LISTEN TO HIM!
COME *WITH* ME, BROO.
COME WITH ME AND BE WHAT YOU WERE ALWAYS *MEANT* TO BE.

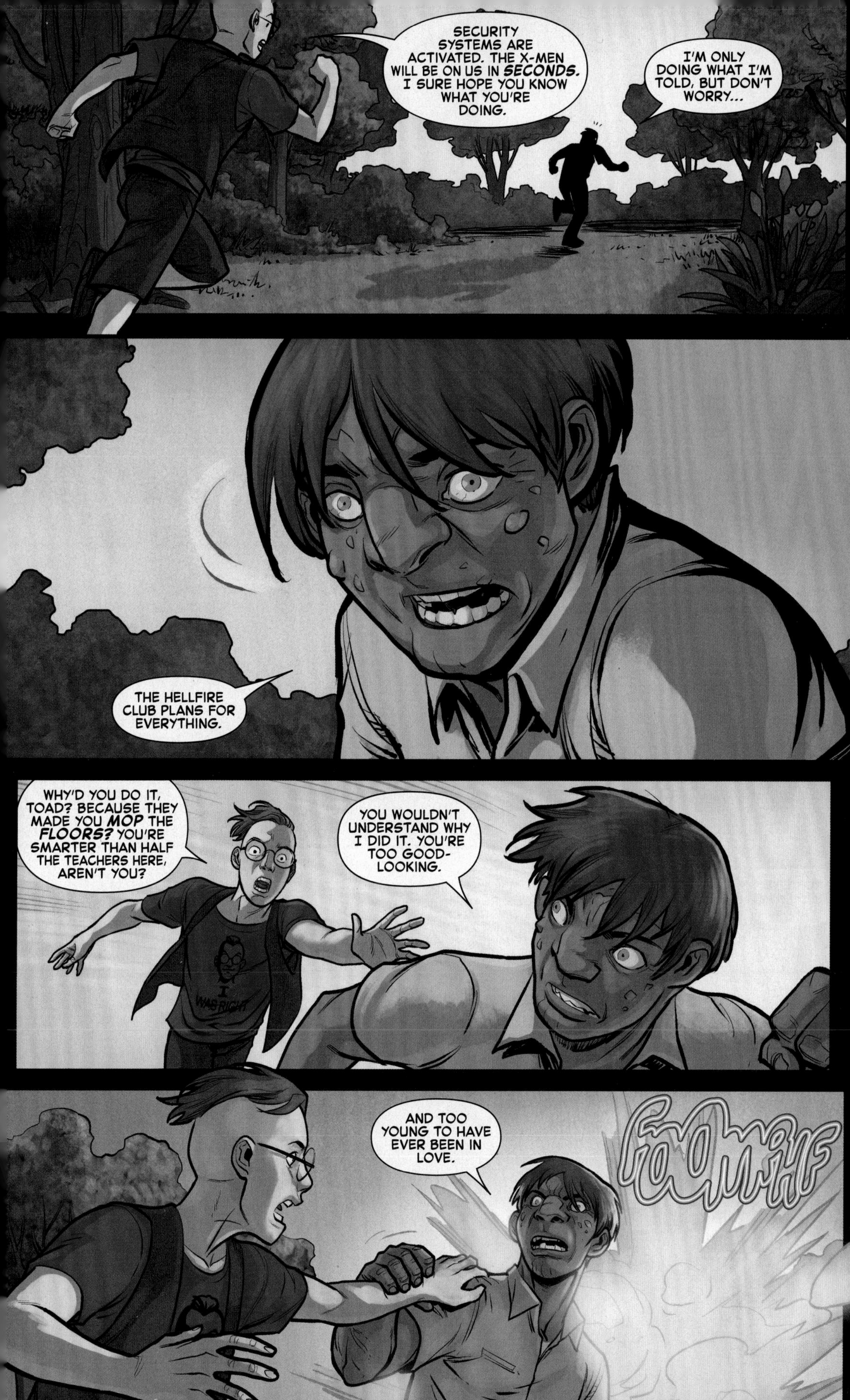

SECURITY SYSTEMS ARE ACTIVATED. THE X-MEN WILL BE ON US IN *SECONDS.* I SURE HOPE YOU KNOW WHAT YOU'RE DOING.
I'M ONLY DOING WHAT I'M TOLD, BUT DON'T WORRY...
THE HELLFIRE CLUB PLANS FOR EVERYTHING.
WHY'D YOU DO IT, TOAD? BECAUSE THEY MADE YOU *MOP* THE *FLOORS?* YOU'RE SMARTER THAN HALF THE TEACHERS HERE, AREN'T YOU?
YOU WOULDN'T UNDERSTAND WHY I DID IT. YOU'RE TOO GOOD-LOOKING.
AND TOO YOUNG TO HAVE EVER BEEN IN LOVE.

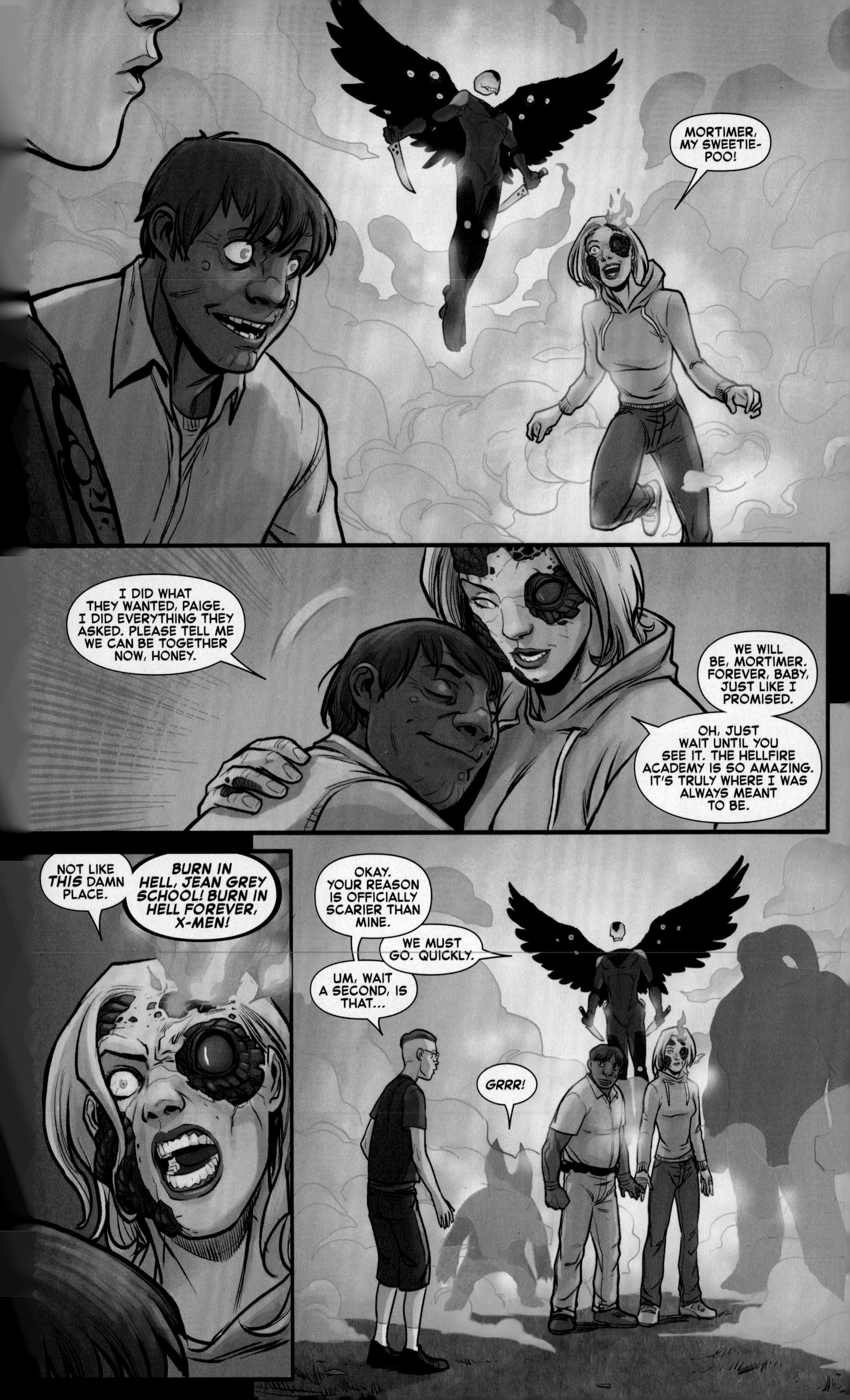
MORTIMER, MY SWEETIE-POO!
I DID WHAT THEY WANTED, PAIGE. I DID EVERYTHING THEY ASKED. PLEASE TELL ME WE CAN BE TOGETHER NOW, HONEY.
WE WILL BE, MORTIMER. FOREVER, BABY, JUST LIKE I PROMISED.
OH, JUST WAIT UNTIL YOU SEE IT. THE HELLFIRE ACADEMY IS SO AMAZING. IT'S TRULY WHERE I WAS ALWAYS MEANT TO BE.
NOT LIKE THIS DAMN PLACE.
BURN IN HELL, JEAN GREY SCHOOL! BURN IN HELL FOREVER, X-MEN!
OKAY. YOUR REASON IS OFFICIALLY SCARIER THAN MINE.
WE MUST GO. QUICKLY.
UM, WAIT A SECOND, IS THAT...
GRRR!

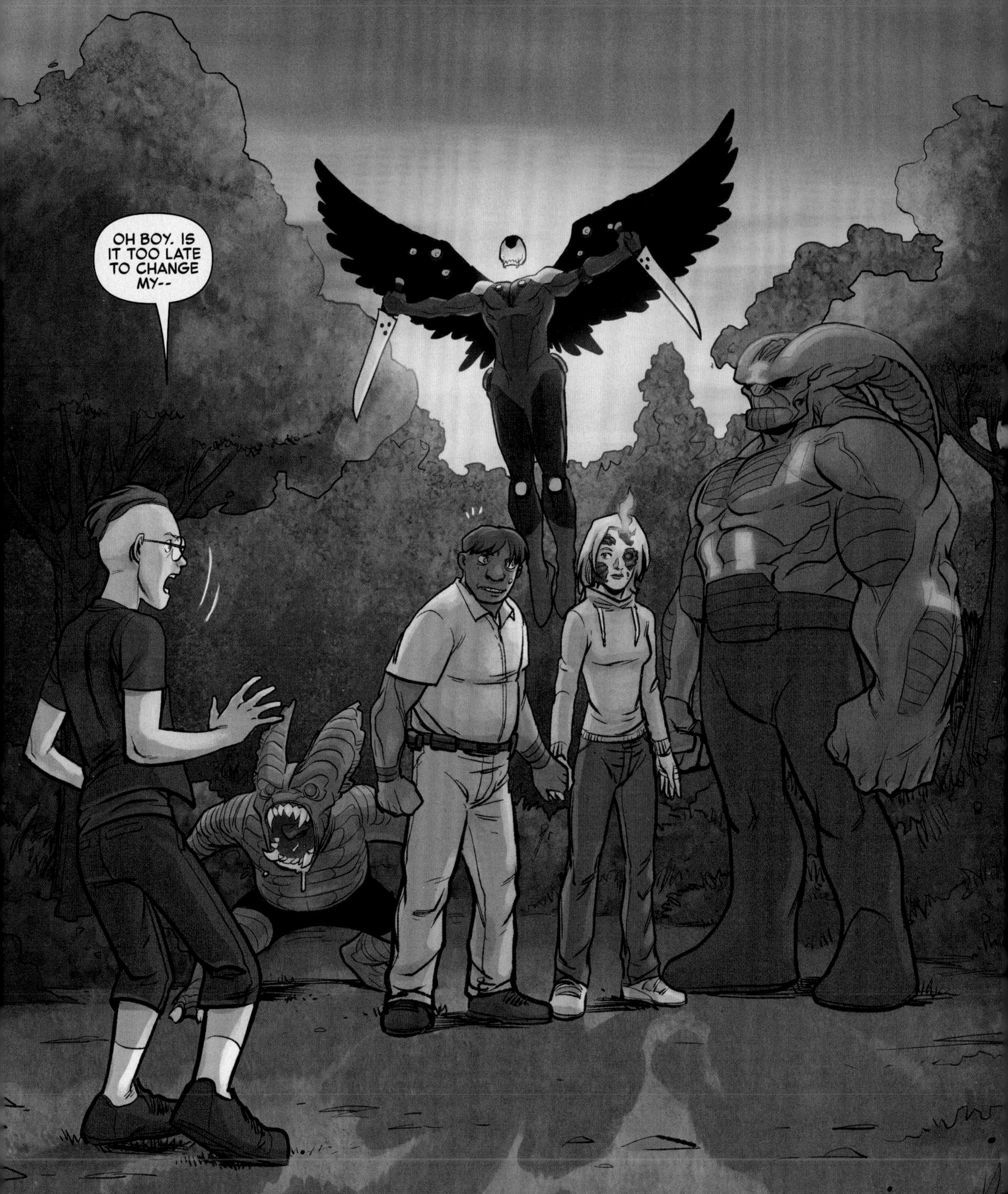
OH BOY. IS IT TOO LATE TO CHANGE MY--

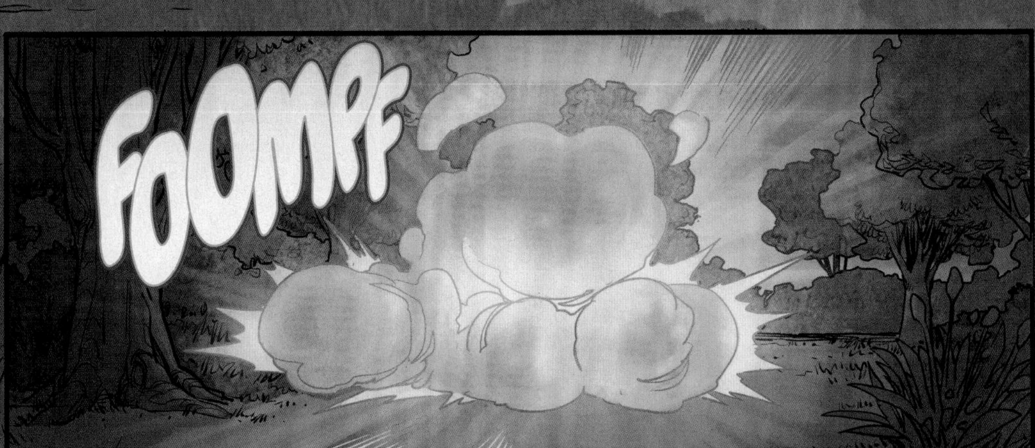
FOOMPF

31 WOLVERINE THROUGH THE AGES VARIANT
BY RYAN STEGMAN, TIM TOWNSEND & MORRY HOLLOWELL

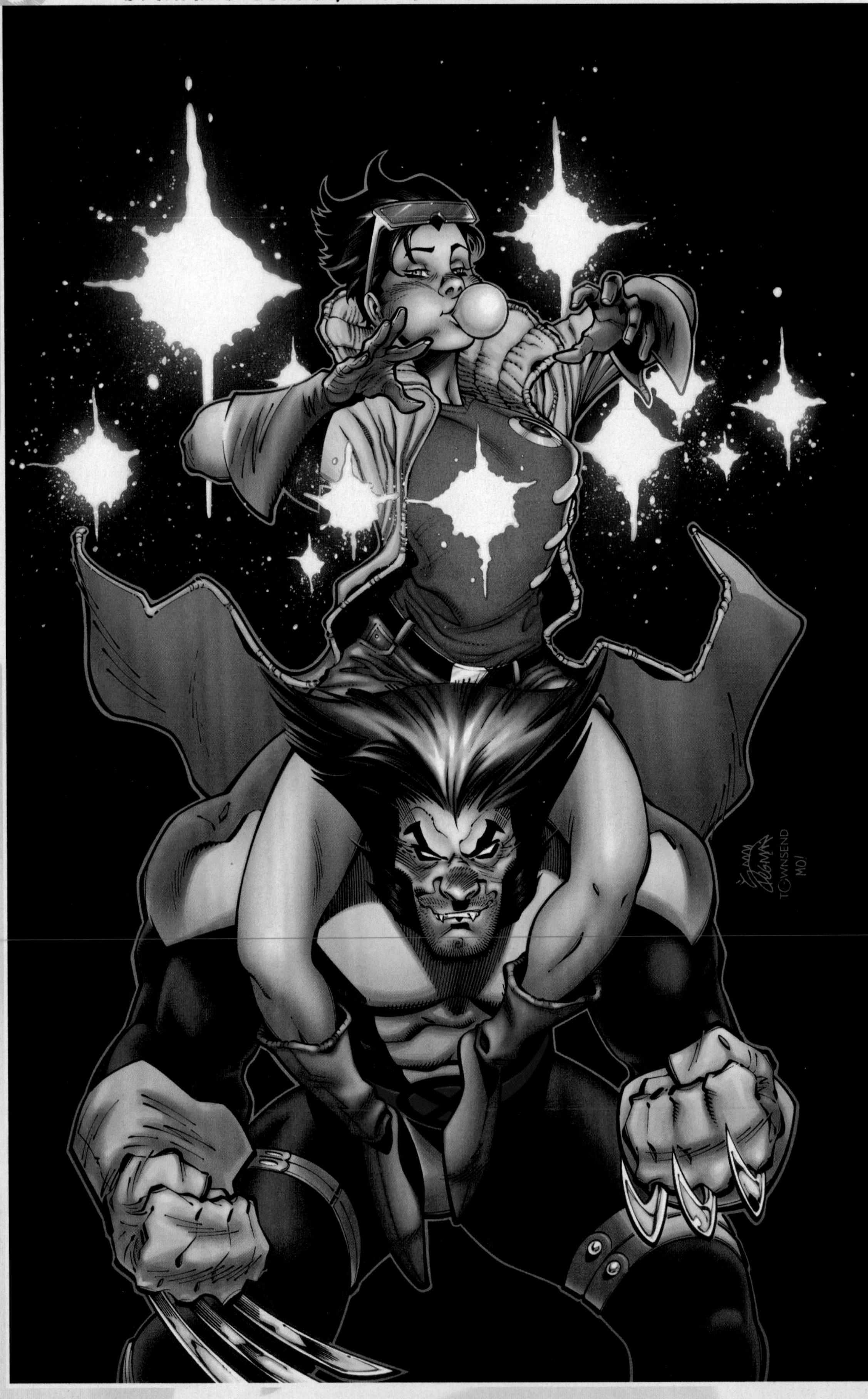
TOWNSEND
MD!

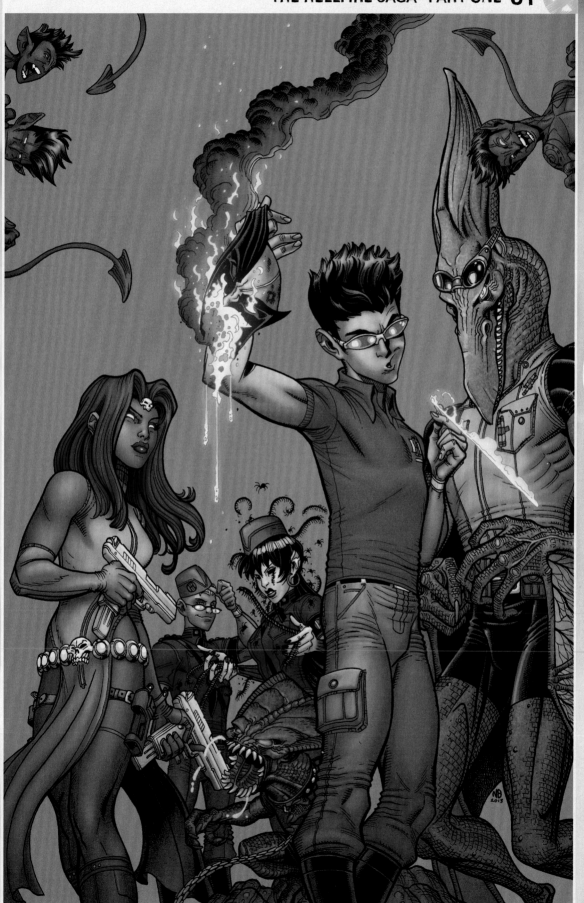

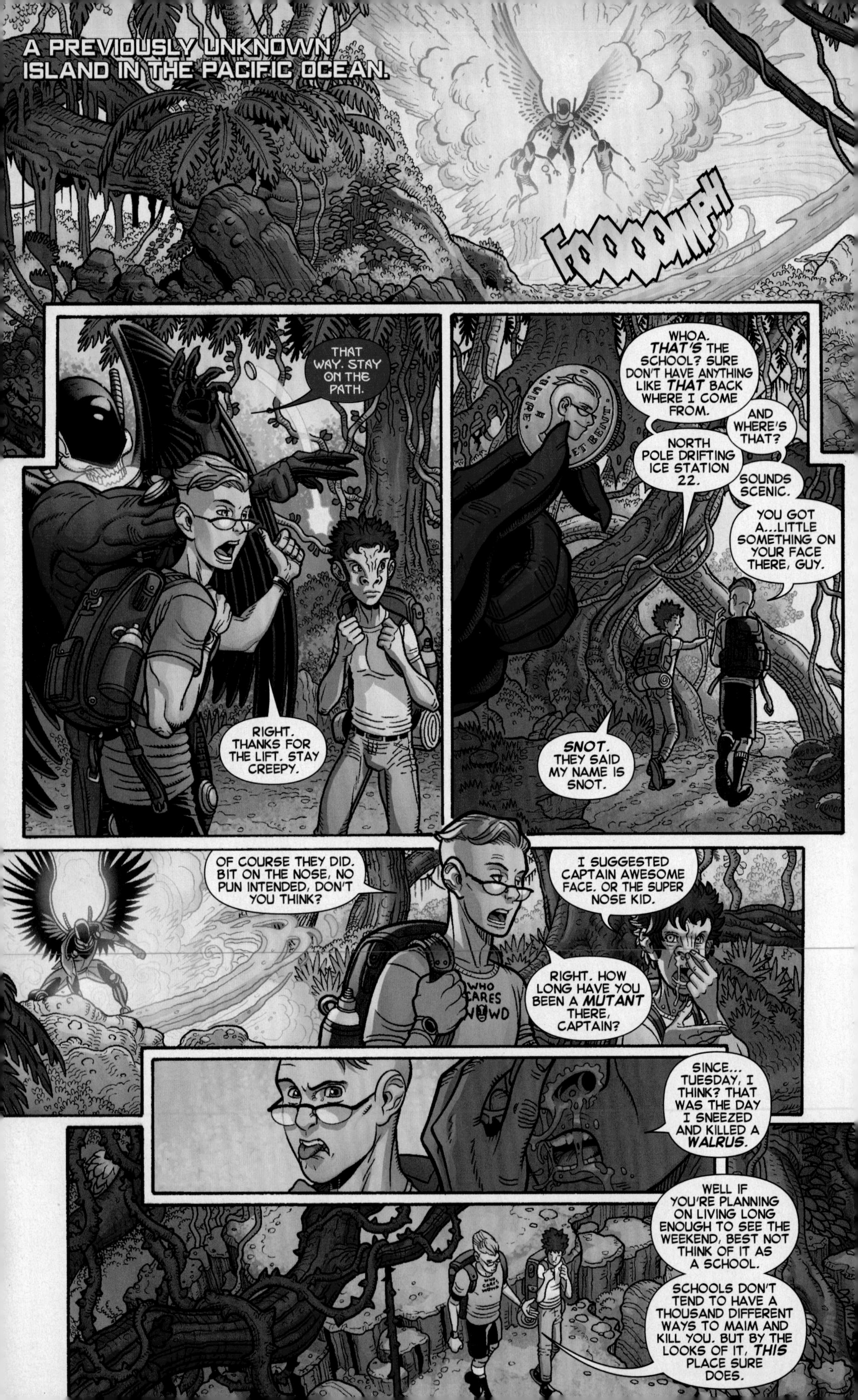
A PREVIOUSLY UNKNOWN ISLAND IN THE PACIFIC OCEAN.
FOOOOMPH
THAT WAY. STAY ON THE PATH.
RIGHT. THANKS FOR THE LIFT. STAY CREEPY.
WHOA. THAT'S THE SCHOOL? SURE DON'T HAVE ANYTHING LIKE THAT BACK WHERE I COME FROM.
AND WHERE'S THAT?
NORTH POLE DRIFTING ICE STATION 22.
SOUNDS SCENIC.
YOU GOT A...LITTLE SOMETHING ON YOUR FACE THERE, GUY.
SNOT. THEY SAID MY NAME IS SNOT.
OF COURSE THEY DID. BIT ON THE NOSE, NO PUN INTENDED, DON'T YOU THINK?
I SUGGESTED CAPTAIN AWESOME FACE. OR THE SUPER NOSE KID.
RIGHT. HOW LONG HAVE YOU BEEN A MUTANT THERE, CAPTAIN?
WHO CARES WWD
SINCE... TUESDAY, I THINK? THAT WAS THE DAY I SNEEZED AND KILLED A WALRUS.
WELL IF YOU'RE PLANNING ON LIVING LONG ENOUGH TO SEE THE WEEKEND, BEST NOT THINK OF IT AS A SCHOOL.
SCHOOLS DON'T TEND TO HAVE A THOUSAND DIFFERENT WAYS TO MAIM AND KILL YOU. BUT BY THE LOOKS OF IT, THIS PLACE SURE DOES.

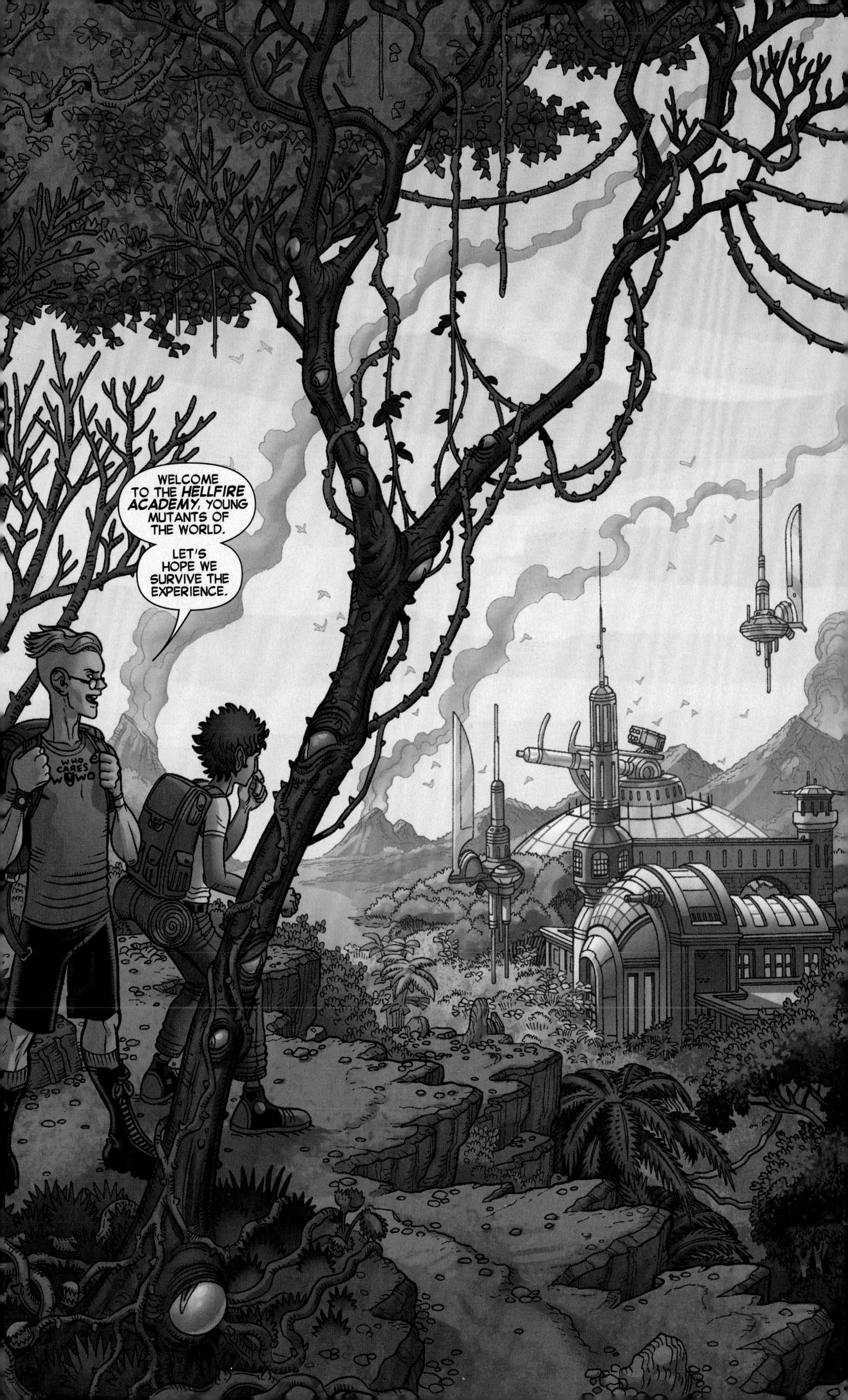
WELCOME TO THE *HELLFIRE ACADEMY*, YOUNG MUTANTS OF THE WORLD.
LET'S HOPE WE SURVIVE THE EXPERIENCE.
WHO CARES WOWO

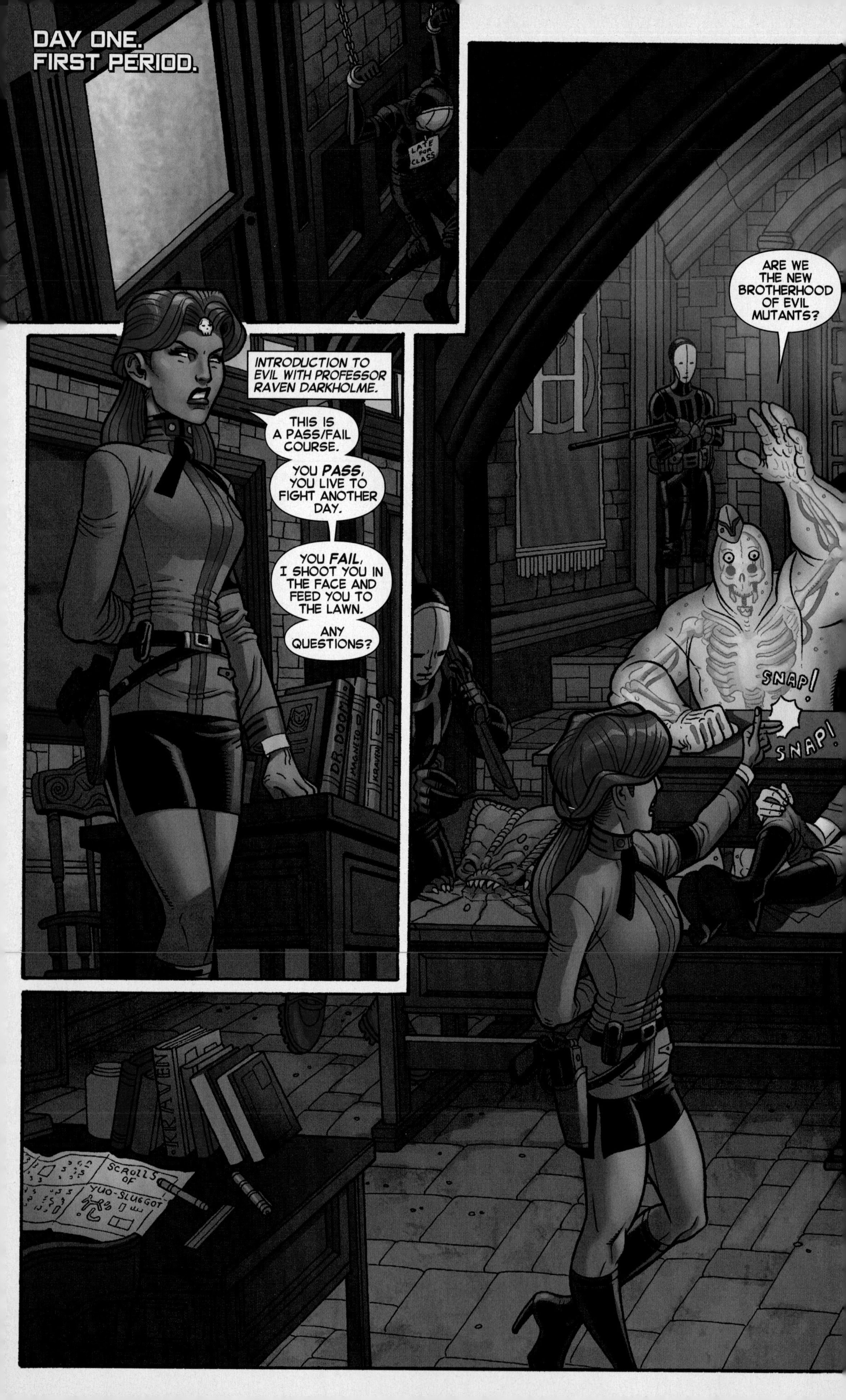
DAY ONE.
FIRST PERIOD.
LATE FOR CLASS
INTRODUCTION TO EVIL WITH PROFESSOR RAVEN DARKHOLME.
THIS IS A PASS/FAIL COURSE.
YOU PASS, YOU LIVE TO FIGHT ANOTHER DAY.
YOU FAIL, I SHOOT YOU IN THE FACE AND FEED YOU TO THE LAWN.
ANY QUESTIONS?
DR. DOOM
MAGNETO
KRAVEN
ARE WE THE NEW BROTHERHOOD OF EVIL MUTANTS?
SNAP!
SNAP!
KRAVEN
SCROLLS OF YUO-SLUGGOT

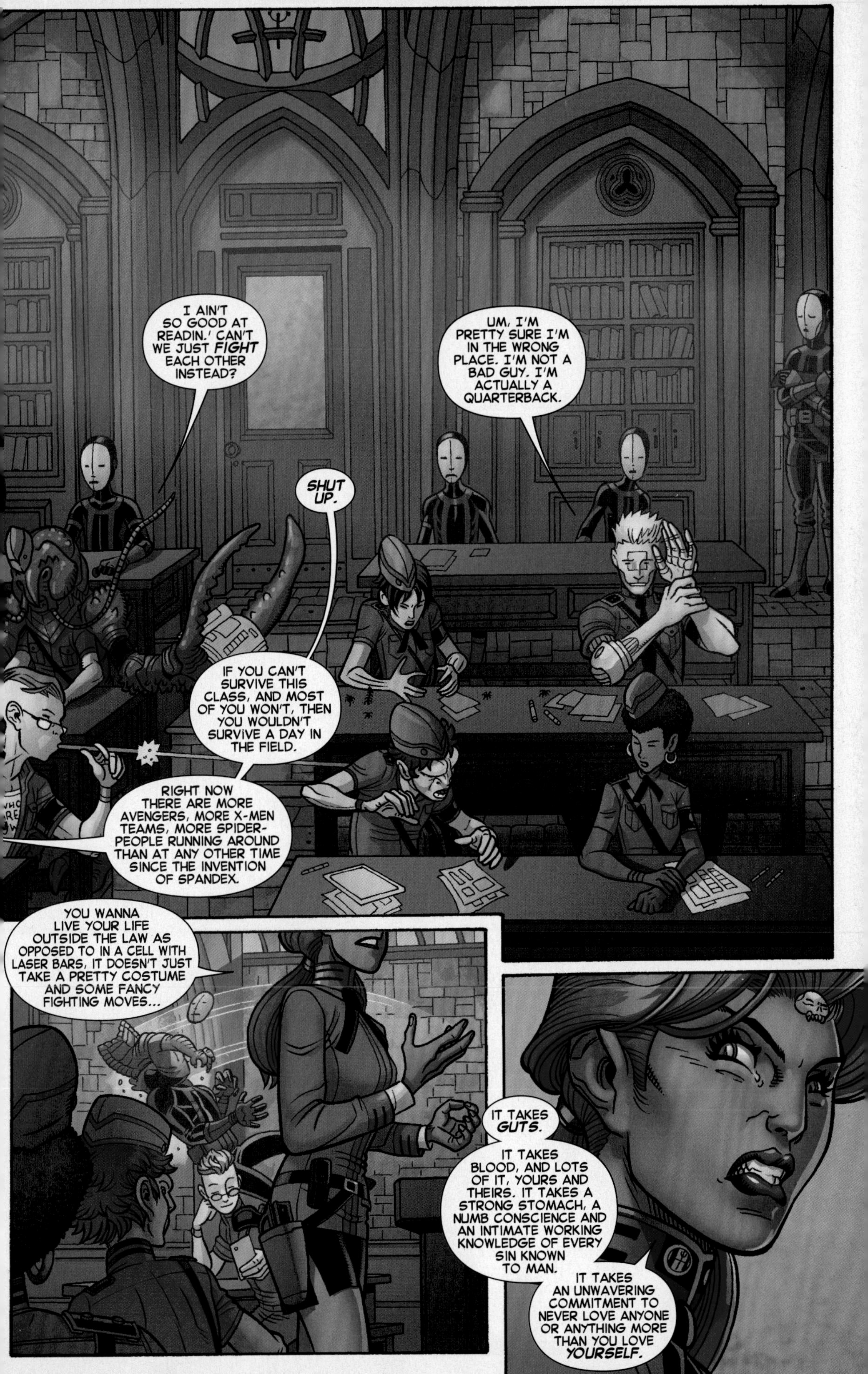
I AIN'T SO GOOD AT READIN.' CAN'T WE JUST FIGHT EACH OTHER INSTEAD?
UM, I'M PRETTY SURE I'M IN THE WRONG PLACE. I'M NOT A BAD GUY. I'M ACTUALLY A QUARTERBACK.
SHUT UP.
IF YOU CAN'T SURVIVE THIS CLASS, AND MOST OF YOU WON'T, THEN YOU WOULDN'T SURVIVE A DAY IN THE FIELD.
RIGHT NOW THERE ARE MORE AVENGERS, MORE X-MEN TEAMS, MORE SPIDER-PEOPLE RUNNING AROUND THAN AT ANY OTHER TIME SINCE THE INVENTION OF SPANDEX.
YOU WANNA LIVE YOUR LIFE OUTSIDE THE LAW AS OPPOSED TO IN A CELL WITH LASER BARS, IT DOESN'T JUST TAKE A PRETTY COSTUME AND SOME FANCY FIGHTING MOVES...
IT TAKES GUTS.
IT TAKES BLOOD, AND LOTS OF IT, YOURS AND THEIRS. IT TAKES A STRONG STOMACH, A NUMB CONSCIENCE AND AN INTIMATE WORKING KNOWLEDGE OF EVERY SIN KNOWN TO MAN.
IT TAKES AN UNWAVERING COMMITMENT TO NEVER LOVE ANYONE OR ANYTHING MORE THAN YOU LOVE YOURSELF.

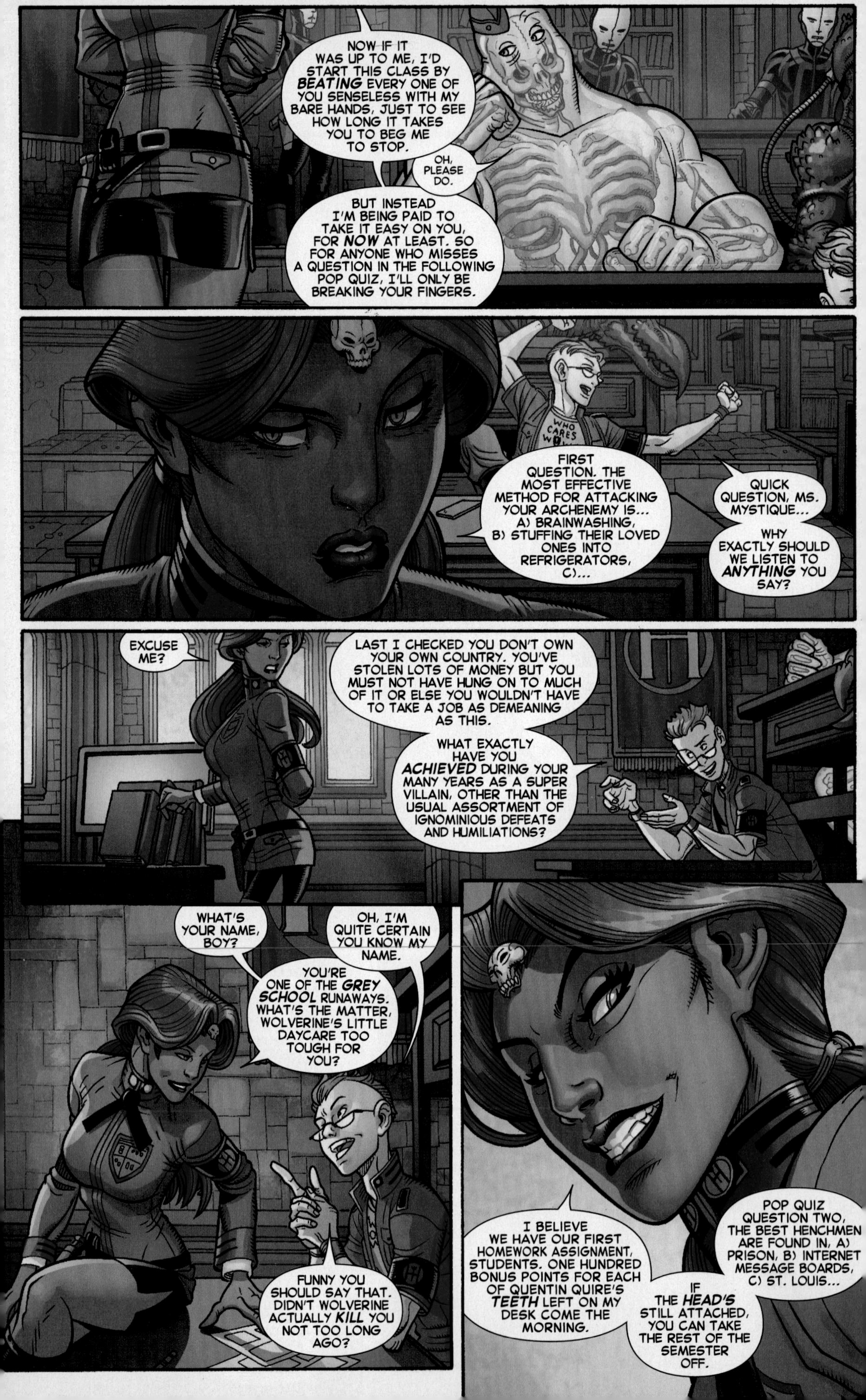
NOW IF IT WAS UP TO ME, I'D START THIS CLASS BY BEATING EVERY ONE OF YOU SENSELESS WITH MY BARE HANDS, JUST TO SEE HOW LONG IT TAKES YOU TO BEG ME TO STOP.
OH, PLEASE DO.
BUT INSTEAD I'M BEING PAID TO TAKE IT EASY ON YOU, FOR NOW AT LEAST. SO FOR ANYONE WHO MISSES A QUESTION IN THE FOLLOWING POP QUIZ, I'LL ONLY BE BREAKING YOUR FINGERS.
WHO CARES
FIRST QUESTION. THE MOST EFFECTIVE METHOD FOR ATTACKING YOUR ARCHENEMY IS... A) BRAINWASHING, B) STUFFING THEIR LOVED ONES INTO REFRIGERATORS, C)...
QUICK QUESTION, MS. MYSTIQUE...
WHY EXACTLY SHOULD WE LISTEN TO ANYTHING YOU SAY?
EXCUSE ME?
LAST I CHECKED YOU DON'T OWN YOUR OWN COUNTRY. YOU'VE STOLEN LOTS OF MONEY BUT YOU MUST NOT HAVE HUNG ON TO MUCH OF IT OR ELSE YOU WOULDN'T HAVE TO TAKE A JOB AS DEMEANING AS THIS.
WHAT EXACTLY HAVE YOU ACHIEVED DURING YOUR MANY YEARS AS A SUPER VILLAIN, OTHER THAN THE USUAL ASSORTMENT OF IGNOMINIOUS DEFEATS AND HUMILIATIONS?
WHAT'S YOUR NAME, BOY?
OH, I'M QUITE CERTAIN YOU KNOW MY NAME.
YOU'RE ONE OF THE GREY SCHOOL RUNAWAYS. WHAT'S THE MATTER, WOLVERINE'S LITTLE DAYCARE TOO TOUGH FOR YOU?
FUNNY YOU SHOULD SAY THAT. DIDN'T WOLVERINE ACTUALLY KILL YOU NOT TOO LONG AGO?
POP QUIZ QUESTION TWO, THE BEST HENCHMEN ARE FOUND IN, A) PRISON, B) INTERNET MESSAGE BOARDS, C) ST. LOUIS...
I BELIEVE WE HAVE OUR FIRST HOMEWORK ASSIGNMENT, STUDENTS. ONE HUNDRED BONUS POINTS FOR EACH OF QUENTIN QUIRE'S TEETH LEFT ON MY DESK COME THE MORNING.
IF THE HEAD'S STILL ATTACHED, YOU CAN TAKE THE REST OF THE SEMESTER OFF.

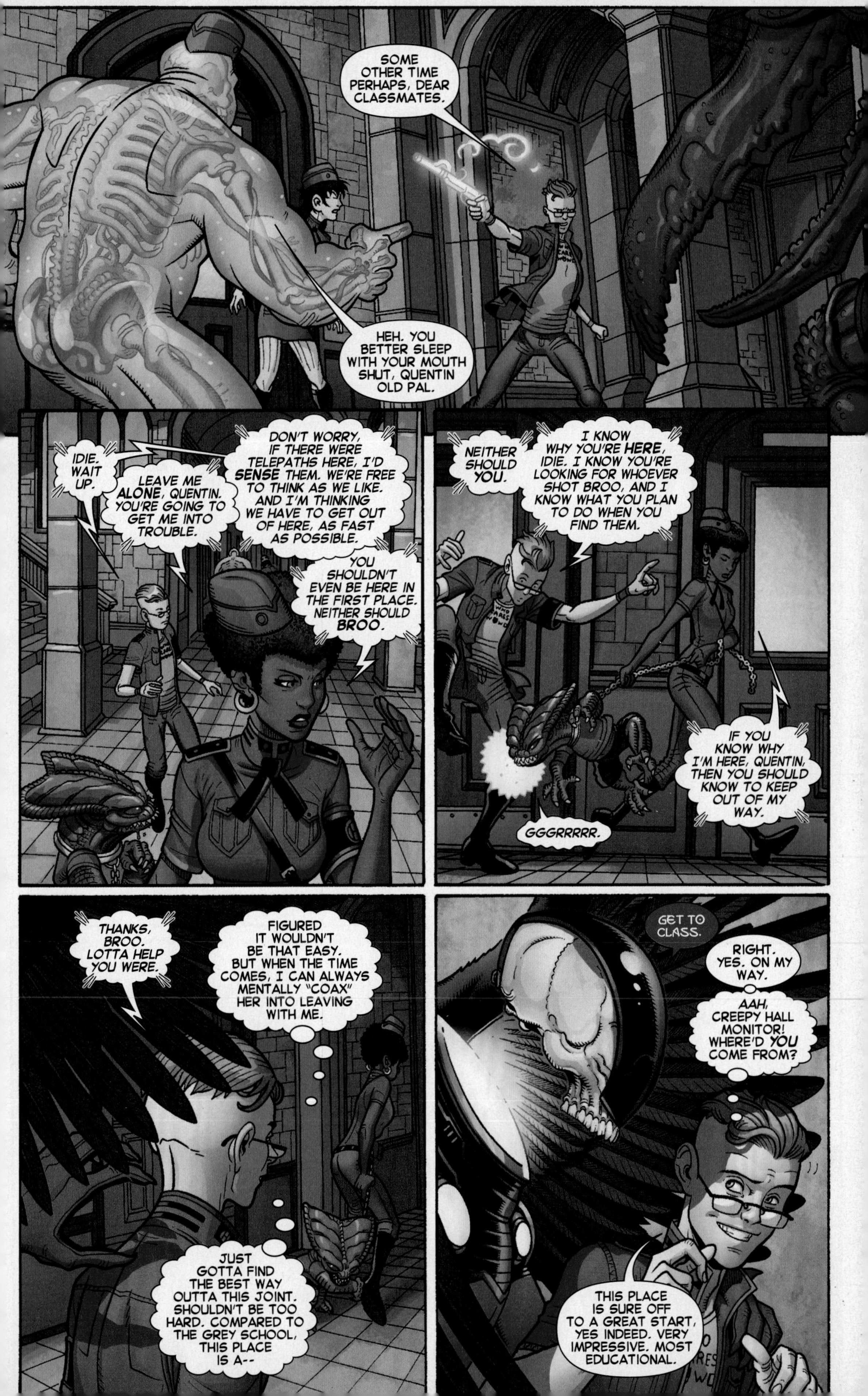
SOME OTHER TIME PERHAPS, DEAR CLASSMATES.
HEH. YOU BETTER SLEEP WITH YOUR MOUTH SHUT, QUENTIN OLD PAL.
IDIE. WAIT UP.
LEAVE ME ALONE, QUENTIN. YOU'RE GOING TO GET ME INTO TROUBLE.
DON'T WORRY, IF THERE WERE TELEPATHS HERE, I'D SENSE THEM. WE'RE FREE TO THINK AS WE LIKE. AND I'M THINKING WE HAVE TO GET OUT OF HERE, AS FAST AS POSSIBLE.
YOU SHOULDN'T EVEN BE HERE IN THE FIRST PLACE. NEITHER SHOULD BROO.
NEITHER SHOULD YOU.
I KNOW WHY YOU'RE HERE, IDIE. I KNOW YOU'RE LOOKING FOR WHOEVER SHOT BROO, AND I KNOW WHAT YOU PLAN TO DO WHEN YOU FIND THEM.
IF YOU KNOW WHY I'M HERE, QUENTIN, THEN YOU SHOULD KNOW TO KEEP OUT OF MY WAY.
GGGRRRRR.
THANKS, BROO. LOTTA HELP YOU WERE.
FIGURED IT WOULDN'T BE THAT EASY. BUT WHEN THE TIME COMES, I CAN ALWAYS MENTALLY "COAX" HER INTO LEAVING WITH ME.
JUST GOTTA FIND THE BEST WAY OUTTA THIS JOINT. SHOULDN'T BE TOO HARD. COMPARED TO THE GREY SCHOOL, THIS PLACE IS A--
GET TO CLASS.
RIGHT. YES. ON MY WAY.
AAH, CREEPY HALL MONITOR! WHERE'D YOU COME FROM?
THIS PLACE IS SURE OFF TO A GREAT START, YES INDEED. VERY IMPRESSIVE. MOST EDUCATIONAL.

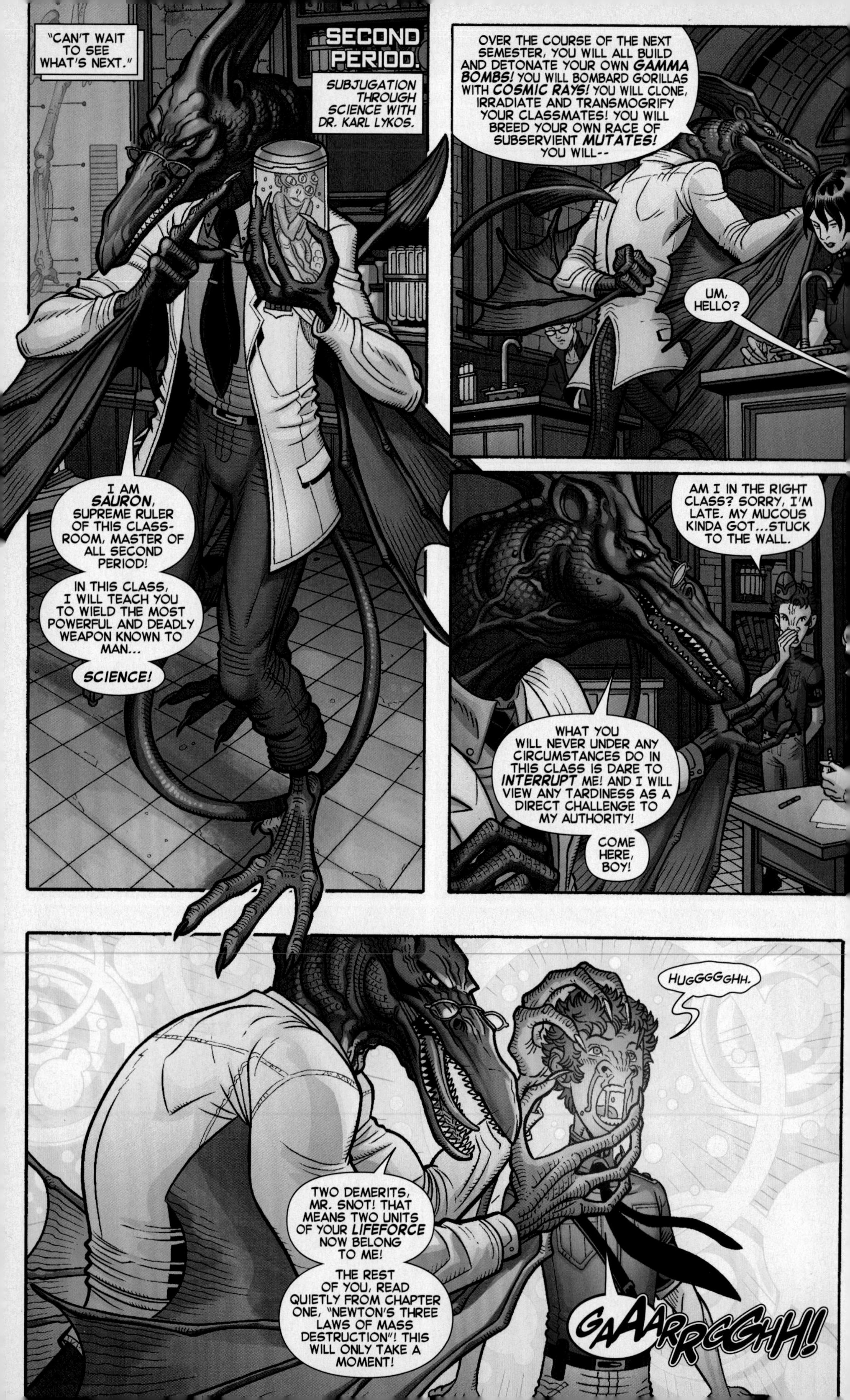
"CAN'T WAIT TO SEE WHAT'S NEXT."
SECOND PERIOD.
SUBJUGATION THROUGH SCIENCE WITH DR. KARL LYKOS.
I AM SAURON, SUPREME RULER OF THIS CLASS-ROOM, MASTER OF ALL SECOND PERIOD!
IN THIS CLASS, I WILL TEACH YOU TO WIELD THE MOST POWERFUL AND DEADLY WEAPON KNOWN TO MAN...
SCIENCE!
OVER THE COURSE OF THE NEXT SEMESTER, YOU WILL ALL BUILD AND DETONATE YOUR OWN GAMMA BOMBS! YOU WILL BOMBARD GORILLAS WITH COSMIC RAYS! YOU WILL CLONE, IRRADIATE AND TRANSMOGRIFY YOUR CLASSMATES! YOU WILL BREED YOUR OWN RACE OF SUBSERVIENT MUTATES! YOU WILL--
UM, HELLO?
AM I IN THE RIGHT CLASS? SORRY, I'M LATE. MY MUCOUS KINDA GOT...STUCK TO THE WALL.
WHAT YOU WILL NEVER UNDER ANY CIRCUMSTANCES DO IN THIS CLASS IS DARE TO INTERRUPT ME! AND I WILL VIEW ANY TARDINESS AS A DIRECT CHALLENGE TO MY AUTHORITY!
COME HERE, BOY!
HUGGGGGHH.
TWO DEMERITS, MR. SNOT! THAT MEANS TWO UNITS OF YOUR LIFEFORCE NOW BELONG TO ME!
THE REST OF YOU, READ QUIETLY FROM CHAPTER ONE, "NEWTON'S THREE LAWS OF MASS DESTRUCTION"! THIS WILL ONLY TAKE A MOMENT!
GAAARRGGHH!

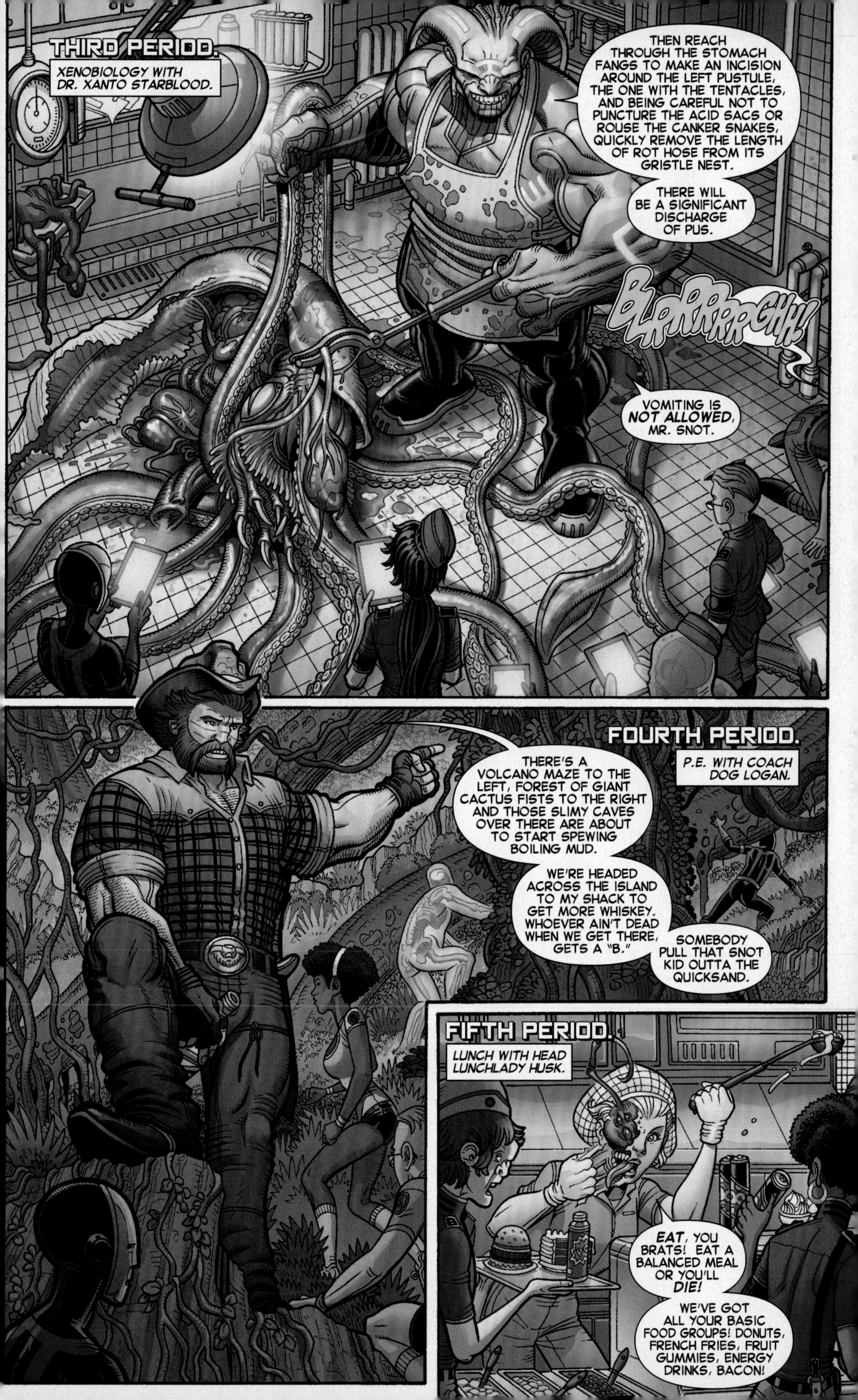
THIRD PERIOD.
XENOBIOLOGY WITH DR. XANTO STARBLOOD.
THEN REACH THROUGH THE STOMACH FANGS TO MAKE AN INCISION AROUND THE LEFT PUSTULE, THE ONE WITH THE TENTACLES, AND BEING CAREFUL NOT TO PUNCTURE THE ACID SACS OR ROUSE THE CANKER SNAKES, QUICKLY REMOVE THE LENGTH OF ROT HOSE FROM ITS GRISTLE NEST.
THERE WILL BE A SIGNIFICANT DISCHARGE OF PUS.
BLRRRRRRGHH!
VOMITING IS NOT ALLOWED, MR. SNOT.
FOURTH PERIOD.
P.E. WITH COACH DOG LOGAN.
THERE'S A VOLCANO MAZE TO THE LEFT, FOREST OF GIANT CACTUS FISTS TO THE RIGHT AND THOSE SLIMY CAVES OVER THERE ARE ABOUT TO START SPEWING BOILING MUD.
WE'RE HEADED ACROSS THE ISLAND TO MY SHACK TO GET MORE WHISKEY. WHOEVER AIN'T DEAD WHEN WE GET THERE, GETS A "B."
SOMEBODY PULL THAT SNOT KID OUTTA THE QUICKSAND.
FIFTH PERIOD.
LUNCH WITH HEAD LUNCHLADY HUSK.
EAT, YOU BRATS! EAT A BALANCED MEAL OR YOU'LL DIE!
WE'VE GOT ALL YOUR BASIC FOOD GROUPS! DONUTS, FRENCH FRIES, FRUIT GUMMIES, ENERGY DRINKS, BACON!

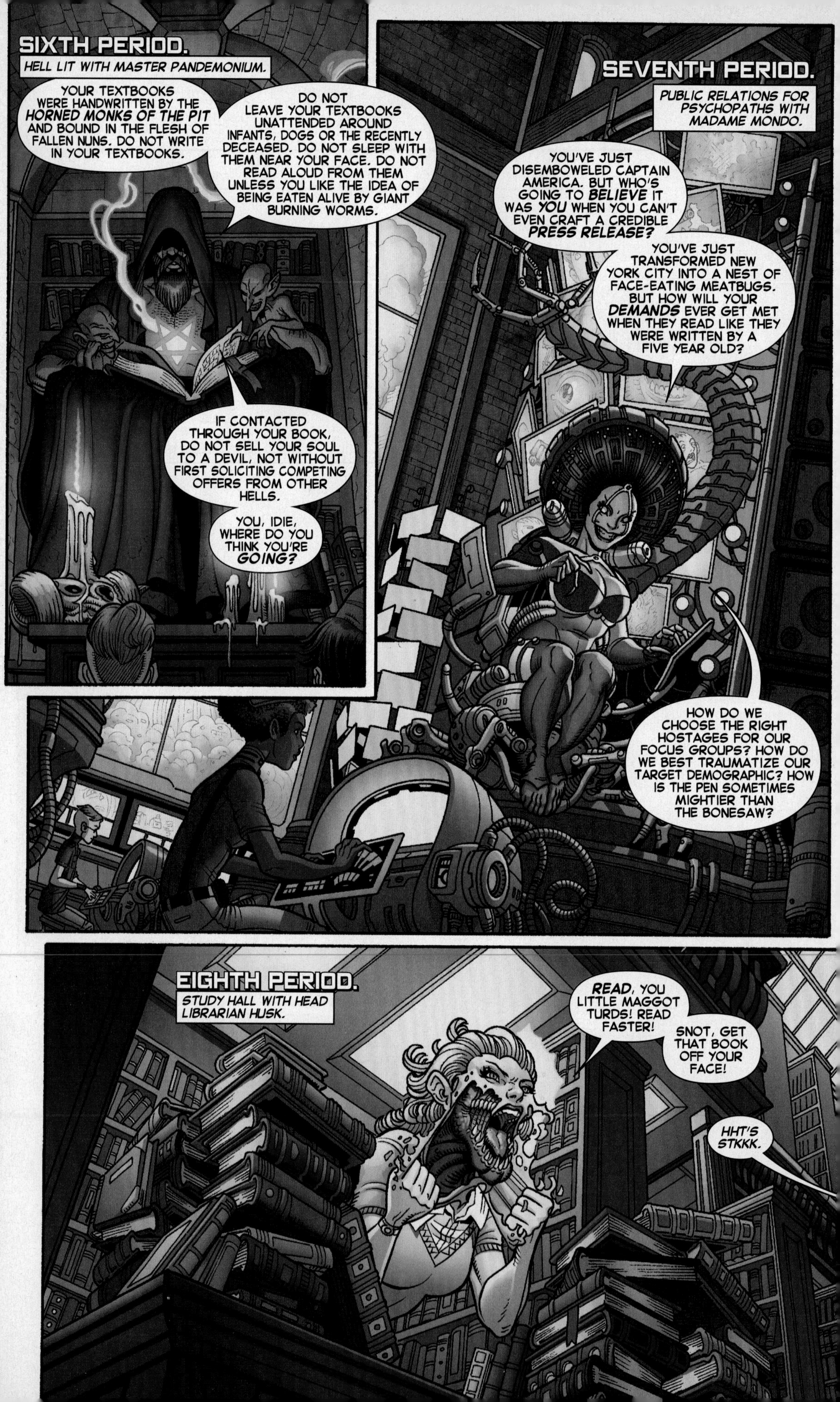
SIXTH PERIOD.
HELL LIT WITH MASTER PANDEMONIUM.
YOUR TEXTBOOKS WERE HANDWRITTEN BY THE HORNED MONKS OF THE PIT AND BOUND IN THE FLESH OF FALLEN NUNS. DO NOT WRITE IN YOUR TEXTBOOKS.
DO NOT LEAVE YOUR TEXTBOOKS UNATTENDED AROUND INFANTS, DOGS OR THE RECENTLY DECEASED. DO NOT SLEEP WITH THEM NEAR YOUR FACE. DO NOT READ ALOUD FROM THEM UNLESS YOU LIKE THE IDEA OF BEING EATEN ALIVE BY GIANT BURNING WORMS.
IF CONTACTED THROUGH YOUR BOOK, DO NOT SELL YOUR SOUL TO A DEVIL, NOT WITHOUT FIRST SOLICITING COMPETING OFFERS FROM OTHER HELLS.
YOU, IDIE, WHERE DO YOU THINK YOU'RE GOING?
SEVENTH PERIOD.
PUBLIC RELATIONS FOR PSYCHOPATHS WITH MADAME MONDO.
YOU'VE JUST DISEMBOWELED CAPTAIN AMERICA. BUT WHO'S GOING TO BELIEVE IT WAS YOU WHEN YOU CAN'T EVEN CRAFT A CREDIBLE PRESS RELEASE?
YOU'VE JUST TRANSFORMED NEW YORK CITY INTO A NEST OF FACE-EATING MEATBUGS. BUT HOW WILL YOUR DEMANDS EVER GET MET WHEN THEY READ LIKE THEY WERE WRITTEN BY A FIVE YEAR OLD?
HOW DO WE CHOOSE THE RIGHT HOSTAGES FOR OUR FOCUS GROUPS? HOW DO WE BEST TRAUMATIZE OUR TARGET DEMOGRAPHIC? HOW IS THE PEN SOMETIMES MIGHTIER THAN THE BONESAW?
EIGHTH PERIOD.
STUDY HALL WITH HEAD LIBRARIAN HUSK.
READ, YOU LITTLE MAGGOT TURDS! READ FASTER!
SNOT, GET THAT BOOK OFF YOUR FACE!
HHT'S STKKK.

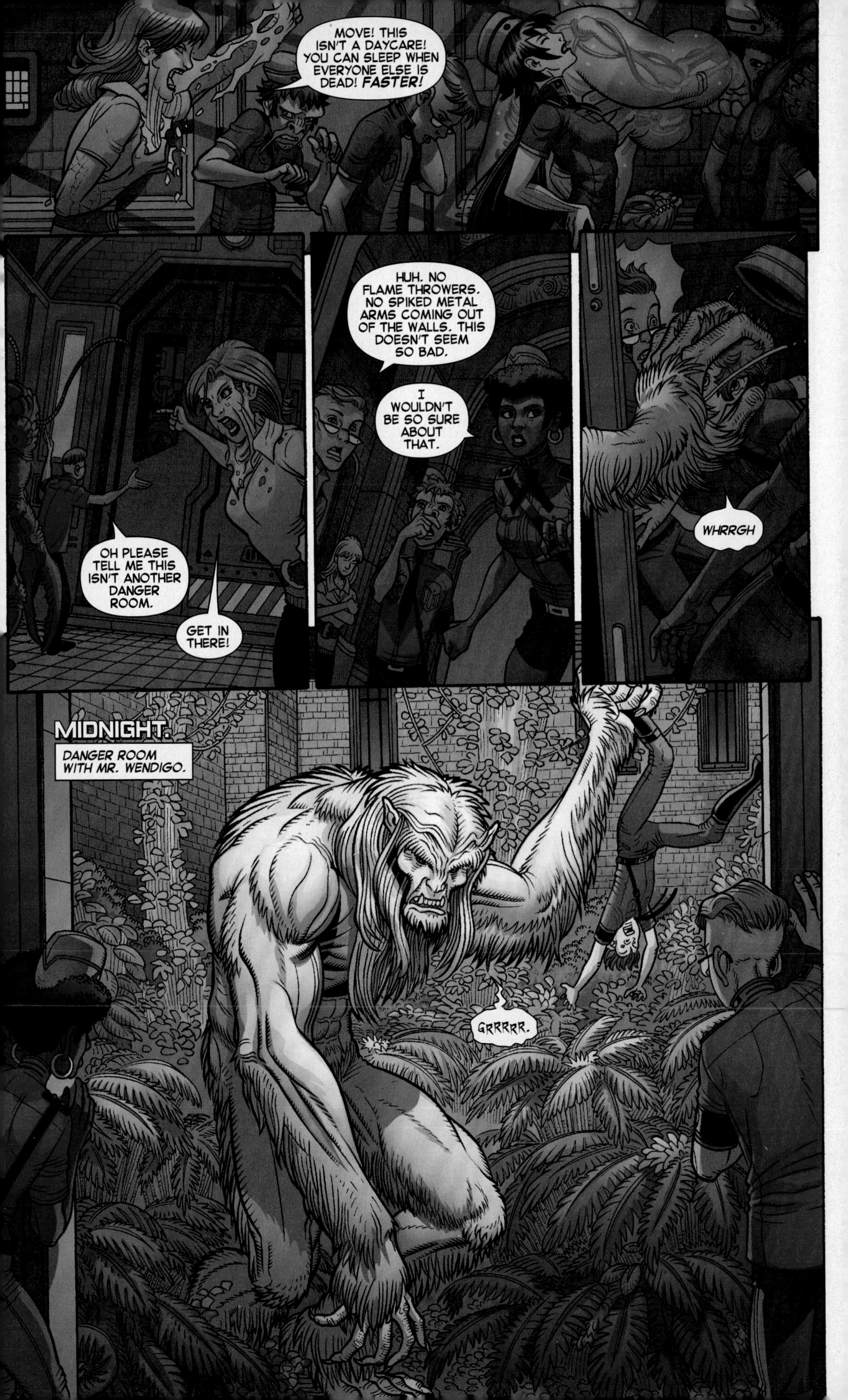
MOVE! THIS ISN'T A DAYCARE! YOU CAN SLEEP WHEN EVERYONE ELSE IS DEAD! *FASTER!*
OH PLEASE TELL ME THIS ISN'T ANOTHER DANGER ROOM.
GET IN THERE!
HUH. NO FLAME THROWERS. NO SPIKED METAL ARMS COMING OUT OF THE WALLS. THIS DOESN'T SEEM SO BAD.
I WOULDN'T BE SO SURE ABOUT THAT.
WHRRGH
MIDNIGHT.
DANGER ROOM WITH MR. WENDIGO.
GRRRRR.

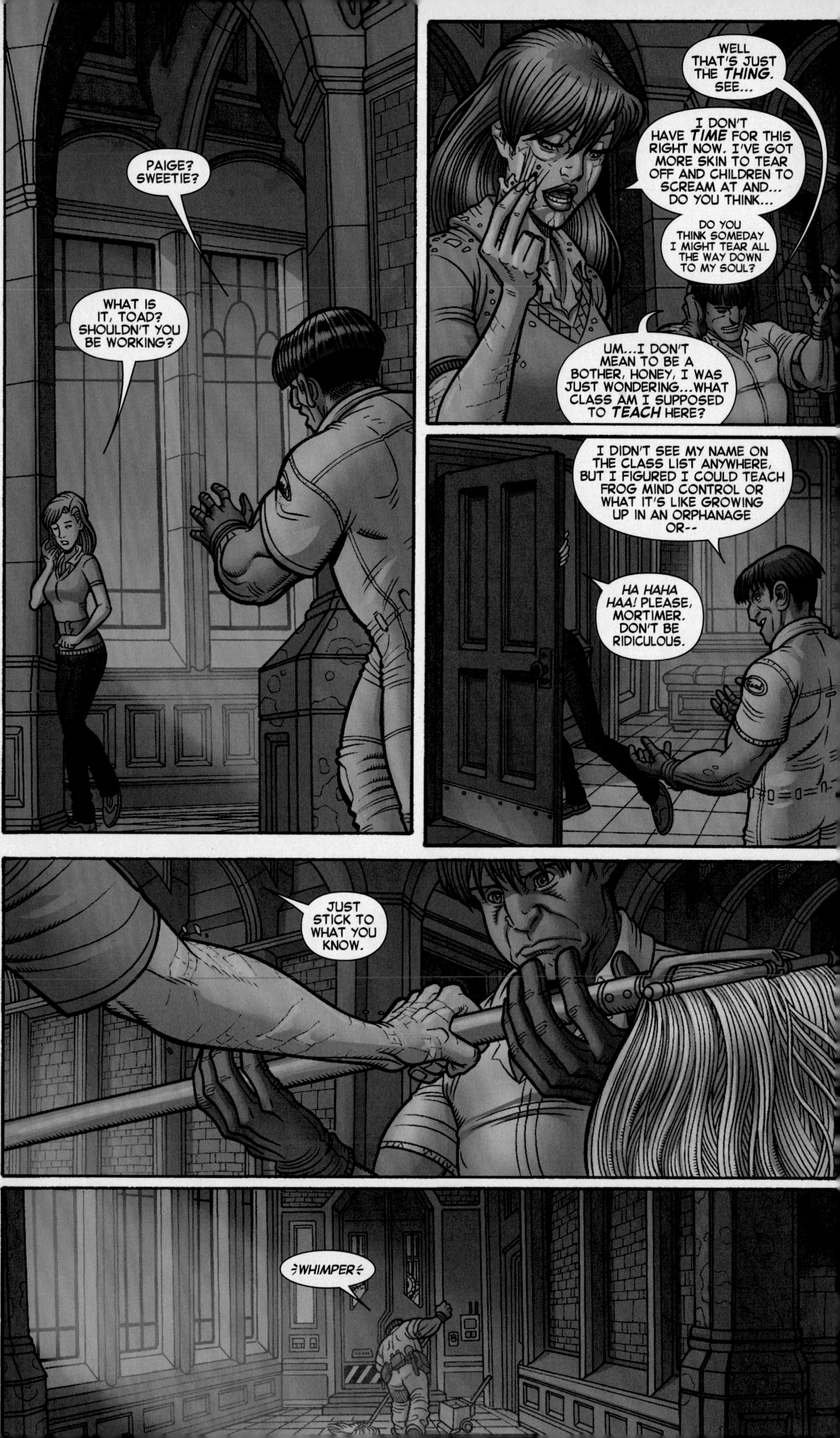
PAIGE? SWEETIE?
WHAT IS IT, TOAD? SHOULDN'T YOU BE WORKING?
WELL THAT'S JUST THE *THING*. SEE...
I DON'T HAVE *TIME* FOR THIS RIGHT NOW. I'VE GOT MORE SKIN TO TEAR OFF AND CHILDREN TO SCREAM AT AND... DO YOU THINK...
DO YOU THINK SOMEDAY I MIGHT TEAR ALL THE WAY DOWN TO MY SOUL?
UM...I DON'T MEAN TO BE A BOTHER, HONEY, I WAS JUST WONDERING...WHAT CLASS AM I SUPPOSED TO *TEACH* HERE?
I DIDN'T SEE MY NAME ON THE CLASS LIST ANYWHERE, BUT I FIGURED I COULD TEACH FROG MIND CONTROL OR WHAT IT'S LIKE GROWING UP IN AN ORPHANAGE OR--
HA HAHA HAA! PLEASE, MORTIMER. DON'T BE RIDICULOUS.
JUST STICK TO WHAT YOU KNOW.
WHIMPER

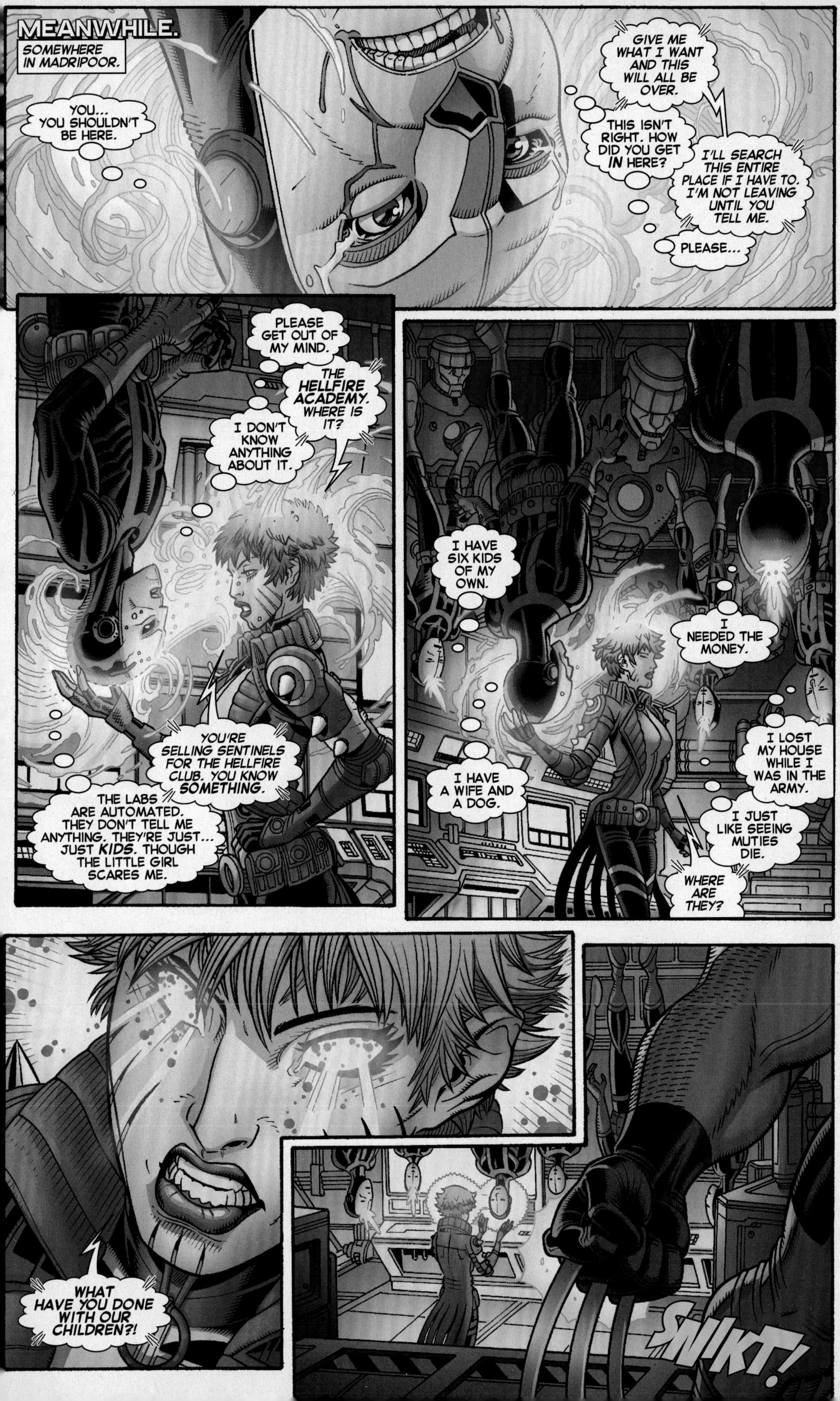
MEANWHILE.
SOMEWHERE IN MADRIPOOR.
YOU... YOU SHOULDN'T BE HERE.
GIVE ME WHAT I WANT AND THIS WILL ALL BE OVER.
THIS ISN'T RIGHT. HOW DID YOU GET IN HERE?
I'LL SEARCH THIS ENTIRE PLACE IF I HAVE TO. I'M NOT LEAVING UNTIL YOU TELL ME.
PLEASE...
PLEASE GET OUT OF MY MIND.
THE HELLFIRE ACADEMY. WHERE IS IT?
I DON'T KNOW ANYTHING ABOUT IT.
YOU'RE SELLING SENTINELS FOR THE HELLFIRE CLUB. YOU KNOW SOMETHING.
THE LABS ARE AUTOMATED. THEY DON'T TELL ME ANYTHING. THEY'RE JUST... JUST KIDS. THOUGH THE LITTLE GIRL SCARES ME.
I HAVE SIX KIDS OF MY OWN.
I NEEDED THE MONEY.
I HAVE A WIFE AND A DOG.
I LOST MY HOUSE WHILE I WAS IN THE ARMY.
I JUST LIKE SEEING MUTIES DIE.
WHERE ARE THEY?
WHAT HAVE YOU DONE WITH OUR CHILDREN?!
SNIKT!

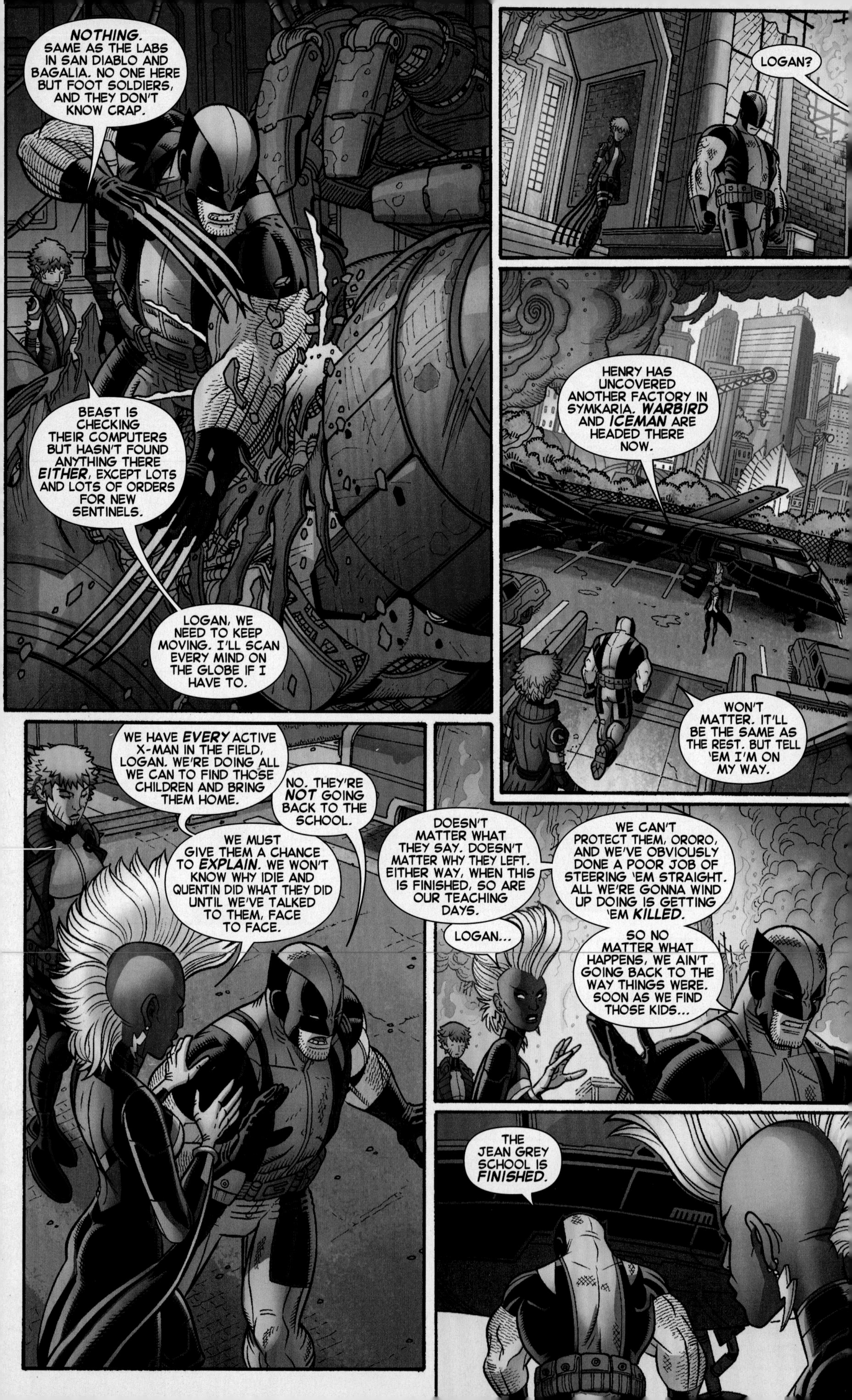
NOTHING. SAME AS THE LABS IN SAN DIABLO AND BAGALIA. NO ONE HERE BUT FOOT SOLDIERS, AND THEY DON'T KNOW CRAP.
BEAST IS CHECKING THEIR COMPUTERS BUT HASN'T FOUND ANYTHING THERE EITHER, EXCEPT LOTS AND LOTS OF ORDERS FOR NEW SENTINELS.
LOGAN, WE NEED TO KEEP MOVING. I'LL SCAN EVERY MIND ON THE GLOBE IF I HAVE TO.
LOGAN?
HENRY HAS UNCOVERED ANOTHER FACTORY IN SYMKARIA. WARBIRD AND ICEMAN ARE HEADED THERE NOW.
WON'T MATTER. IT'LL BE THE SAME AS THE REST. BUT TELL 'EM I'M ON MY WAY.
WE HAVE EVERY ACTIVE X-MAN IN THE FIELD, LOGAN. WE'RE DOING ALL WE CAN TO FIND THOSE CHILDREN AND BRING THEM HOME.
NO. THEY'RE NOT GOING BACK TO THE SCHOOL.
WE MUST GIVE THEM A CHANCE TO EXPLAIN. WE WON'T KNOW WHY IDIE AND QUENTIN DID WHAT THEY DID UNTIL WE'VE TALKED TO THEM, FACE TO FACE.
DOESN'T MATTER WHAT THEY SAY. DOESN'T MATTER WHY THEY LEFT. EITHER WAY, WHEN THIS IS FINISHED, SO ARE OUR TEACHING DAYS.
WE CAN'T PROTECT THEM, ORORO, AND WE'VE OBVIOUSLY DONE A POOR JOB OF STEERING 'EM STRAIGHT. ALL WE'RE GONNA WIND UP DOING IS GETTING 'EM KILLED.
LOGAN...
SO NO MATTER WHAT HAPPENS, WE AIN'T GOING BACK TO THE WAY THINGS WERE. SOON AS WE FIND THOSE KIDS...
THE JEAN GREY SCHOOL IS FINISHED.

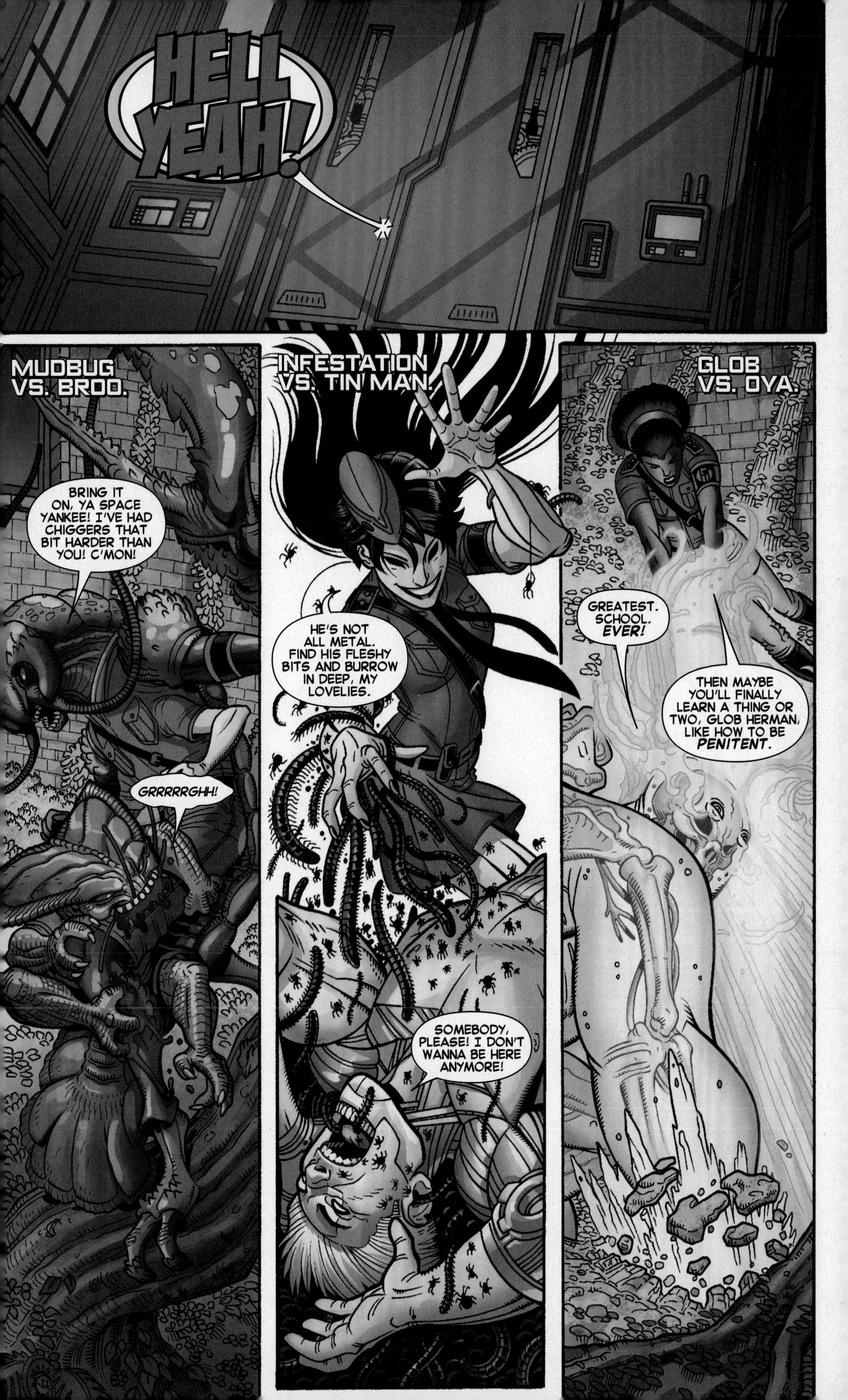
HELL YEAH!
MUDBUG VS. BROO.
BRING IT ON, YA SPACE YANKEE! I'VE HAD CHIGGERS THAT BIT HARDER THAN YOU! C'MON!
GRRRRRGHH!
INFESTATION VS. TIN MAN.
HE'S NOT ALL METAL. FIND HIS FLESHY BITS AND BURROW IN DEEP, MY LOVELIES.
SOMEBODY, PLEASE! I DON'T WANNA BE HERE ANYMORE!
GLOB VS. OYA.
GREATEST. SCHOOL. *EVER!*
THEN MAYBE YOU'LL FINALLY LEARN A THING OR TWO, GLOB HERMAN, LIKE HOW TO BE *PENITENT*.

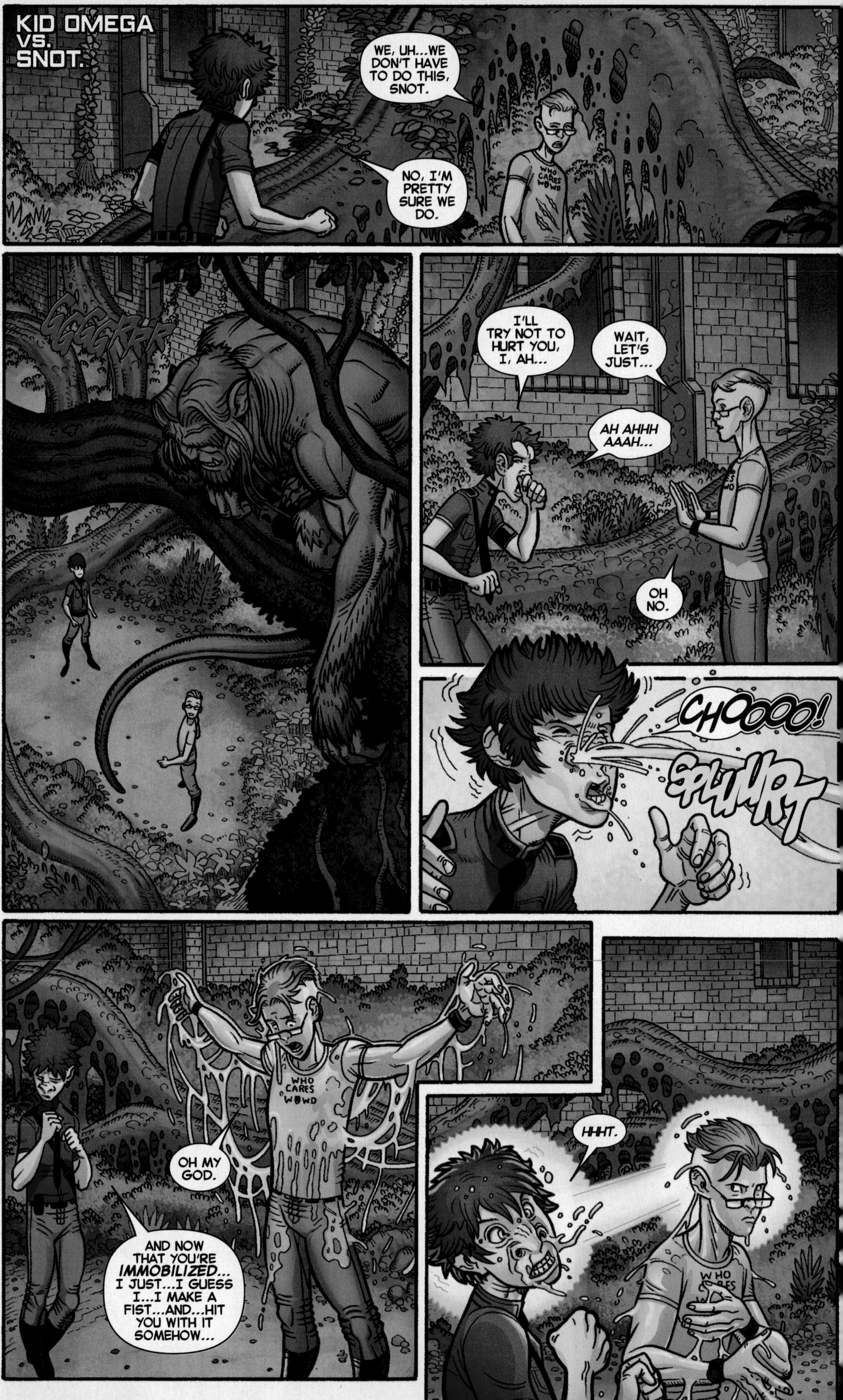
KID OMEGA VS. SNOT.
WE, UH...WE DON'T HAVE TO DO THIS, SNOT.
NO, I'M PRETTY SURE WE DO.
GGGGRRR
I'LL TRY NOT TO HURT YOU, I, AH...
WAIT, LET'S JUST...
AH AHHH AAAH...
OH NO.
CHOOOOO!
SPLURT
OH MY GOD.
AND NOW THAT YOU'RE IMMOBILIZED... I JUST...I GUESS I...I MAKE A FIST...AND...HIT YOU WITH IT SOMEHOW...
HHHT.

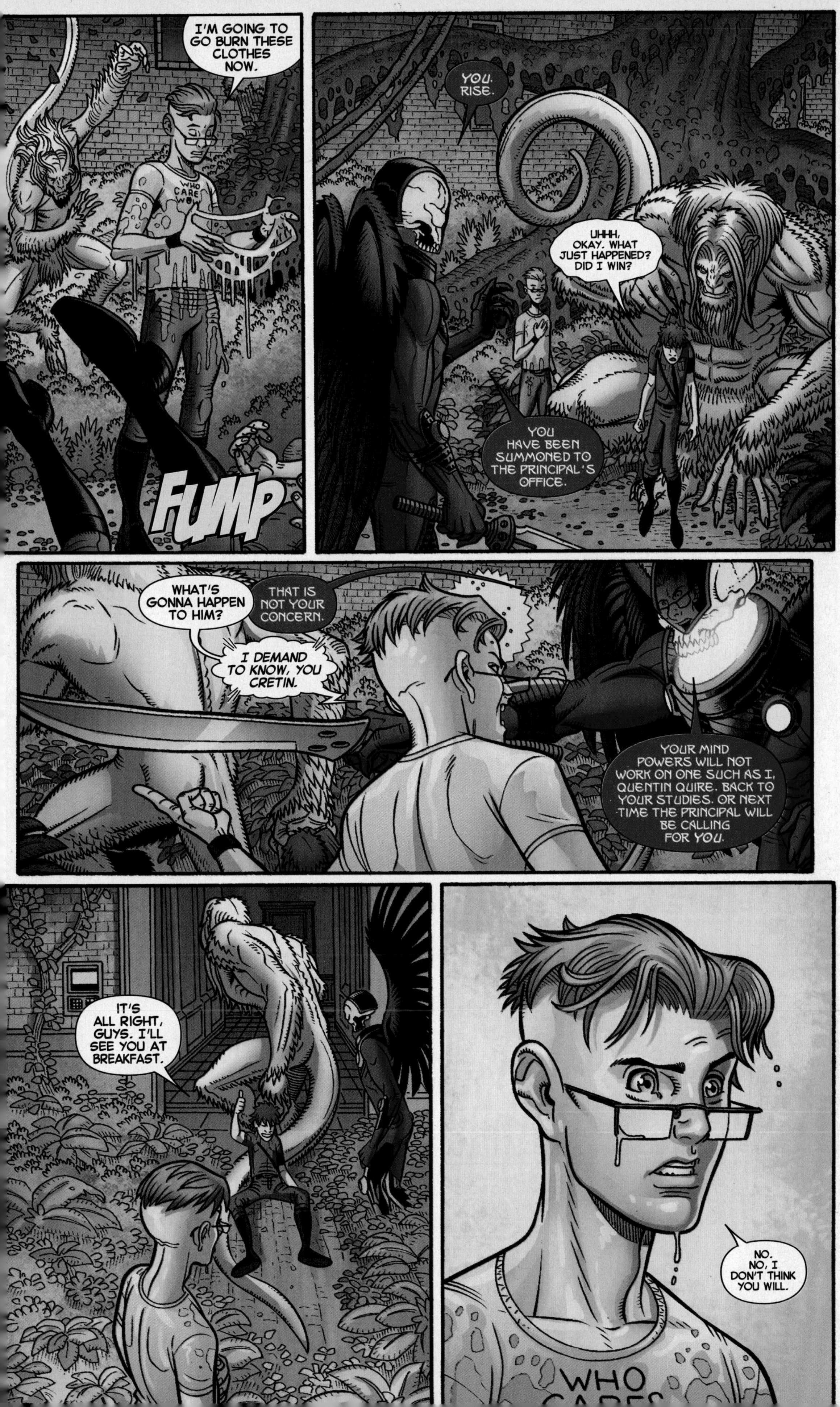
I'M GOING TO GO BURN THESE CLOTHES NOW.
FUMP
YOU. RISE.
UHHH, OKAY. WHAT JUST HAPPENED? DID I WIN?
YOU HAVE BEEN SUMMONED TO THE PRINCIPAL'S OFFICE.
WHAT'S GONNA HAPPEN TO HIM?
THAT IS NOT YOUR CONCERN.
I DEMAND TO KNOW, YOU CRETIN.
YOUR MIND POWERS WILL NOT WORK ON ONE SUCH AS I, QUENTIN QUIRE. BACK TO YOUR STUDIES. OR NEXT TIME THE PRINCIPAL WILL BE CALLING FOR YOU.
IT'S ALL RIGHT, GUYS. I'LL SEE YOU AT BREAKFAST.
NO. NO, I DON'T THINK YOU WILL.

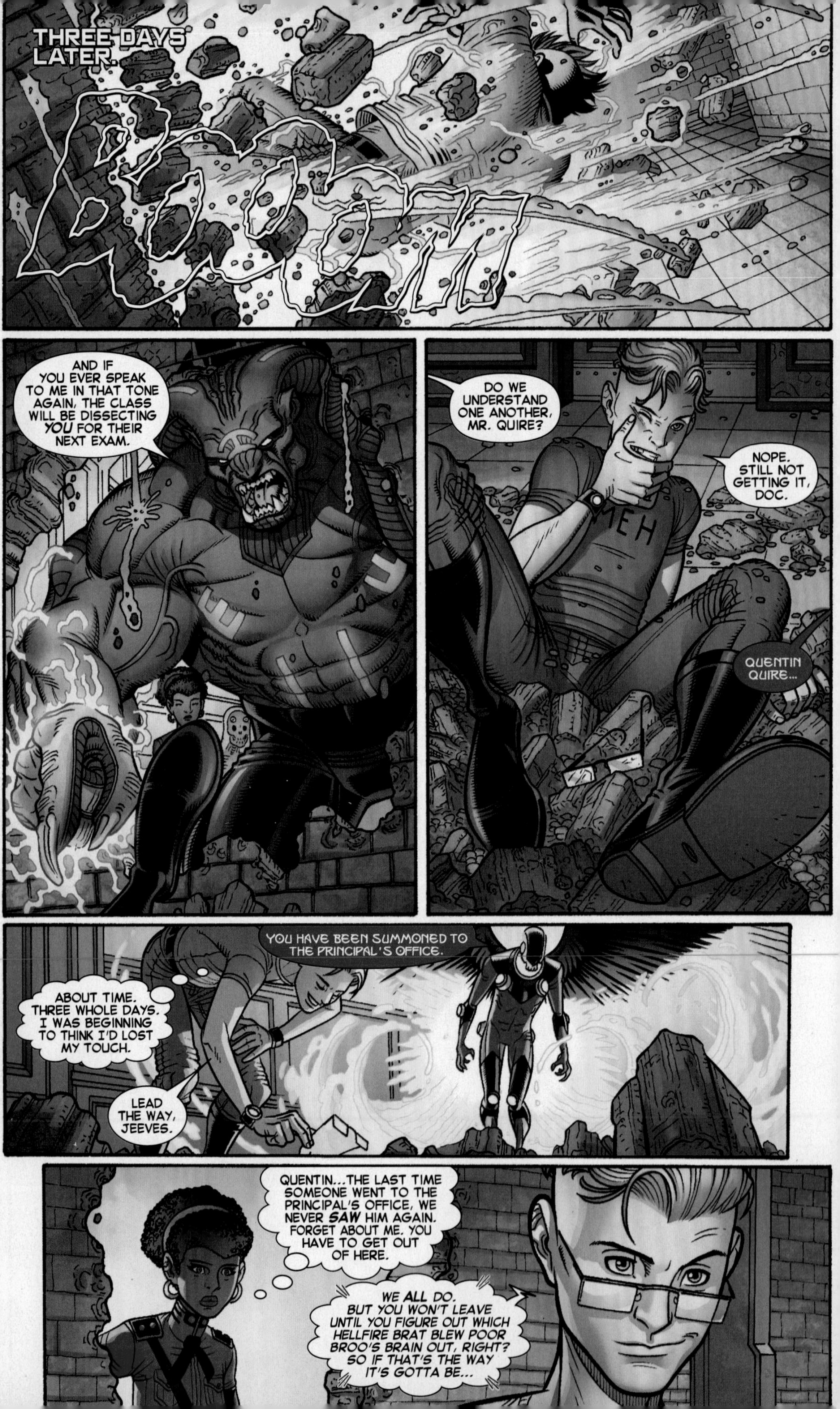
THREE DAYS LATER.
BOOOM
AND IF YOU EVER SPEAK TO ME IN THAT TONE AGAIN, THE CLASS WILL BE DISSECTING YOU FOR THEIR NEXT EXAM.
DO WE UNDERSTAND ONE ANOTHER, MR. QUIRE?
NOPE. STILL NOT GETTING IT, DOC.
MEH
QUENTIN QUIRE...
YOU HAVE BEEN SUMMONED TO THE PRINCIPAL'S OFFICE.
ABOUT TIME. THREE WHOLE DAYS. I WAS BEGINNING TO THINK I'D LOST MY TOUCH.
LEAD THE WAY, JEEVES.
QUENTIN...THE LAST TIME SOMEONE WENT TO THE PRINCIPAL'S OFFICE, WE NEVER SAW HIM AGAIN. FORGET ABOUT ME. YOU HAVE TO GET OUT OF HERE.
WE ALL DO. BUT YOU WON'T LEAVE UNTIL YOU FIGURE OUT WHICH HELLFIRE BRAT BLEW POOR BROO'S BRAIN OUT, RIGHT? SO IF THAT'S THE WAY IT'S GOTTA BE...

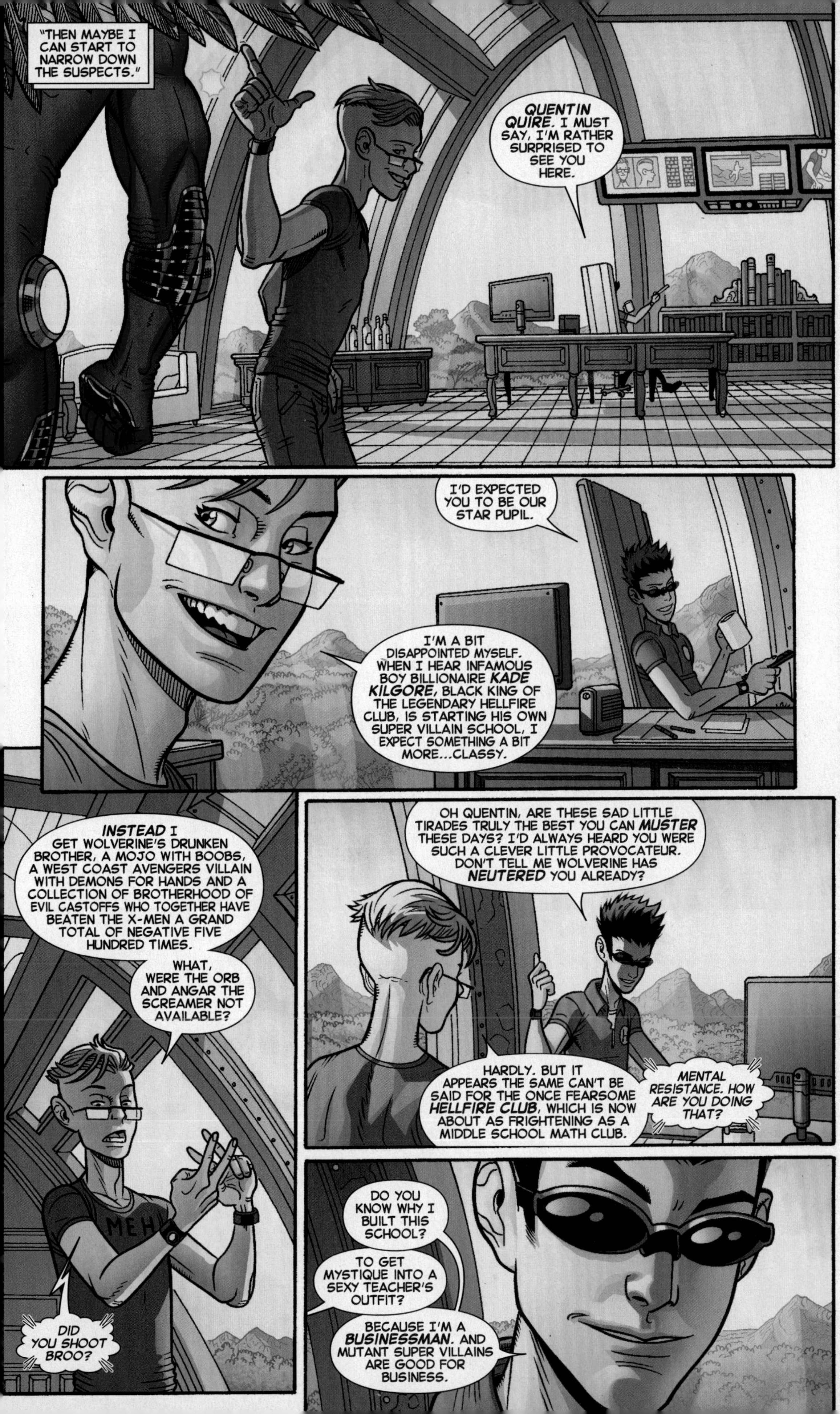

"THEN MAYBE I CAN START TO NARROW DOWN THE SUSPECTS."
QUENTIN QUIRE. I MUST SAY, I'M RATHER SURPRISED TO SEE YOU HERE.
I'D EXPECTED YOU TO BE OUR STAR PUPIL.
I'M A BIT DISAPPOINTED MYSELF. WHEN I HEAR INFAMOUS BOY BILLIONAIRE KADE KILGORE, BLACK KING OF THE LEGENDARY HELLFIRE CLUB, IS STARTING HIS OWN SUPER VILLAIN SCHOOL, I EXPECT SOMETHING A BIT MORE...CLASSY.
INSTEAD I GET WOLVERINE'S DRUNKEN BROTHER, A MOJO WITH BOOBS, A WEST COAST AVENGERS VILLAIN WITH DEMONS FOR HANDS AND A COLLECTION OF BROTHERHOOD OF EVIL CASTOFFS WHO TOGETHER HAVE BEATEN THE X-MEN A GRAND TOTAL OF NEGATIVE FIVE HUNDRED TIMES.
WHAT, WERE THE ORB AND ANGAR THE SCREAMER NOT AVAILABLE?
MEH
DID YOU SHOOT BROO?
OH QUENTIN, ARE THESE SAD LITTLE TIRADES TRULY THE BEST YOU CAN MUSTER THESE DAYS? I'D ALWAYS HEARD YOU WERE SUCH A CLEVER LITTLE PROVOCATEUR. DON'T TELL ME WOLVERINE HAS NEUTERED YOU ALREADY?
HARDLY. BUT IT APPEARS THE SAME CAN'T BE SAID FOR THE ONCE FEARSOME HELLFIRE CLUB, WHICH IS NOW ABOUT AS FRIGHTENING AS A MIDDLE SCHOOL MATH CLUB.
MENTAL RESISTANCE. HOW ARE YOU DOING THAT?
DO YOU KNOW WHY I BUILT THIS SCHOOL?
TO GET MYSTIQUE INTO A SEXY TEACHER'S OUTFIT?
BECAUSE I'M A BUSINESSMAN. AND MUTANT SUPER VILLAINS ARE GOOD FOR BUSINESS.

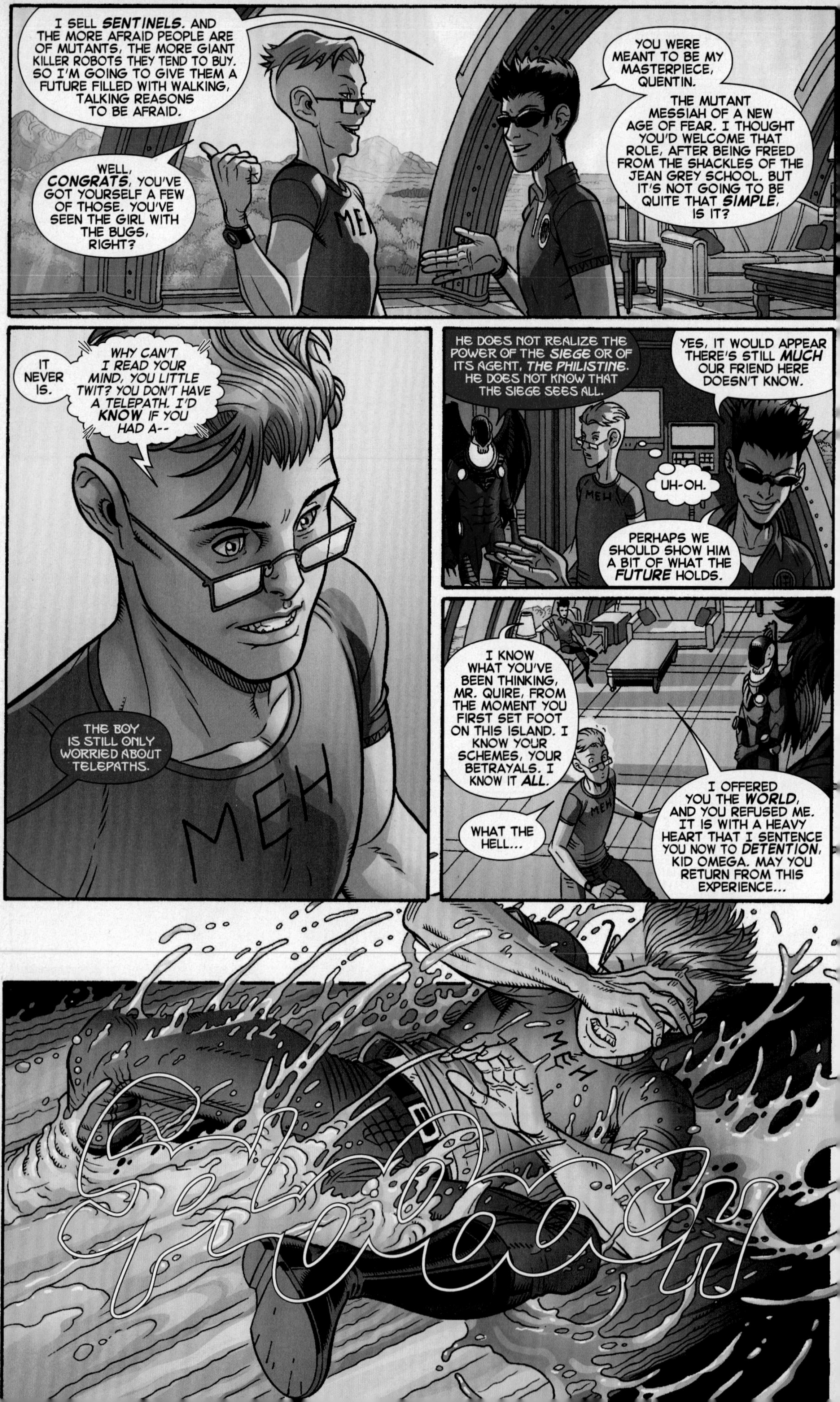
I SELL SENTINELS. AND THE MORE AFRAID PEOPLE ARE OF MUTANTS, THE MORE GIANT KILLER ROBOTS THEY TEND TO BUY. SO I'M GOING TO GIVE THEM A FUTURE FILLED WITH WALKING, TALKING REASONS TO BE AFRAID.
WELL, CONGRATS, YOU'VE GOT YOURSELF A FEW OF THOSE. YOU'VE SEEN THE GIRL WITH THE BUGS, RIGHT?
YOU WERE MEANT TO BE MY MASTERPIECE, QUENTIN.
THE MUTANT MESSIAH OF A NEW AGE OF FEAR. I THOUGHT YOU'D WELCOME THAT ROLE, AFTER BEING FREED FROM THE SHACKLES OF THE JEAN GREY SCHOOL. BUT IT'S NOT GOING TO BE QUITE THAT SIMPLE, IS IT?
IT NEVER IS.
WHY CAN'T I READ YOUR MIND, YOU LITTLE TWIT? YOU DON'T HAVE A TELEPATH. I'D KNOW IF YOU HAD A--
THE BOY IS STILL ONLY WORRIED ABOUT TELEPATHS.
HE DOES NOT REALIZE THE POWER OF THE SIEGE OR OF ITS AGENT, THE PHILISTINE. HE DOES NOT KNOW THAT THE SIEGE SEES ALL.
YES, IT WOULD APPEAR THERE'S STILL MUCH OUR FRIEND HERE DOESN'T KNOW.
UH-OH.
PERHAPS WE SHOULD SHOW HIM A BIT OF WHAT THE FUTURE HOLDS.
I KNOW WHAT YOU'VE BEEN THINKING, MR. QUIRE, FROM THE MOMENT YOU FIRST SET FOOT ON THIS ISLAND. I KNOW YOUR SCHEMES, YOUR BETRAYALS. I KNOW IT ALL.
WHAT THE HELL...
I OFFERED YOU THE WORLD, AND YOU REFUSED ME. IT IS WITH A HEAVY HEART THAT I SENTENCE YOU NOW TO DETENTION, KID OMEGA. MAY YOU RETURN FROM THIS EXPERIENCE...
SPLOOSH

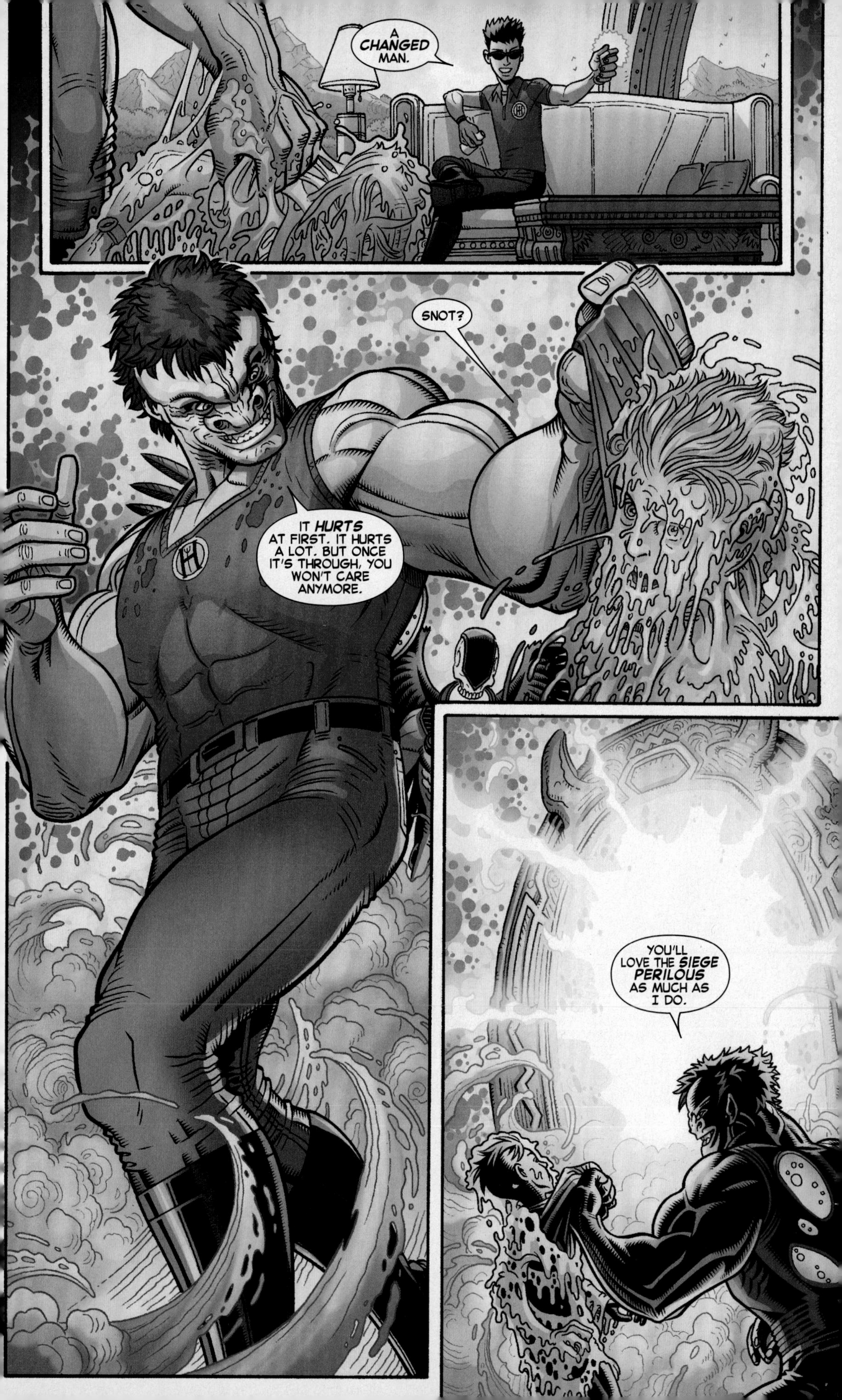
A CHANGED MAN.
SNOT?
IT HURTS AT FIRST. IT HURTS A LOT. BUT ONCE IT'S THROUGH, YOU WON'T CARE ANYMORE.
YOU'LL LOVE THE SIEGE PERILOUS AS MUCH AS I DO.

HELLFIRE ACADEMY

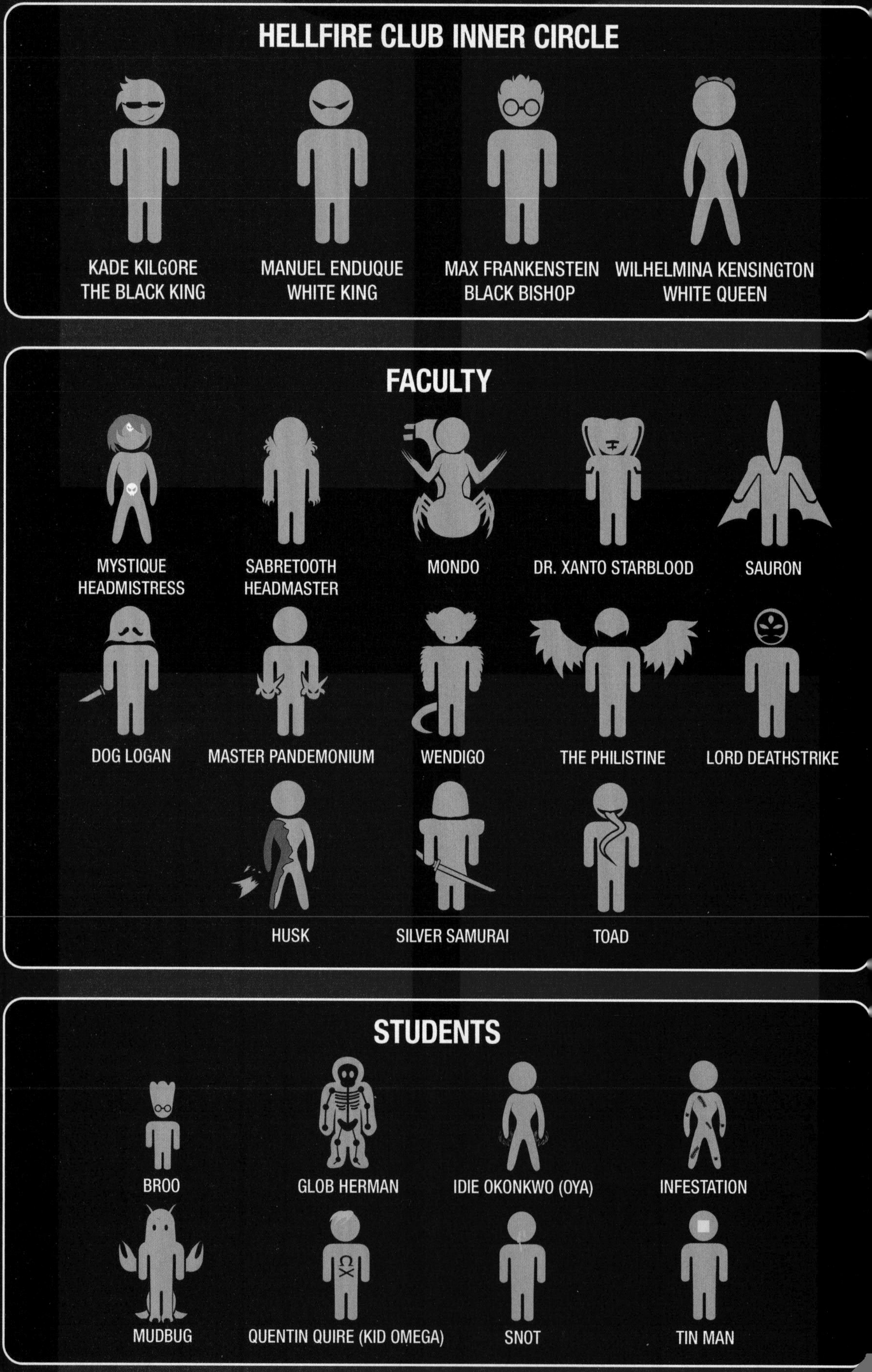
HELLFIRE CLUB INNER CIRCLE
KADE KILGORE
THE BLACK KING
MANUEL ENDUQUE
WHITE KING
MAX FRANKENSTEIN
BLACK BISHOP
WILHELMINA KENSINGTON
WHITE QUEEN
FACULTY
MYSTIQUE
HEADMISTRESS
SABRETOOTH
HEADMASTER
MONDO
DR. XANTO STARBLOOD
SAURON
DOG LOGAN
MASTER PANDEMONIUM
WENDIGO
THE PHILISTINE
LORD DEATHSTRIKE
HUSK
SILVER SAMURAI
TOAD
STUDENTS
BROO
GLOB HERMAN
IDIE OKONKWO (OYA)
INFESTATION
MUDBUG
QUENTIN QUIRE (KID OMEGA)
SNOT
TIN MAN

HELLFIRE ACADEMY

"FAIS CE QUE TU VOUDRAS."

HELLFIRE ACADEMY CLASS LIST

Ethics 101: Do What Thou Wilt, with Professor Raven Darkholme

Hell Lit: Reading the Infernal Classics, from the Darkhold to the Necronomicon, with Master Pandemonium

Defying the Will of God: The Titillating Thrill of Genetic Manipulation, with Dr. Karl Lykos

Science and Weaponry: Better Living Through Superior Firepower, with Dr. Xanto Starblood

Physical Education: The Krakoa Survival Hour, with Coach Dog Logan

Danger Room, with Mr. Wendigo

Public Relations for Psychopaths: The Marketing of Terror, with Madame Mondo

Public Speaking for Super Villains: Delivering the Perfect Soliloquy, with Madame Mondo

Subjugation Through Science: Experiments So Simple Even An Absolute Moron Like You Can Do Them, with Dr. Karl Lyko

Dealing with the Devil: How to Get the Most In Exchange for Your Soul, with Master Pandemonium

Xenobiology and the Art of Evisceration, with Dr. Xanto Starblood

The Art of Trolling: Using Social Media for Evil, with Madame Mondo

Senseless Destruction of Property, with Mr. Wendigo

99 Reasons to Hate Wolverine, with Coach Dog Logan

Coming Back From the Dead: It's Easier Than You Might Think, with Professor Darkholme

EXTRACARICULAR ACTIVITIES

Necromancer Club, with Maximilian Frankenstein

High Stakes Poker Club, with Manuel Enduque

Killing and Eating Other Mammals Club, with Mr. Wendigo

Debate Team! With Husk!! Prepare to be screamed at!!!

Movie Club, with Madame Mondo, reviewing the films of Welles, Kurosawa, Kubrick and Mojo

Dolphin Shooting Club, with Lord Deathstrike

SPECIAL EVENTS

"Stabbing for Fun and Profit." A guest lecture by Victor Creed

Ritual seppuku demonstration, with the Silver Samurai (volunteers needed)

First Annual Little Miss Hellfire Beauty Pageant/Swordfighting Competition, Featuring the White Queen, Wilhelmina Kensington (NOTE: No other entries allowed)

"Driving on the Highway to Hell." A guest lecture by The Highwayman

A special sneak-peek of the Fall Munitions Catalogue from Kilgore Arms

And mandatory field trips to Planet Sin, Mole Man's Subterranea, Madripoor's Lowtown, Monster Island, the Negative Zone, Isla Des Demonas, the Frostbite Mountains of Jotunheim and a Latverian soccer match.

32 "THE HELLFIRE SAGA" PART TWO

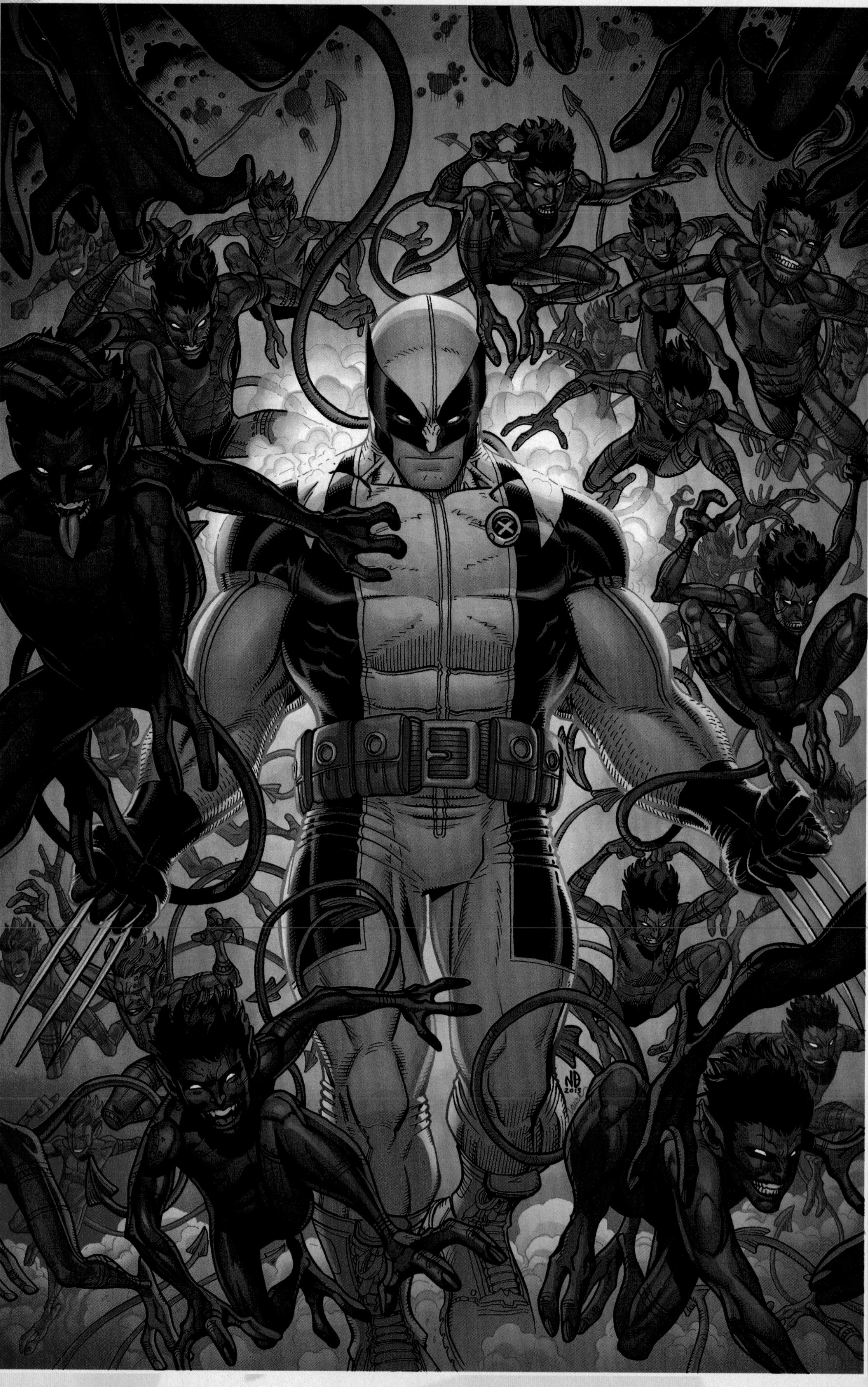

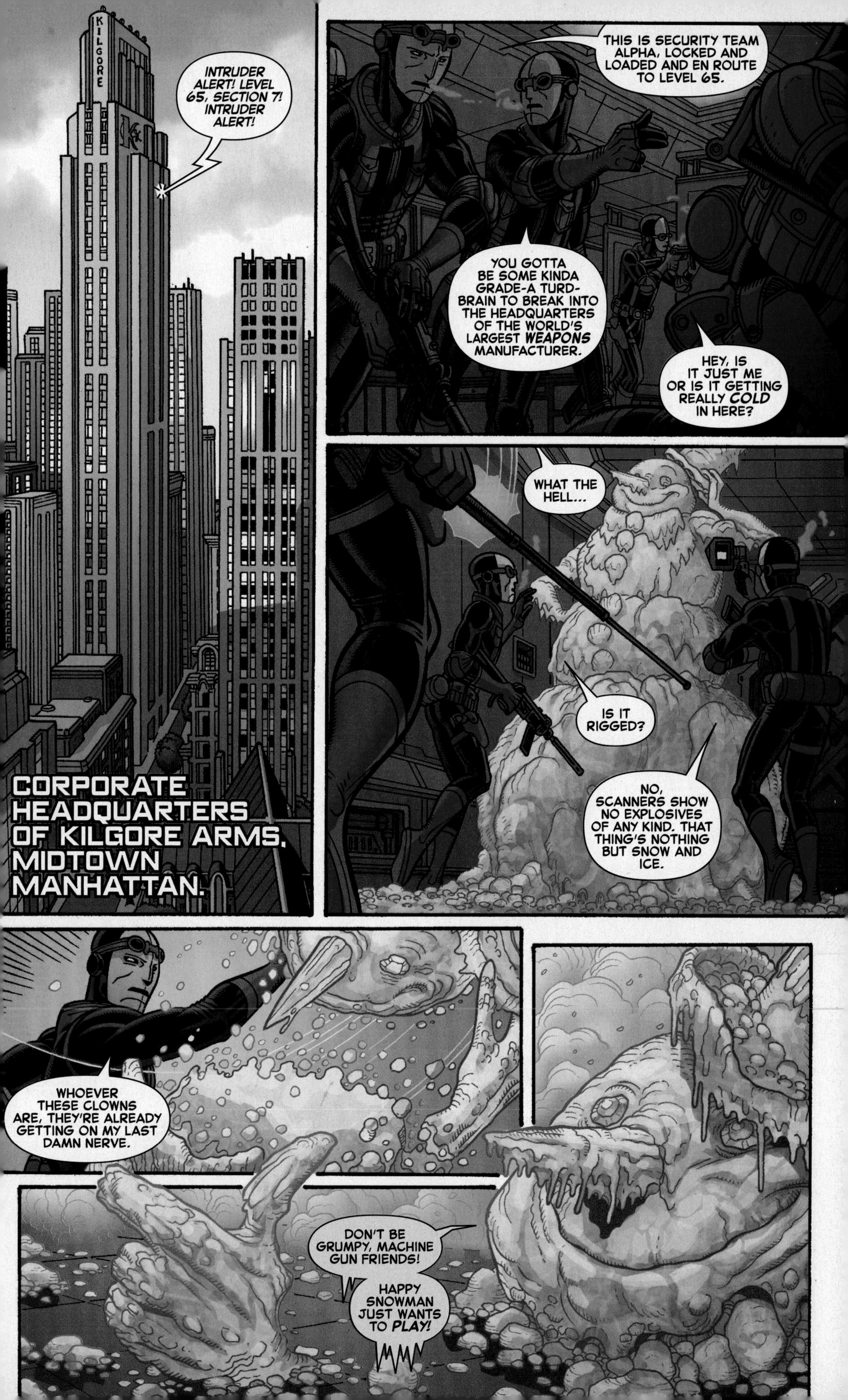
INTRUDER ALERT! LEVEL 65, SECTION 7! INTRUDER ALERT!
CORPORATE HEADQUARTERS OF KILGORE ARMS, MIDTOWN MANHATTAN.
THIS IS SECURITY TEAM ALPHA, LOCKED AND LOADED AND EN ROUTE TO LEVEL 65.
YOU GOTTA BE SOME KINDA GRADE-A TURD-BRAIN TO BREAK INTO THE HEADQUARTERS OF THE WORLD'S LARGEST WEAPONS MANUFACTURER.
HEY, IS IT JUST ME OR IS IT GETTING REALLY COLD IN HERE?
WHAT THE HELL...
IS IT RIGGED?
NO, SCANNERS SHOW NO EXPLOSIVES OF ANY KIND. THAT THING'S NOTHING BUT SNOW AND ICE.
WHOEVER THESE CLOWNS ARE, THEY'RE ALREADY GETTING ON MY LAST DAMN NERVE.
DON'T BE GRUMPY, MACHINE GUN FRIENDS!
HAPPY SNOWMAN JUST WANTS TO PLAY!

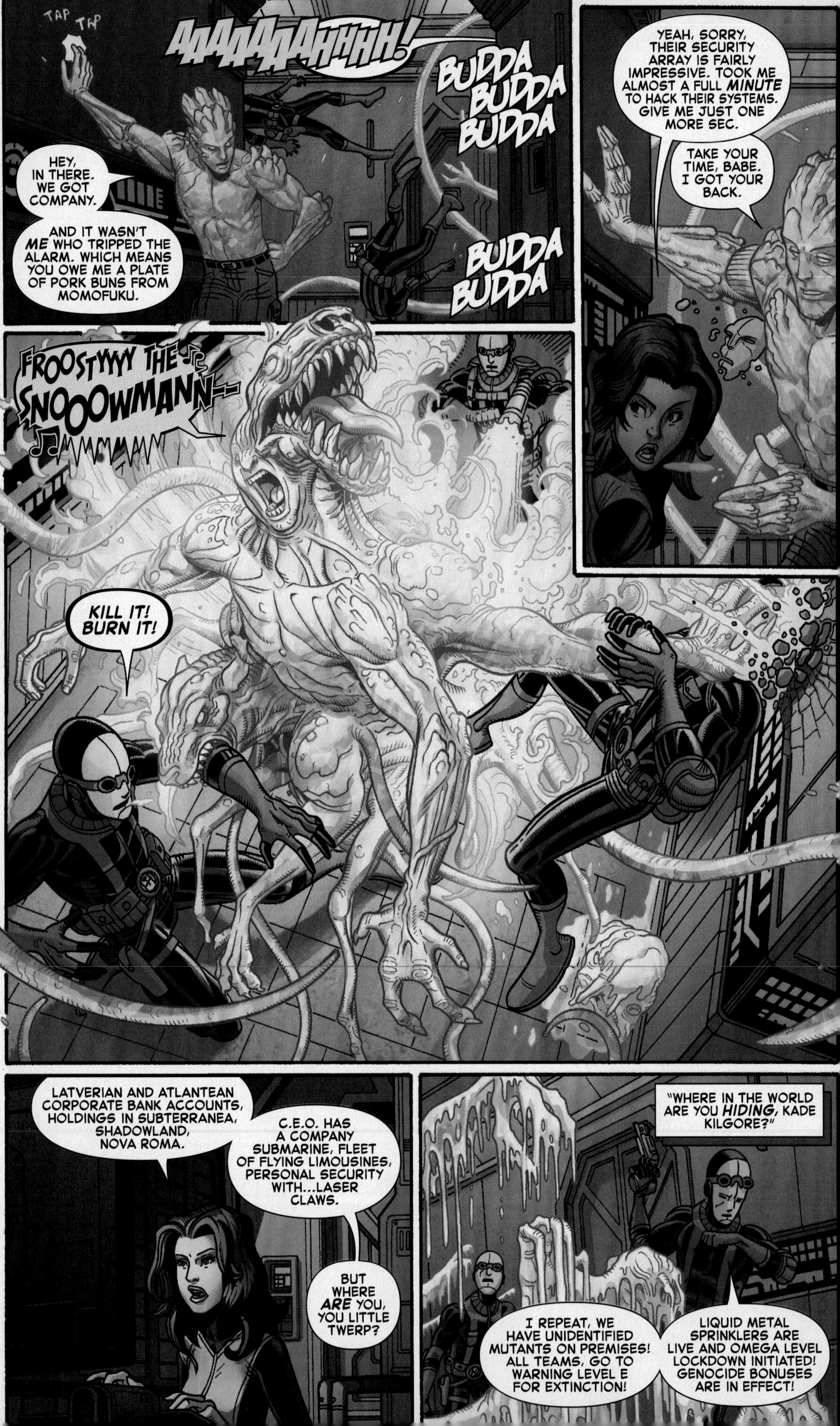
TAP TAP
AAAAAAAAHHHH!
BUDDA BUDDA BUDDA
HEY, IN THERE. WE GOT COMPANY.
AND IT WASN'T ME WHO TRIPPED THE ALARM. WHICH MEANS YOU OWE ME A PLATE OF PORK BUNS FROM MOMOFUKU.
BUDDA BUDDA
YEAH, SORRY, THEIR SECURITY ARRAY IS FAIRLY IMPRESSIVE. TOOK ME ALMOST A FULL MINUTE TO HACK THEIR SYSTEMS. GIVE ME JUST ONE MORE SEC.
TAKE YOUR TIME, BABE. I GOT YOUR BACK.
FROOSTYYYY THE SNOOOWMANN--
KILL IT! BURN IT!
LATVERIAN AND ATLANTEAN CORPORATE BANK ACCOUNTS, HOLDINGS IN SUBTERRANEA, SHADOWLAND, NOVA ROMA.
C.E.O. HAS A COMPANY SUBMARINE, FLEET OF FLYING LIMOUSINES, PERSONAL SECURITY WITH...LASER CLAWS.
BUT WHERE ARE YOU, YOU LITTLE TWERP?
"WHERE IN THE WORLD ARE YOU HIDING, KADE KILGORE?"
I REPEAT, WE HAVE UNIDENTIFIED MUTANTS ON PREMISES! ALL TEAMS, GO TO WARNING LEVEL E FOR EXTINCTION!
LIQUID METAL SPRINKLERS ARE LIVE AND OMEGA LEVEL LOCKDOWN INITIATED! GENOCIDE BONUSES ARE IN EFFECT!

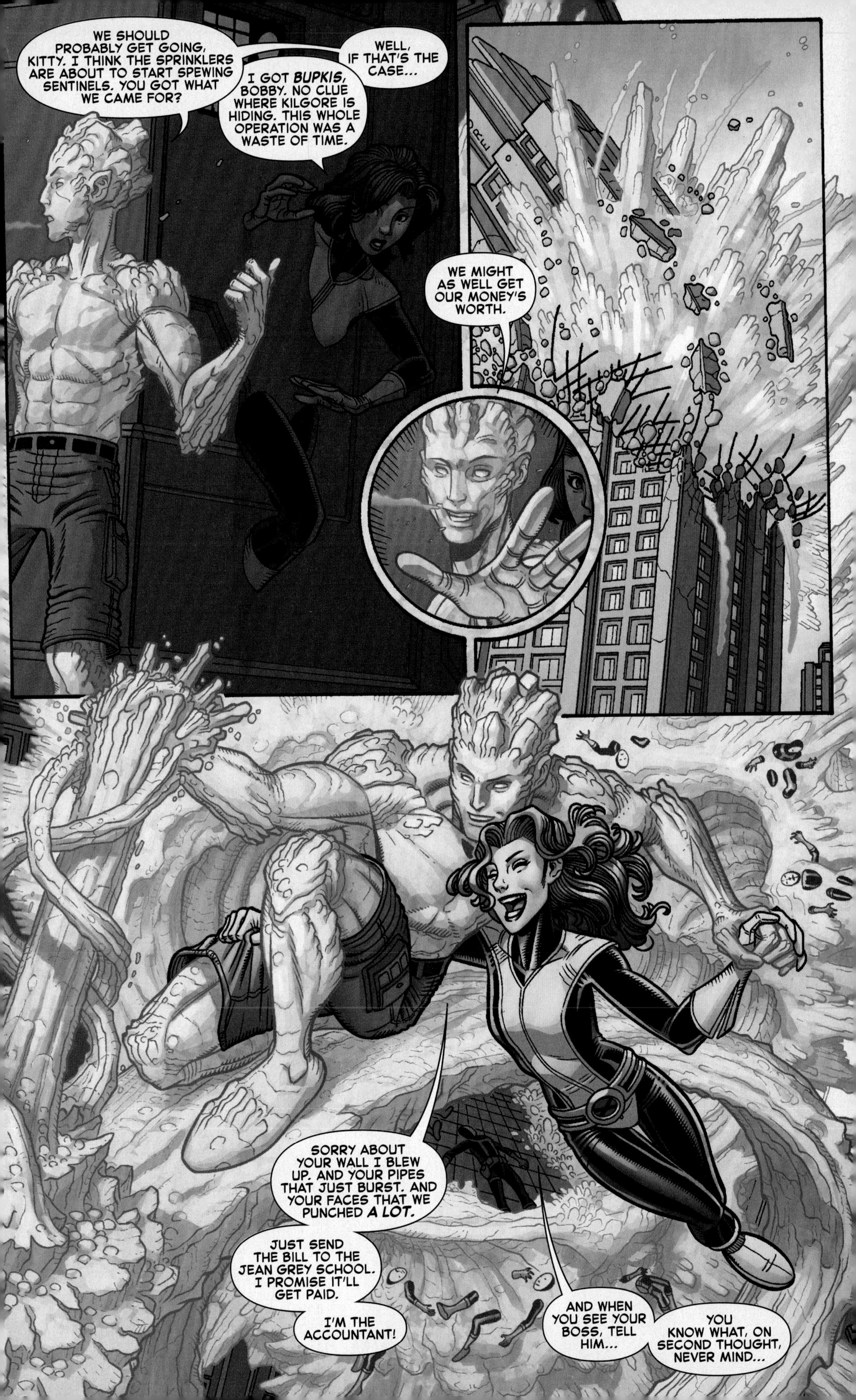
WE SHOULD PROBABLY GET GOING, KITTY. I THINK THE SPRINKLERS ARE ABOUT TO START SPEWING SENTINELS. YOU GOT WHAT WE CAME FOR?
I GOT BUPKIS, BOBBY. NO CLUE WHERE KILGORE IS HIDING. THIS WHOLE OPERATION WAS A WASTE OF TIME.
WELL, IF THAT'S THE CASE...
WE MIGHT AS WELL GET OUR MONEY'S WORTH.
SORRY ABOUT YOUR WALL I BLEW UP. AND YOUR PIPES THAT JUST BURST. AND YOUR FACES THAT WE PUNCHED A LOT.
JUST SEND THE BILL TO THE JEAN GREY SCHOOL. I PROMISE IT'LL GET PAID.
I'M THE ACCOUNTANT!
AND WHEN YOU SEE YOUR BOSS, TELL HIM...
YOU KNOW WHAT, ON SECOND THOUGHT, NEVER MIND...

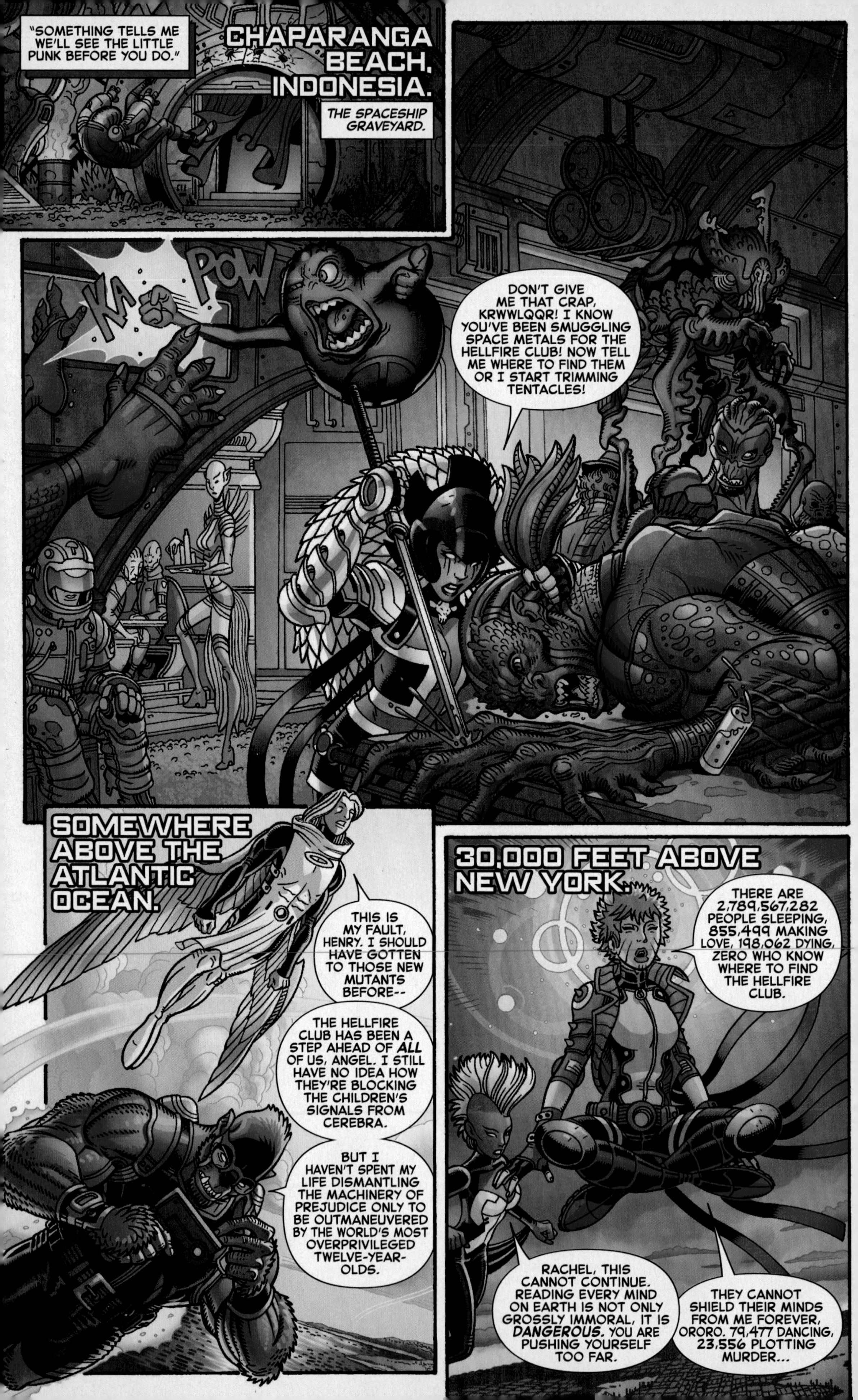
"SOMETHING TELLS ME WE'LL SEE THE LITTLE PUNK BEFORE YOU DO."
CHAPARANGA BEACH, INDONESIA.
THE SPACESHIP GRAVEYARD.
KA POW
DON'T GIVE ME THAT CRAP, KRWWLQQR! I KNOW YOU'VE BEEN SMUGGLING SPACE METALS FOR THE HELLFIRE CLUB! NOW TELL ME WHERE TO FIND THEM OR I START TRIMMING TENTACLES!
SOMEWHERE ABOVE THE ATLANTIC OCEAN.
THIS IS MY FAULT, HENRY. I SHOULD HAVE GOTTEN TO THOSE NEW MUTANTS BEFORE--
THE HELLFIRE CLUB HAS BEEN A STEP AHEAD OF ALL OF US, ANGEL. I STILL HAVE NO IDEA HOW THEY'RE BLOCKING THE CHILDREN'S SIGNALS FROM CEREBRA.
BUT I HAVEN'T SPENT MY LIFE DISMANTLING THE MACHINERY OF PREJUDICE ONLY TO BE OUTMANEUVERED BY THE WORLD'S MOST OVERPRIVILEGED TWELVE-YEAR-OLDS.
30,000 FEET ABOVE NEW YORK.
THERE ARE 2,789,567,282 PEOPLE SLEEPING, 855,499 MAKING LOVE, 198,062 DYING, ZERO WHO KNOW WHERE TO FIND THE HELLFIRE CLUB.
RACHEL, THIS CANNOT CONTINUE. READING EVERY MIND ON EARTH IS NOT ONLY GROSSLY IMMORAL, IT IS DANGEROUS. YOU ARE PUSHING YOURSELF TOO FAR.
THEY CANNOT SHIELD THEIR MINDS FROM ME FOREVER, ORORO. 79,477 DANCING, 23,556 PLOTTING MURDER...

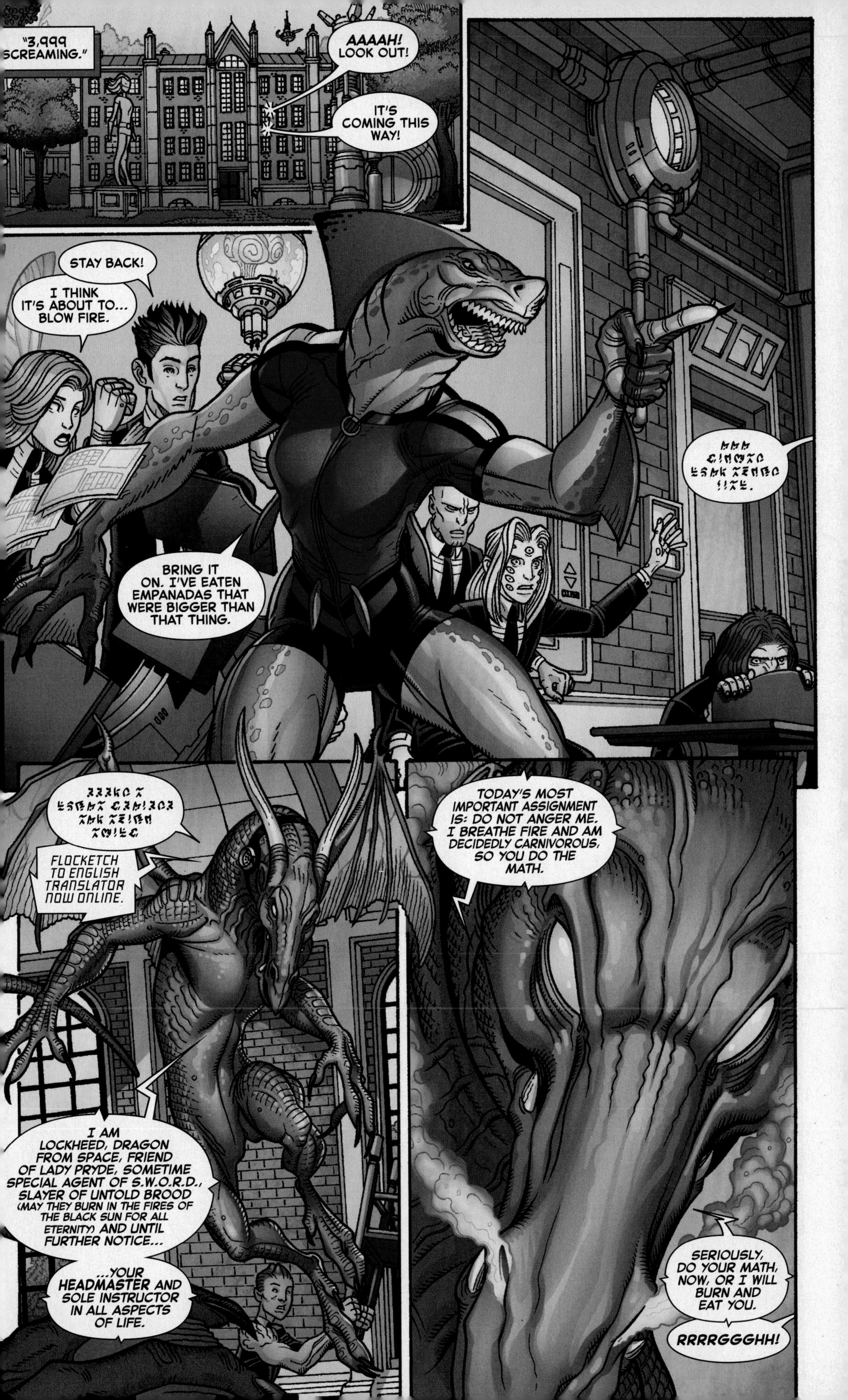
"3,999 SCREAMING."
AAAAH! LOOK OUT!
IT'S COMING THIS WAY!
STAY BACK!
I THINK IT'S ABOUT TO... BLOW FIRE.
BRING IT ON. I'VE EATEN EMPANADAS THAT WERE BIGGER THAN THAT THING.
FLOCKETCH TO ENGLISH TRANSLATOR NOW ONLINE.
TODAY'S MOST IMPORTANT ASSIGNMENT IS: DO NOT ANGER ME. I BREATHE FIRE AND AM DECIDEDLY CARNIVOROUS, SO YOU DO THE MATH.
I AM LOCKHEED, DRAGON FROM SPACE, FRIEND OF LADY PRYDE, SOMETIME SPECIAL AGENT OF S.W.O.R.D., SLAYER OF UNTOLD BROOD (MAY THEY BURN IN THE FIRES OF THE BLACK SUN FOR ALL ETERNITY) AND UNTIL FURTHER NOTICE...
...YOUR HEADMASTER AND SOLE INSTRUCTOR IN ALL ASPECTS OF LIFE.
SERIOUSLY, DO YOUR MATH, NOW, OR I WILL BURN AND EAT YOU.
RRRRGGGHH!

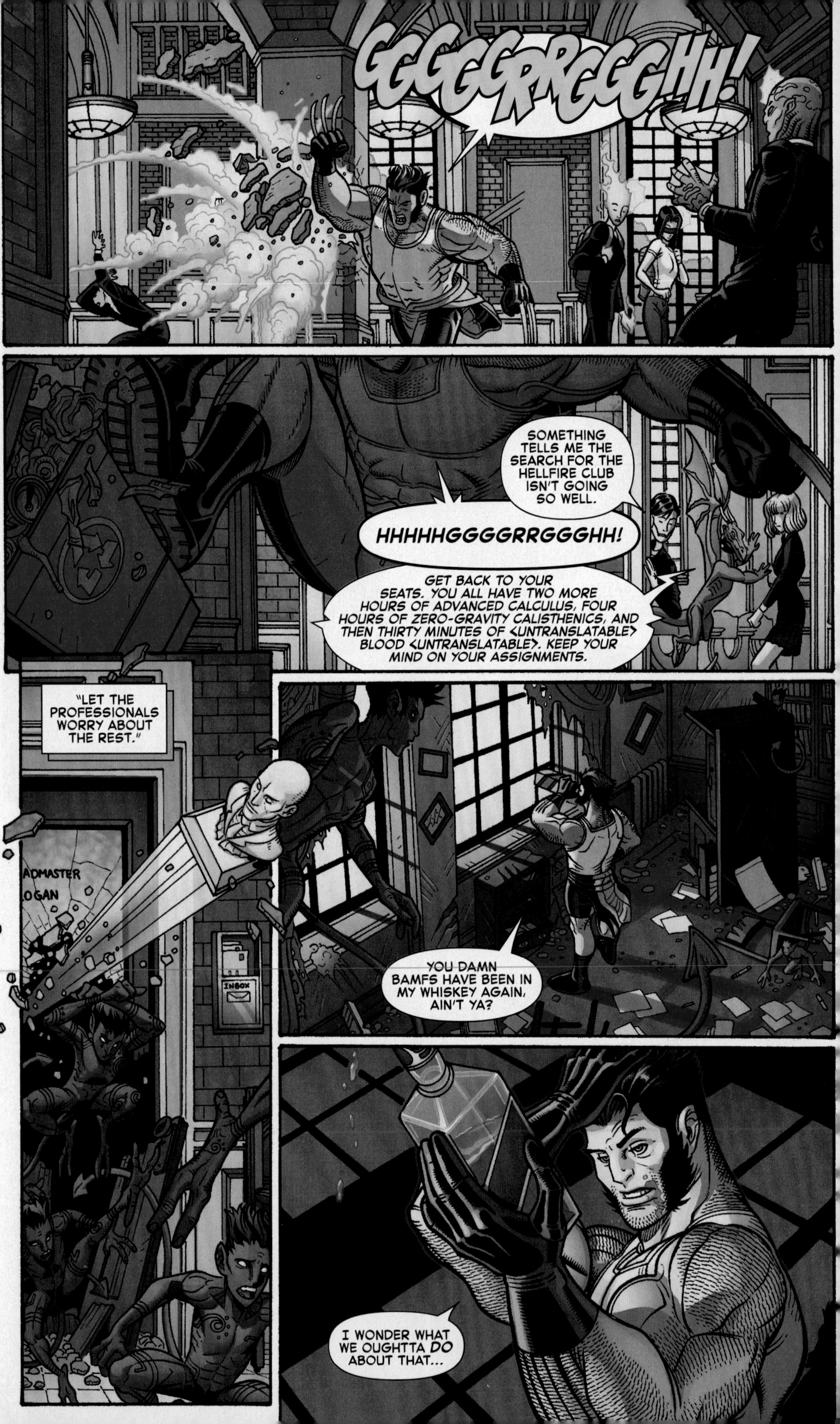
GGGGRRGGGHH!
SOMETHING TELLS ME THE SEARCH FOR THE HELLFIRE CLUB ISN'T GOING SO WELL.
HHHHHGGGGRRGGGHH!
GET BACK TO YOUR SEATS. YOU ALL HAVE TWO MORE HOURS OF ADVANCED CALCULUS, FOUR HOURS OF ZERO-GRAVITY CALISTHENICS, AND THEN THIRTY MINUTES OF <UNTRANSLATABLE> BLOOD <UNTRANSLATABLE>. KEEP YOUR MIND ON YOUR ASSIGNMENTS.
"LET THE PROFESSIONALS WORRY ABOUT THE REST."
ADMASTER
OGAN
INBOX
YOU DAMN BAMFS HAVE BEEN IN MY WHISKEY AGAIN, AIN'T YA?
I WONDER WHAT WE OUGHTTA *DO* ABOUT THAT...

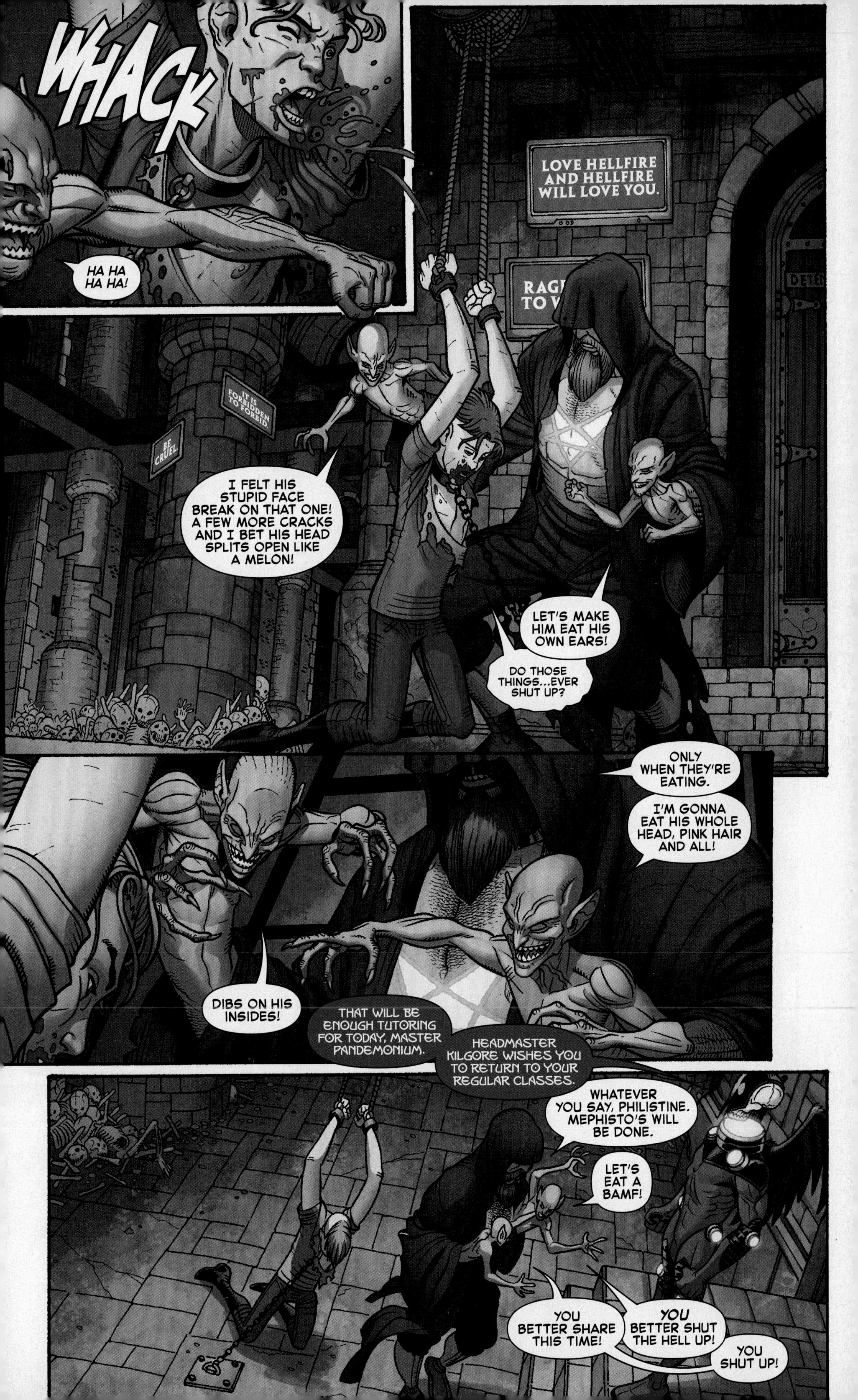
WHACK
HA HA HA HA!
LOVE HELLFIRE AND HELLFIRE WILL LOVE YOU.
IT IS FORBIDDEN TO FORBID.
BE CRUEL.
I FELT HIS STUPID FACE BREAK ON THAT ONE! A FEW MORE CRACKS AND I BET HIS HEAD SPLITS OPEN LIKE A MELON!
LET'S MAKE HIM EAT HIS OWN EARS!
DO THOSE THINGS...EVER SHUT UP?
ONLY WHEN THEY'RE EATING.
I'M GONNA EAT HIS WHOLE HEAD, PINK HAIR AND ALL!
DIBS ON HIS INSIDES!
THAT WILL BE ENOUGH TUTORING FOR TODAY, MASTER PANDEMONIUM.
HEADMASTER KILGORE WISHES YOU TO RETURN TO YOUR REGULAR CLASSES.
WHATEVER YOU SAY, PHILISTINE. MEPHISTO'S WILL BE DONE.
LET'S EAT A BAMF!
YOU BETTER SHARE THIS TIME!
YOU BETTER SHUT THE HELL UP!
YOU SHUT UP!

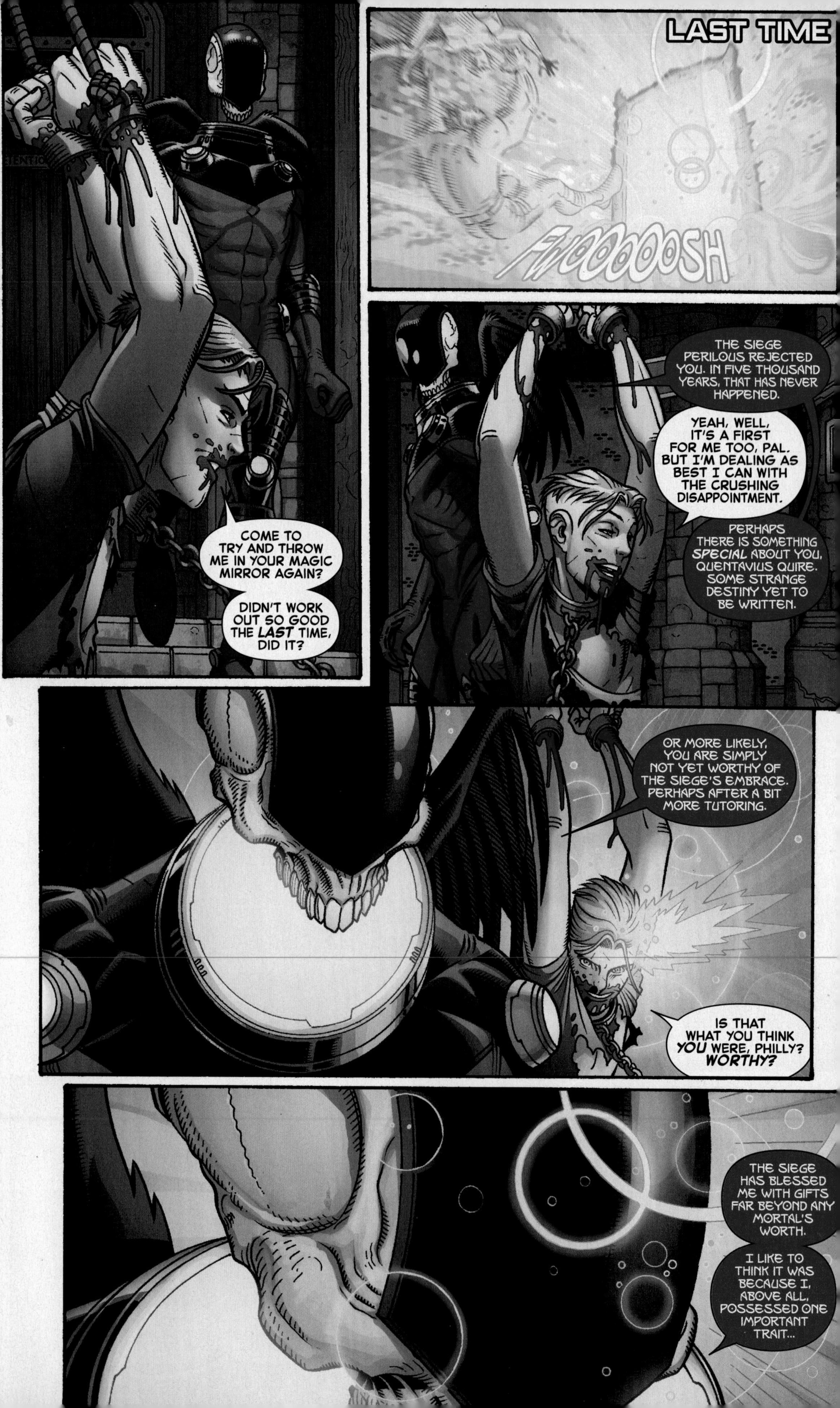
LAST TIME
FWOOOOOOSH
COME TO TRY AND THROW ME IN YOUR MAGIC MIRROR AGAIN?
DIDN'T WORK OUT SO GOOD THE LAST TIME, DID IT?
THE SIEGE PERILOUS REJECTED YOU. IN FIVE THOUSAND YEARS, THAT HAS NEVER HAPPENED.
YEAH, WELL, IT'S A FIRST FOR ME TOO, PAL. BUT I'M DEALING AS BEST I CAN WITH THE CRUSHING DISAPPOINTMENT.
PERHAPS THERE IS SOMETHING SPECIAL ABOUT YOU, QUENTAVIUS QUIRE. SOME STRANGE DESTINY YET TO BE WRITTEN.
OR MORE LIKELY, YOU ARE SIMPLY NOT YET WORTHY OF THE SIEGE'S EMBRACE. PERHAPS AFTER A BIT MORE TUTORING.
IS THAT WHAT YOU THINK YOU WERE, PHILLY? WORTHY?
THE SIEGE HAS BLESSED ME WITH GIFTS FAR BEYOND ANY MORTAL'S WORTH.
I LIKE TO THINK IT WAS BECAUSE I, ABOVE ALL, POSSESSED ONE IMPORTANT TRAIT...

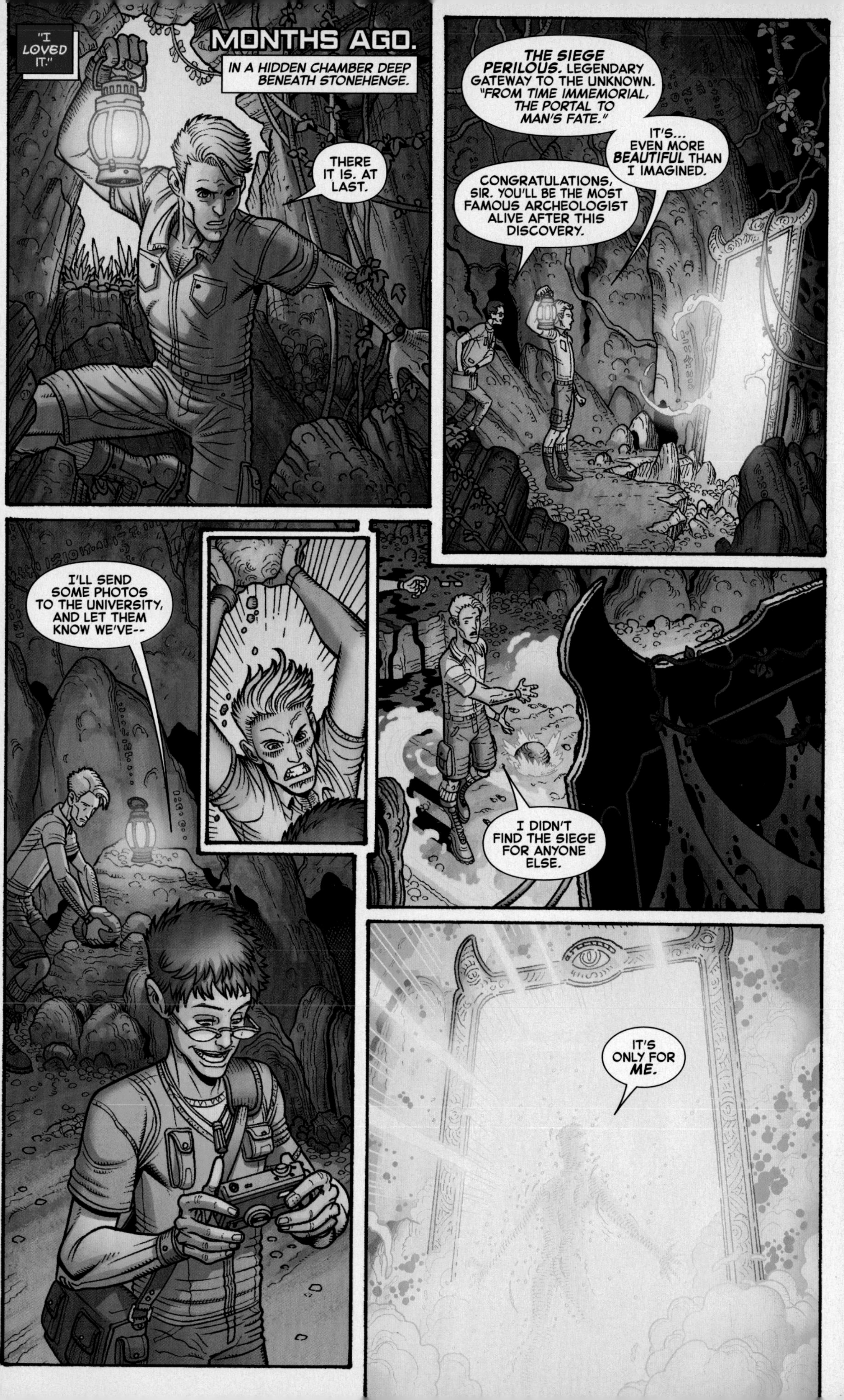
"I LOVED IT."
MONTHS AGO.
IN A HIDDEN CHAMBER DEEP BENEATH STONEHENGE.
THERE IT IS. AT LAST.
THE SIEGE PERILOUS. LEGENDARY GATEWAY TO THE UNKNOWN. "FROM TIME IMMEMORIAL, THE PORTAL TO MAN'S FATE."
IT'S... EVEN MORE BEAUTIFUL THAN I IMAGINED.
CONGRATULATIONS, SIR. YOU'LL BE THE MOST FAMOUS ARCHEOLOGIST ALIVE AFTER THIS DISCOVERY.
I'LL SEND SOME PHOTOS TO THE UNIVERSITY, AND LET THEM KNOW WE'VE--
I DIDN'T FIND THE SIEGE FOR ANYONE ELSE.
IT'S ONLY FOR ME.

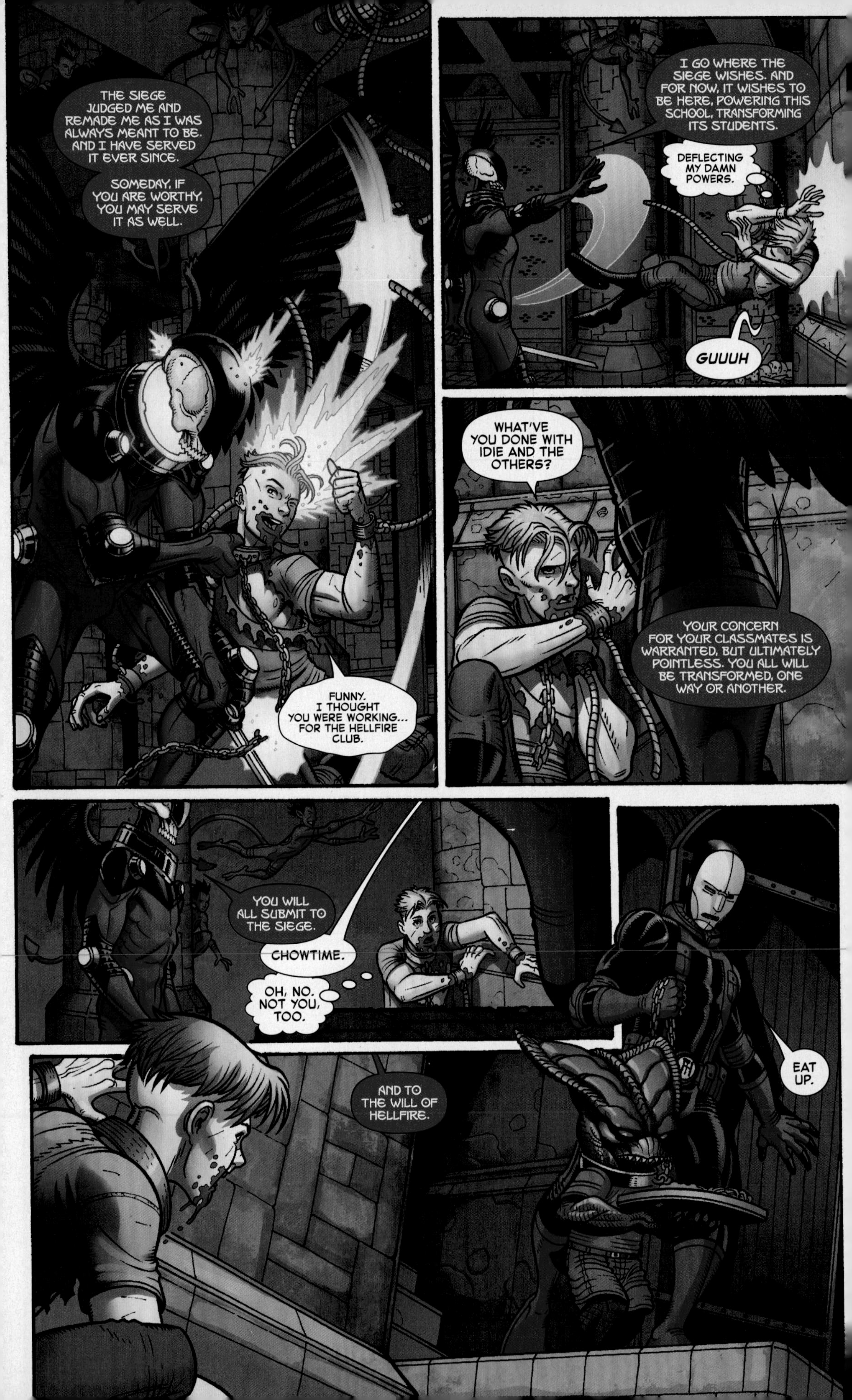
THE SIEGE JUDGED ME AND REMADE ME AS I WAS ALWAYS MEANT TO BE. AND I HAVE SERVED IT EVER SINCE.
SOMEDAY, IF YOU ARE WORTHY, YOU MAY SERVE IT AS WELL.
FUNNY. I THOUGHT YOU WERE WORKING... FOR THE HELLFIRE CLUB.
I GO WHERE THE SIEGE WISHES. AND FOR NOW, IT WISHES TO BE HERE, POWERING THIS SCHOOL, TRANSFORMING ITS STUDENTS.
DEFLECTING MY DAMN POWERS.
GUUUH
WHAT'VE YOU DONE WITH IDIE AND THE OTHERS?
YOUR CONCERN FOR YOUR CLASSMATES IS WARRANTED, BUT ULTIMATELY POINTLESS. YOU ALL WILL BE TRANSFORMED, ONE WAY OR ANOTHER.
YOU WILL ALL SUBMIT TO THE SIEGE.
CHOWTIME.
OH, NO. NOT YOU, TOO.
AND TO THE WILL OF HELLFIRE.
EAT UP.

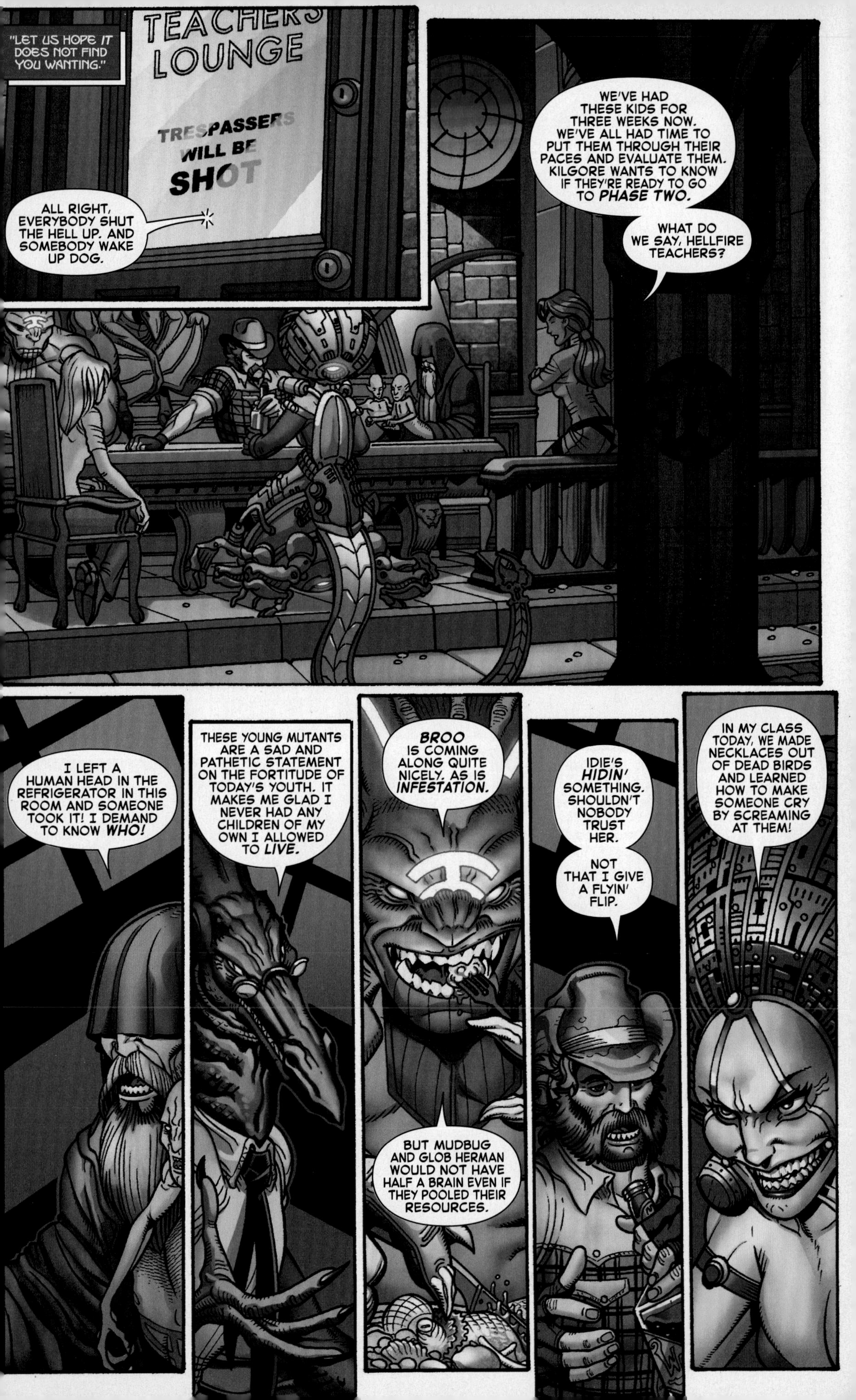
"LET US HOPE IT DOES NOT FIND YOU WANTING."
TEACHERS LOUNGE
TRESPASSERS WILL BE SHOT
ALL RIGHT, EVERYBODY SHUT THE HELL UP. AND SOMEBODY WAKE UP DOG.
WE'VE HAD THESE KIDS FOR THREE WEEKS NOW. WE'VE ALL HAD TIME TO PUT THEM THROUGH THEIR PACES AND EVALUATE THEM. KILGORE WANTS TO KNOW IF THEY'RE READY TO GO TO PHASE TWO.
WHAT DO WE SAY, HELLFIRE TEACHERS?
I LEFT A HUMAN HEAD IN THE REFRIGERATOR IN THIS ROOM AND SOMEONE TOOK IT! I DEMAND TO KNOW WHO!
THESE YOUNG MUTANTS ARE A SAD AND PATHETIC STATEMENT ON THE FORTITUDE OF TODAY'S YOUTH. IT MAKES ME GLAD I NEVER HAD ANY CHILDREN OF MY OWN I ALLOWED TO LIVE.
BROO IS COMING ALONG QUITE NICELY. AS IS INFESTATION.
BUT MUDBUG AND GLOB HERMAN WOULD NOT HAVE HALF A BRAIN EVEN IF THEY POOLED THEIR RESOURCES.
IDIE'S HIDIN' SOMETHING. SHOULDN'T NOBODY TRUST HER.
NOT THAT I GIVE A FLYIN' FLIP.
IN MY CLASS TODAY, WE MADE NECKLACES OUT OF DEAD BIRDS AND LEARNED HOW TO MAKE SOMEONE CRY BY SCREAMING AT THEM!

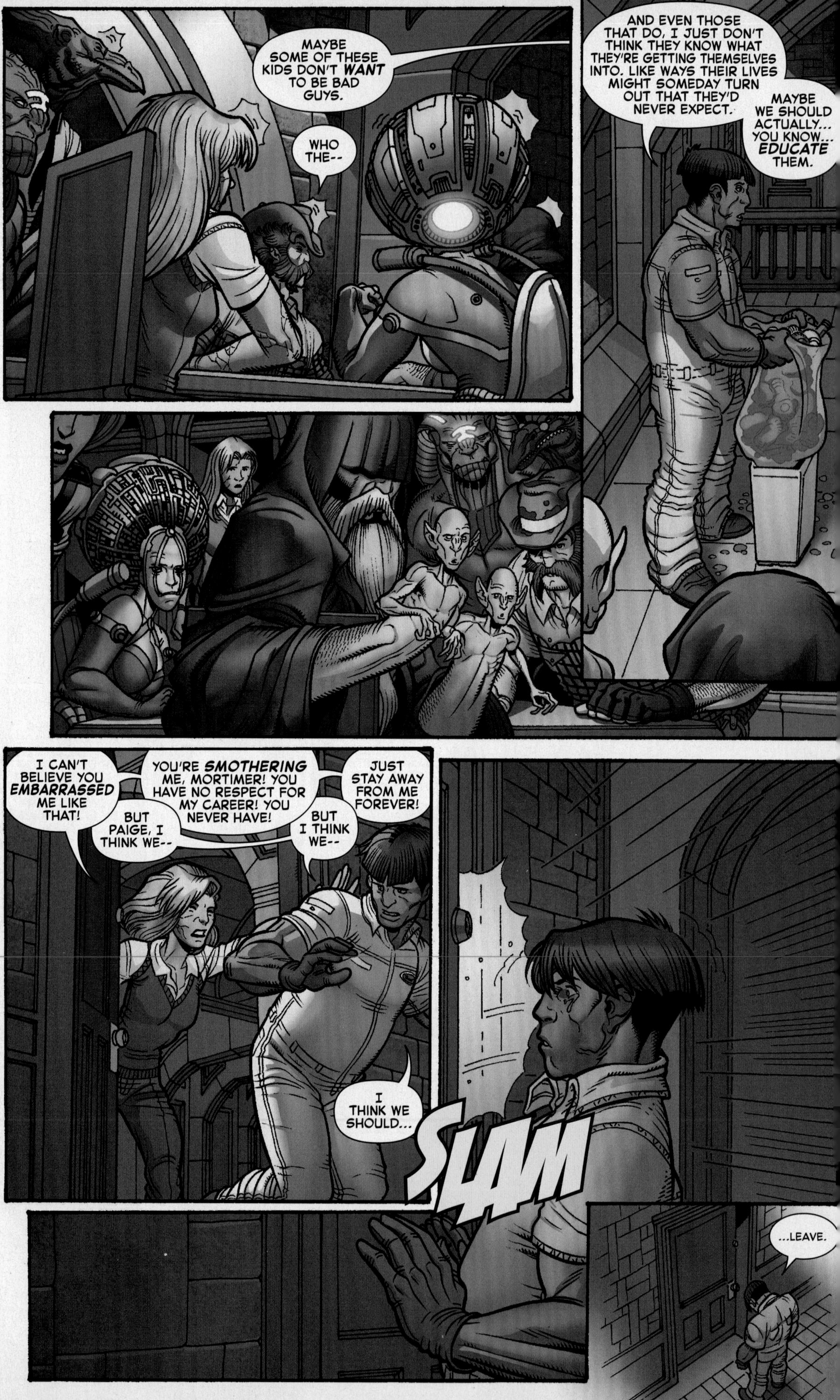
MAYBE SOME OF THESE KIDS DON'T *WANT* TO BE BAD GUYS.
WHO THE--
AND EVEN THOSE THAT DO, I JUST DON'T THINK THEY KNOW WHAT THEY'RE GETTING THEMSELVES INTO. LIKE WAYS THEIR LIVES MIGHT SOMEDAY TURN OUT THAT THEY'D NEVER EXPECT.
MAYBE WE SHOULD ACTUALLY... YOU KNOW... *EDUCATE* THEM.
I CAN'T BELIEVE YOU *EMBARRASSED* ME LIKE THAT!
BUT PAIGE, I THINK WE--
YOU'RE *SMOTHERING* ME, MORTIMER! YOU HAVE NO RESPECT FOR MY CAREER! YOU NEVER HAVE!
BUT I THINK WE--
JUST STAY AWAY FROM ME FOREVER!
I THINK WE SHOULD...
SLAM
...LEAVE.

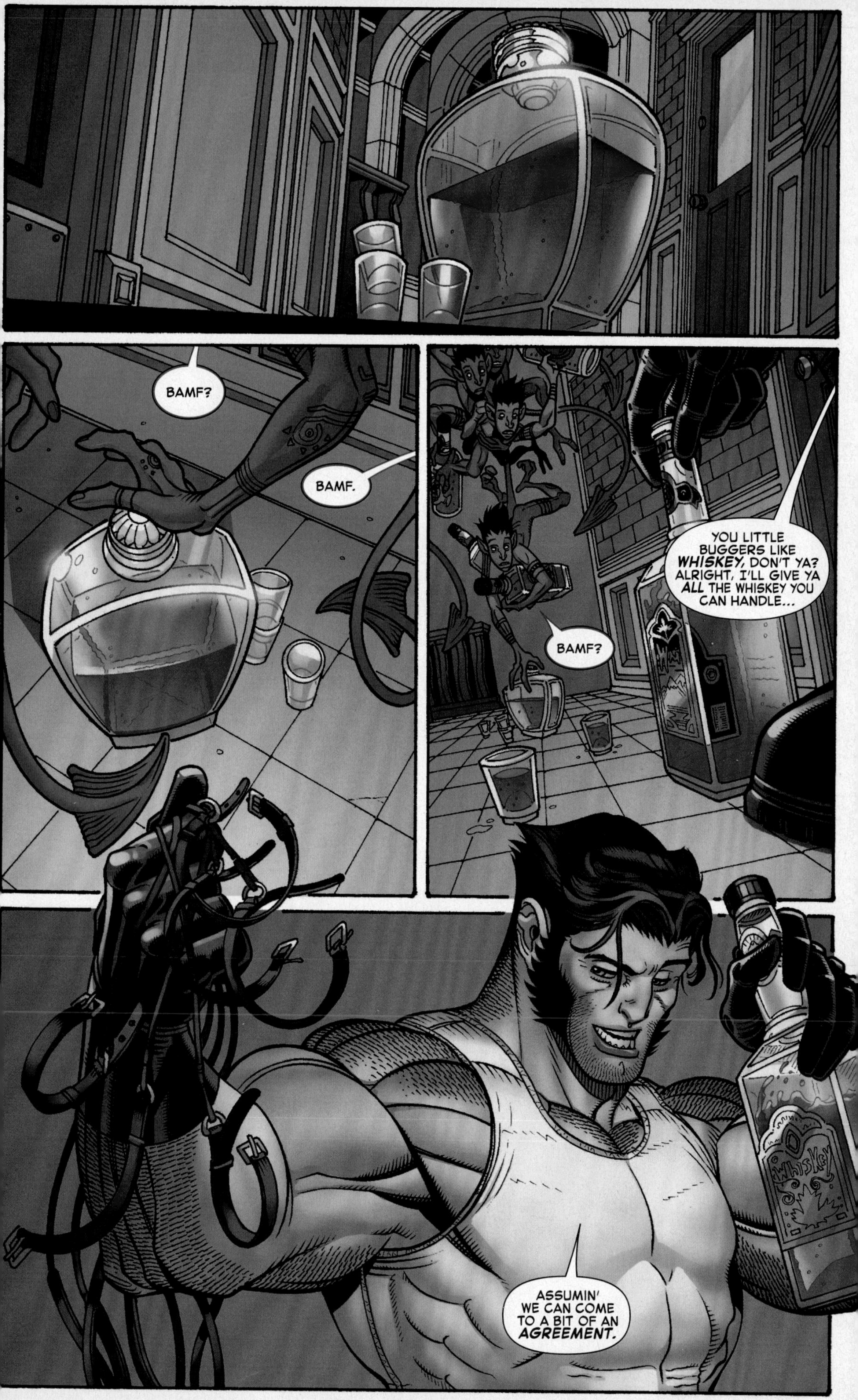
BAMF?
BAMF.
YOU LITTLE BUGGERS LIKE WHISKEY, DON'T YA? ALRIGHT, I'LL GIVE YA ALL THE WHISKEY YOU CAN HANDLE...
BAMF?
ASSUMIN' WE CAN COME TO A BIT OF AN AGREEMENT.

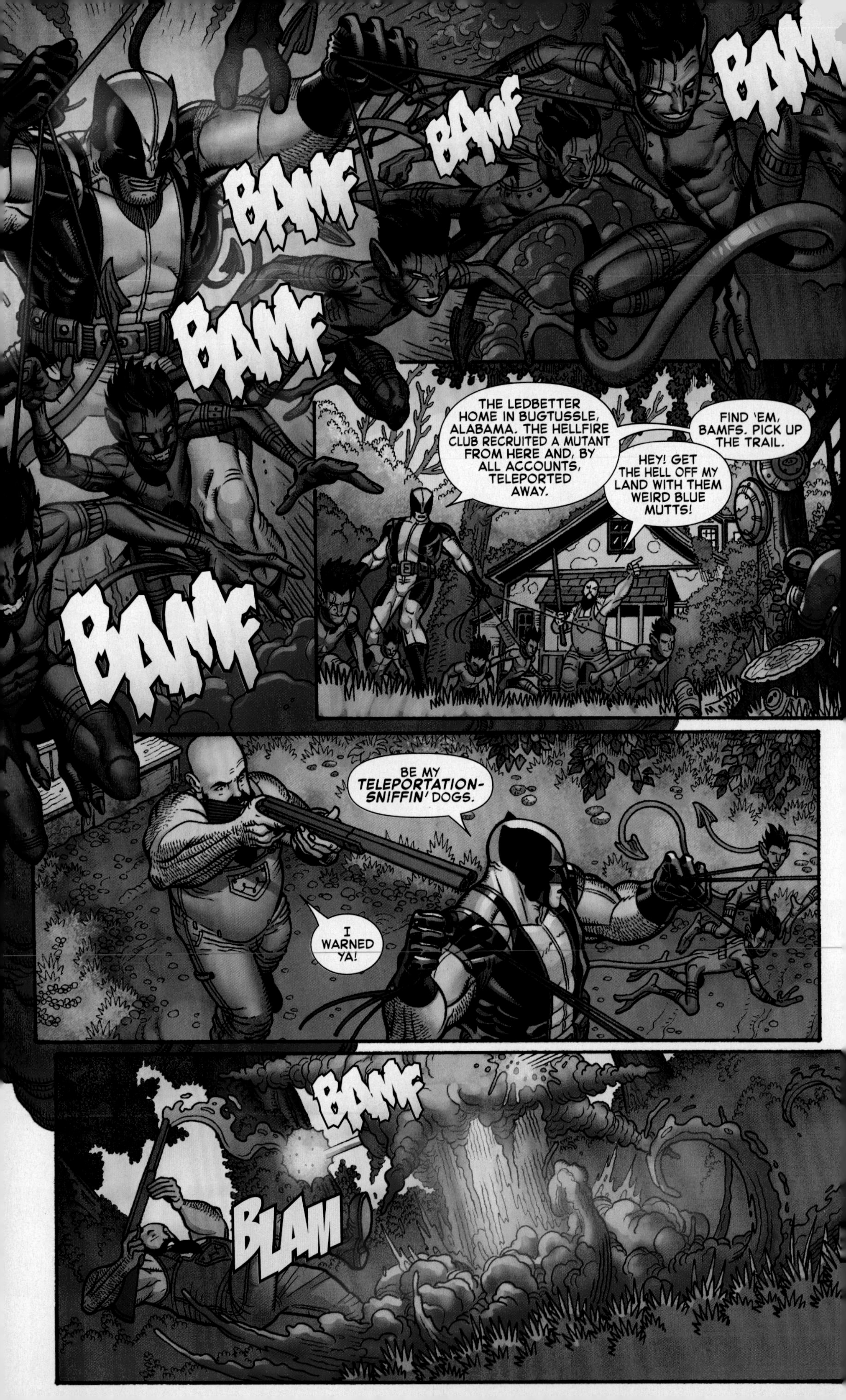
BAMF
BAMF
BAMF
BAMF
BAMF
THE LEDBETTER HOME IN BUGTUSSLE, ALABAMA. THE HELLFIRE CLUB RECRUITED A MUTANT FROM HERE AND, BY ALL ACCOUNTS, TELEPORTED AWAY.
FIND 'EM, BAMFS. PICK UP THE TRAIL.
HEY! GET THE HELL OFF MY LAND WITH THEM WEIRD BLUE MUTTS!
BE MY *TELEPORTATION-SNIFFIN'* DOGS.
I WARNED YA!
BAMF
BLAM

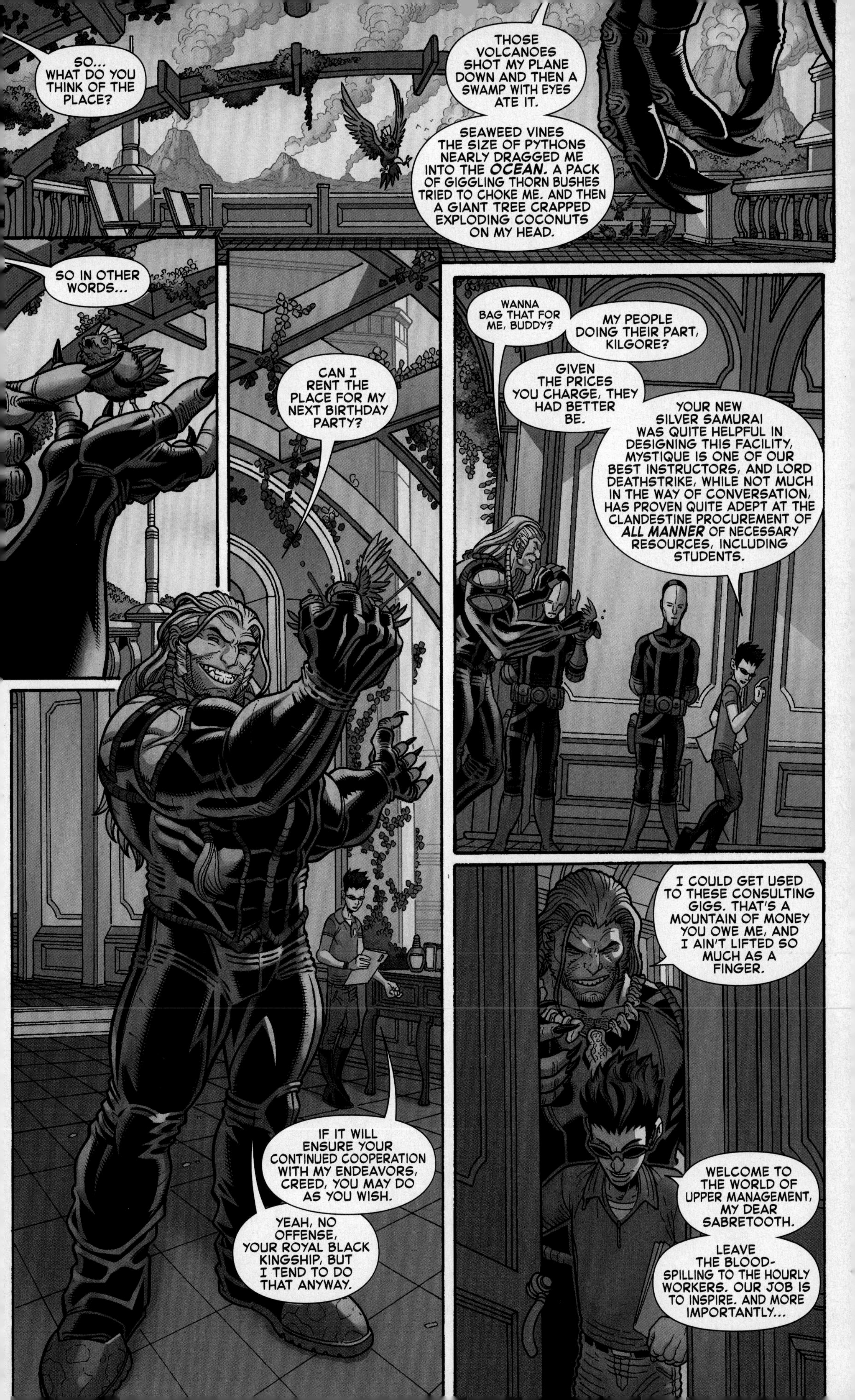
SO... WHAT DO YOU THINK OF THE PLACE?
THOSE VOLCANOES SHOT MY PLANE DOWN AND THEN A SWAMP WITH EYES ATE IT.
SEAWEED VINES THE SIZE OF PYTHONS NEARLY DRAGGED ME INTO THE OCEAN. A PACK OF GIGGLING THORN BUSHES TRIED TO CHOKE ME. AND THEN A GIANT TREE CRAPPED EXPLODING COCONUTS ON MY HEAD.
SO IN OTHER WORDS...
CAN I RENT THE PLACE FOR MY NEXT BIRTHDAY PARTY?
IF IT WILL ENSURE YOUR CONTINUED COOPERATION WITH MY ENDEAVORS, CREED, YOU MAY DO AS YOU WISH.
YEAH, NO OFFENSE, YOUR ROYAL BLACK KINGSHIP, BUT I TEND TO DO THAT ANYWAY.
WANNA BAG THAT FOR ME, BUDDY?
MY PEOPLE DOING THEIR PART, KILGORE?
GIVEN THE PRICES YOU CHARGE, THEY HAD BETTER BE.
YOUR NEW SILVER SAMURAI WAS QUITE HELPFUL IN DESIGNING THIS FACILITY, MYSTIQUE IS ONE OF OUR BEST INSTRUCTORS, AND LORD DEATHSTRIKE, WHILE NOT MUCH IN THE WAY OF CONVERSATION, HAS PROVEN QUITE ADEPT AT THE CLANDESTINE PROCUREMENT OF ALL MANNER OF NECESSARY RESOURCES, INCLUDING STUDENTS.
I COULD GET USED TO THESE CONSULTING GIGS. THAT'S A MOUNTAIN OF MONEY YOU OWE ME, AND I AIN'T LIFTED SO MUCH AS A FINGER.
WELCOME TO THE WORLD OF UPPER MANAGEMENT, MY DEAR SABRETOOTH.
LEAVE THE BLOOD-SPILLING TO THE HOURLY WORKERS. OUR JOB IS TO INSPIRE. AND MORE IMPORTANTLY...

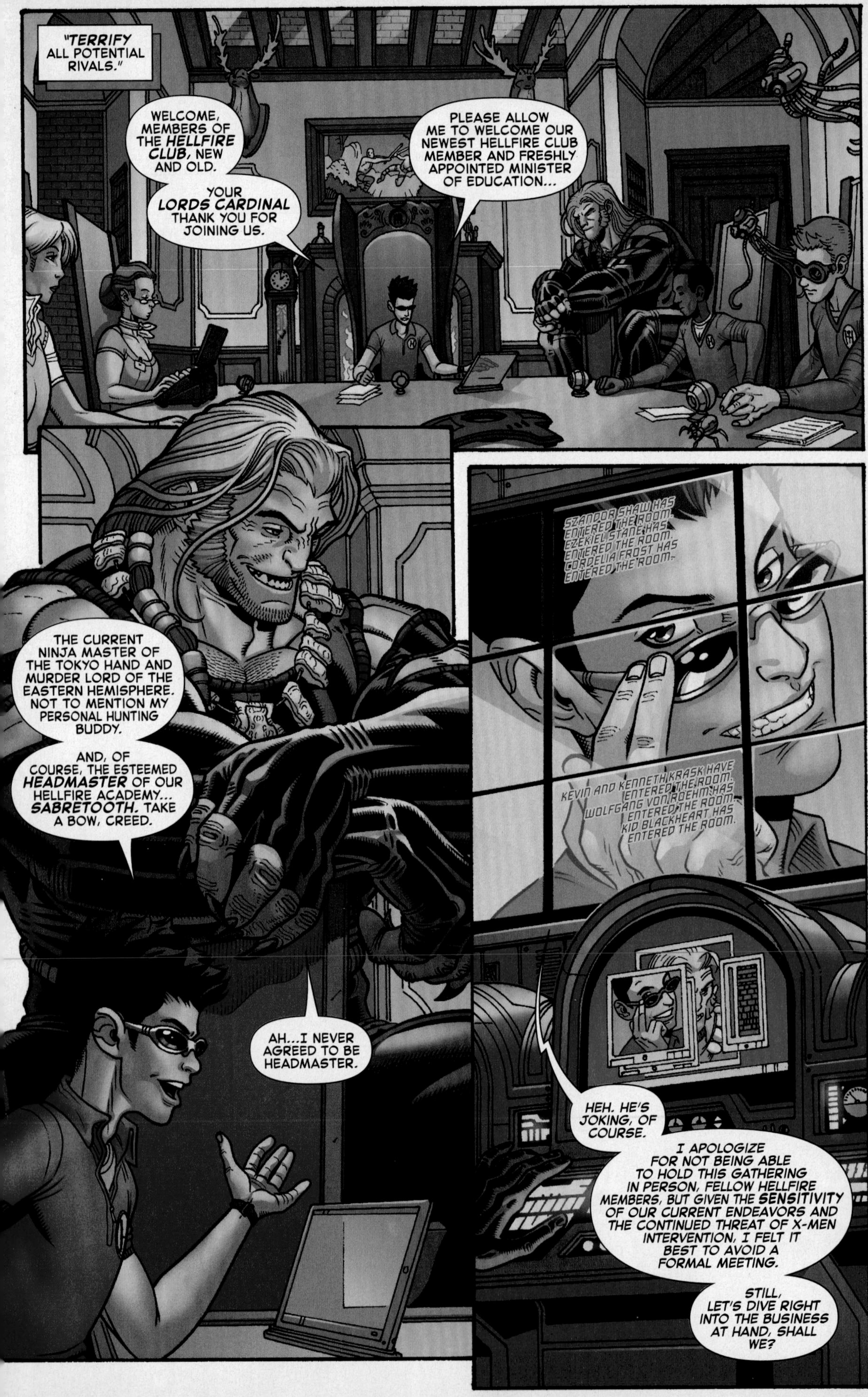
"TERRIFY ALL POTENTIAL RIVALS."
WELCOME, MEMBERS OF THE HELLFIRE CLUB, NEW AND OLD.
YOUR LORDS CARDINAL THANK YOU FOR JOINING US.
PLEASE ALLOW ME TO WELCOME OUR NEWEST HELLFIRE CLUB MEMBER AND FRESHLY APPOINTED MINISTER OF EDUCATION...
SZANDOR SHAW HAS ENTERED THE ROOM. EZEKIEL STANE HAS ENTERED THE ROOM. CORDELIA FROST HAS ENTERED THE ROOM.
KEVIN AND KENNETH KRASK HAVE ENTERED THE ROOM. WOLFGANG VON ROEHM HAS ENTERED THE ROOM. KID BLACKHEART HAS ENTERED THE ROOM.
THE CURRENT NINJA MASTER OF THE TOKYO HAND AND MURDER LORD OF THE EASTERN HEMISPHERE. NOT TO MENTION MY PERSONAL HUNTING BUDDY.
AND, OF COURSE, THE ESTEEMED HEADMASTER OF OUR HELLFIRE ACADEMY... SABRETOOTH. TAKE A BOW, CREED.
AH...I NEVER AGREED TO BE HEADMASTER.
HEH. HE'S JOKING, OF COURSE.
I APOLOGIZE FOR NOT BEING ABLE TO HOLD THIS GATHERING IN PERSON, FELLOW HELLFIRE MEMBERS, BUT GIVEN THE SENSITIVITY OF OUR CURRENT ENDEAVORS AND THE CONTINUED THREAT OF X-MEN INTERVENTION, I FELT IT BEST TO AVOID A FORMAL MEETING.
STILL, LET'S DIVE RIGHT INTO THE BUSINESS AT HAND, SHALL WE?

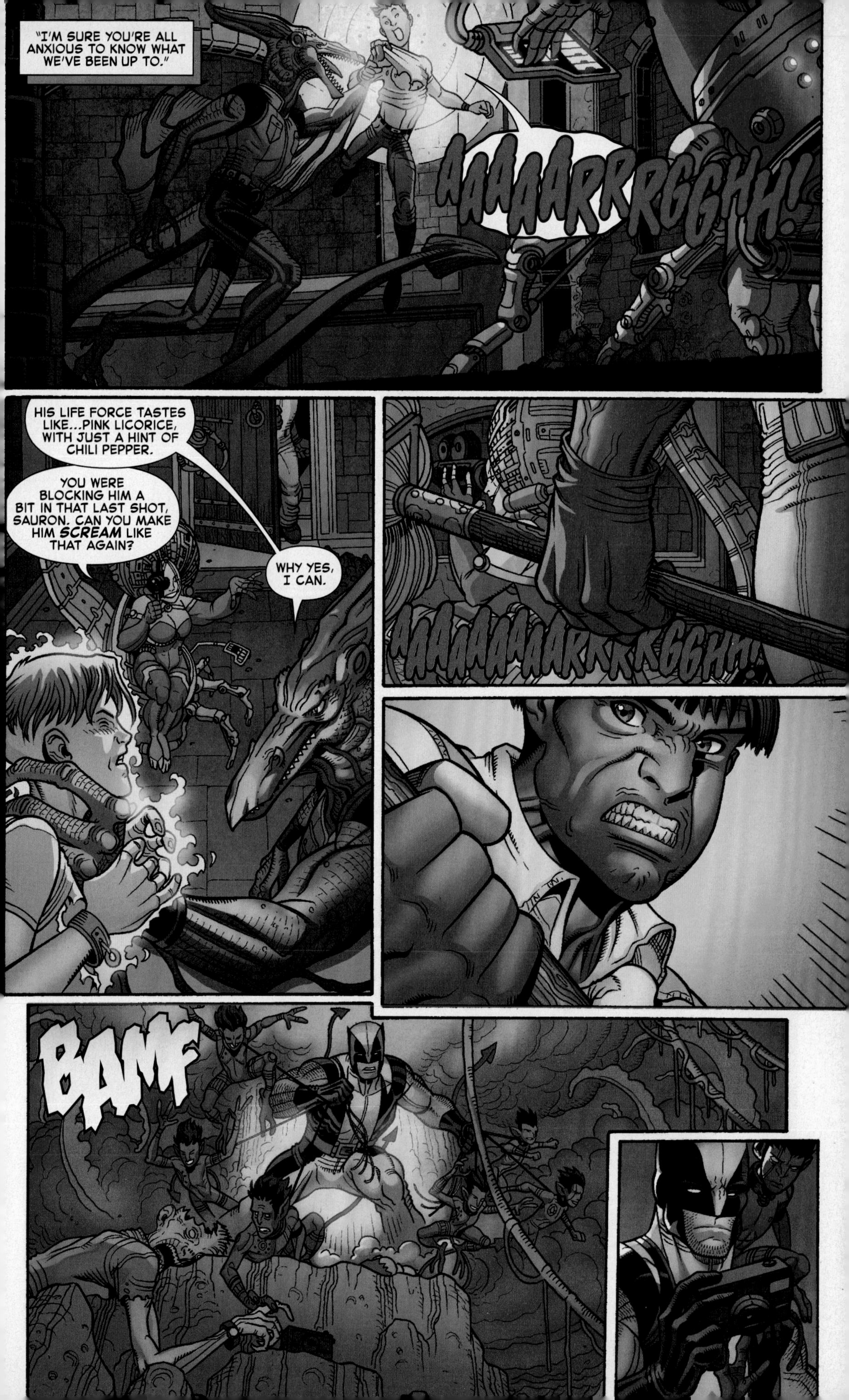
"I'M SURE YOU'RE ALL ANXIOUS TO KNOW WHAT WE'VE BEEN UP TO."
AAAAARRRGGHH!
HIS LIFE FORCE TASTES LIKE...PINK LICORICE, WITH JUST A HINT OF CHILI PEPPER.
YOU WERE BLOCKING HIM A BIT IN THAT LAST SHOT, SAURON. CAN YOU MAKE HIM SCREAM LIKE THAT AGAIN?
WHY YES, I CAN.
AAAAAAAAAARRRRGGHH!
BAMF

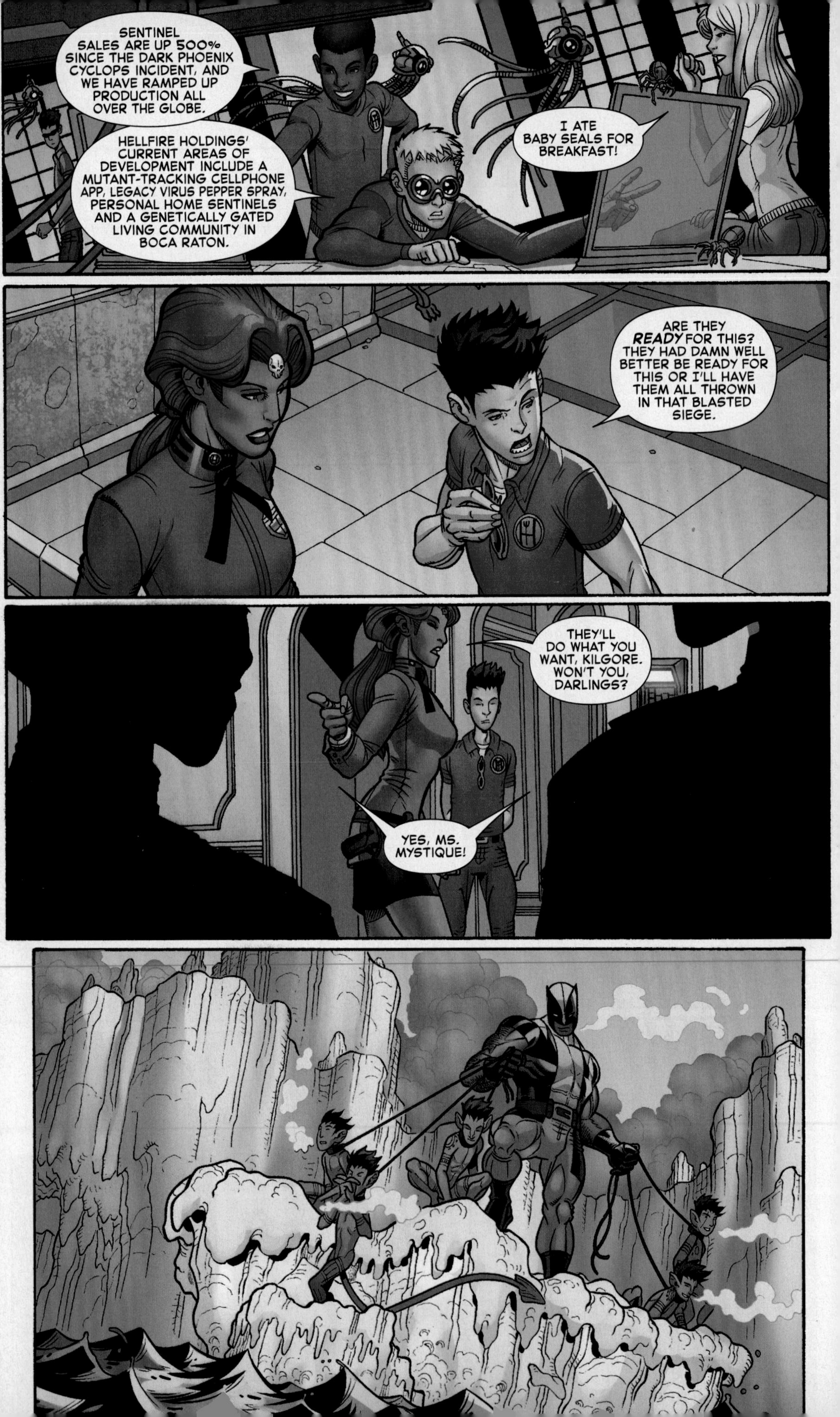
SENTINEL SALES ARE UP 500% SINCE THE DARK PHOENIX CYCLOPS INCIDENT, AND WE HAVE RAMPED UP PRODUCTION ALL OVER THE GLOBE.
HELLFIRE HOLDINGS' CURRENT AREAS OF DEVELOPMENT INCLUDE A MUTANT-TRACKING CELLPHONE APP, LEGACY VIRUS PEPPER SPRAY, PERSONAL HOME SENTINELS AND A GENETICALLY GATED LIVING COMMUNITY IN BOCA RATON.
I ATE BABY SEALS FOR BREAKFAST!
ARE THEY *READY* FOR THIS? THEY HAD DAMN WELL BETTER BE READY FOR THIS OR I'LL HAVE THEM ALL THROWN IN THAT BLASTED SIEGE.
THEY'LL DO WHAT YOU WANT, KILGORE. WON'T YOU, DARLINGS?
YES, MS. MYSTIQUE!

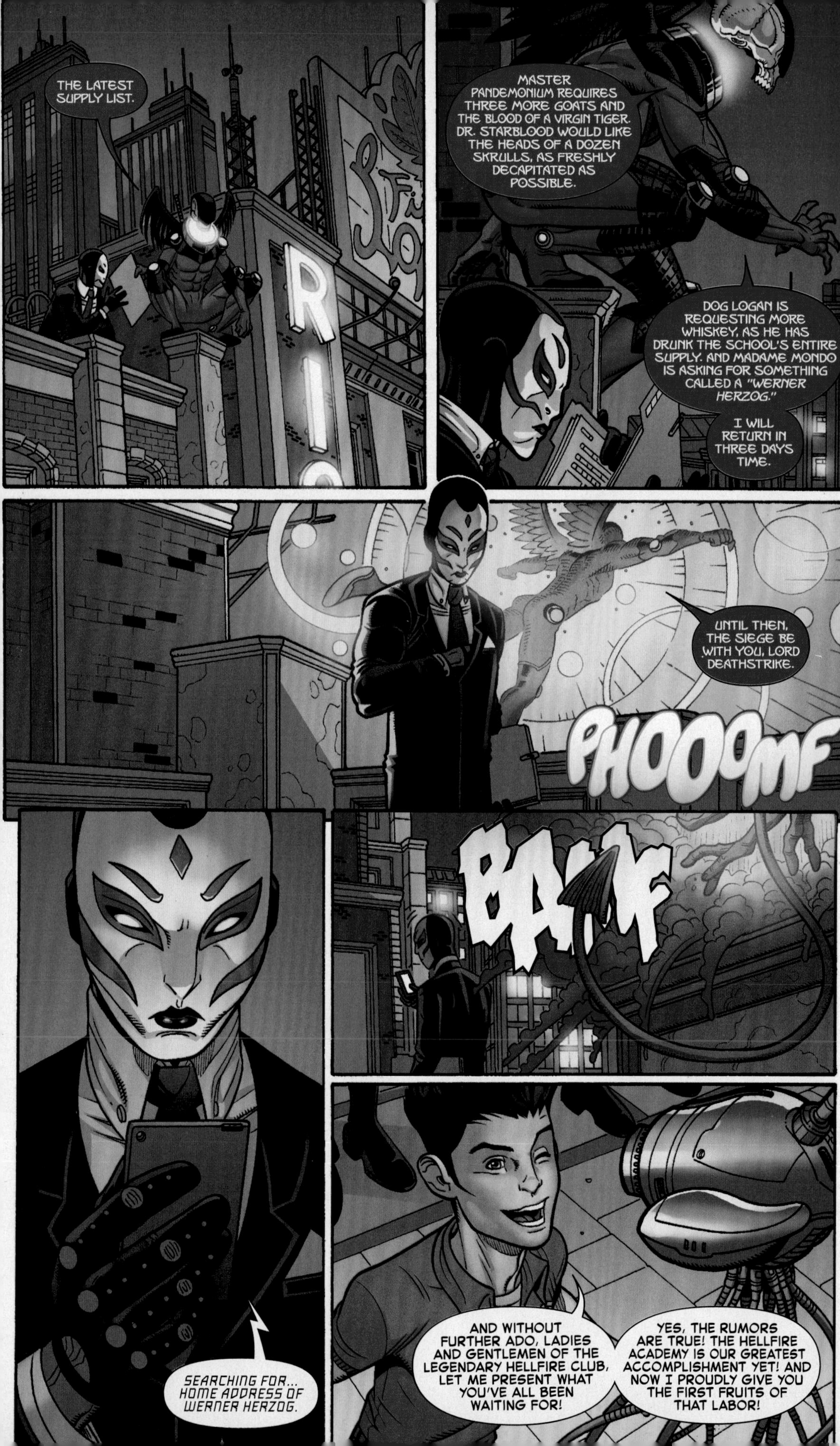
THE LATEST SUPPLY LIST.
MASTER PANDEMONIUM REQUIRES THREE MORE GOATS AND THE BLOOD OF A VIRGIN TIGER. DR. STARBLOOD WOULD LIKE THE HEADS OF A DOZEN SKRULLS, AS FRESHLY DECAPITATED AS POSSIBLE.
DOG LOGAN IS REQUESTING MORE WHISKEY, AS HE HAS DRUNK THE SCHOOL'S ENTIRE SUPPLY. AND MADAME MONDO IS ASKING FOR SOMETHING CALLED A "WERNER HERZOG."
I WILL RETURN IN THREE DAYS TIME.
UNTIL THEN, THE SIEGE BE WITH YOU, LORD DEATHSTRIKE.
PHOOOMF
SEARCHING FOR... HOME ADDRESS OF WERNER HERZOG.
AND WITHOUT FURTHER ADO, LADIES AND GENTLEMEN OF THE LEGENDARY HELLFIRE CLUB, LET ME PRESENT WHAT YOU'VE ALL BEEN WAITING FOR!
YES, THE RUMORS ARE TRUE! THE HELLFIRE ACADEMY IS OUR GREATEST ACCOMPLISHMENT YET! AND NOW I PROUDLY GIVE YOU THE FIRST FRUITS OF THAT LABOR!

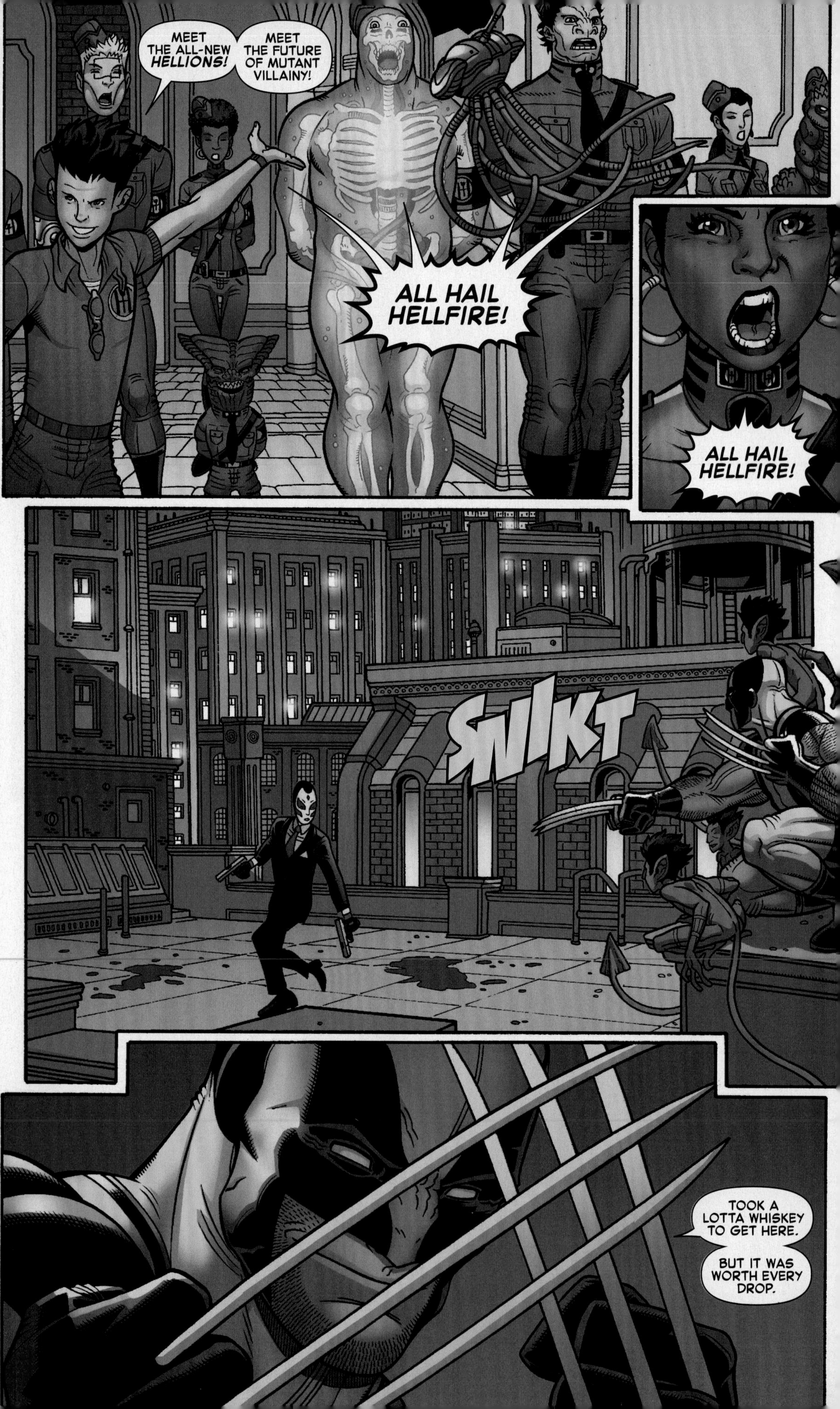
MEET THE ALL-NEW HELLIONS!
MEET THE FUTURE OF MUTANT VILLAINY!
ALL HAIL HELLFIRE!
ALL HAIL HELLFIRE!
SNIKT
TOOK A LOTTA WHISKEY TO GET HERE.
BUT IT WAS WORTH EVERY DROP.

X-MEN 50TH ANNIVERSARY VARIANT
BY CLAY MANN & DAVID CURIEL

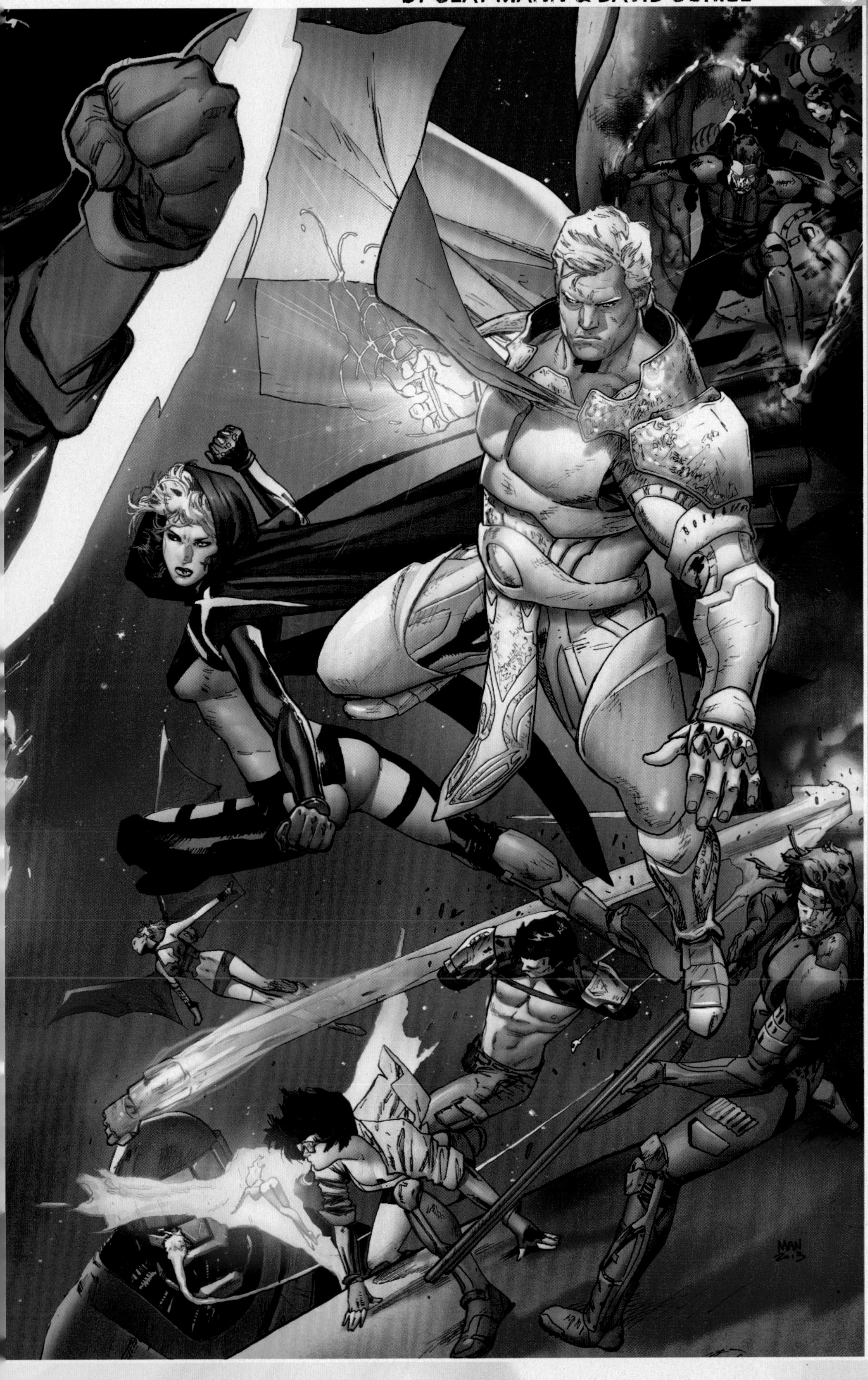

33 "THE HELLFIRE SAGA" PART THREE

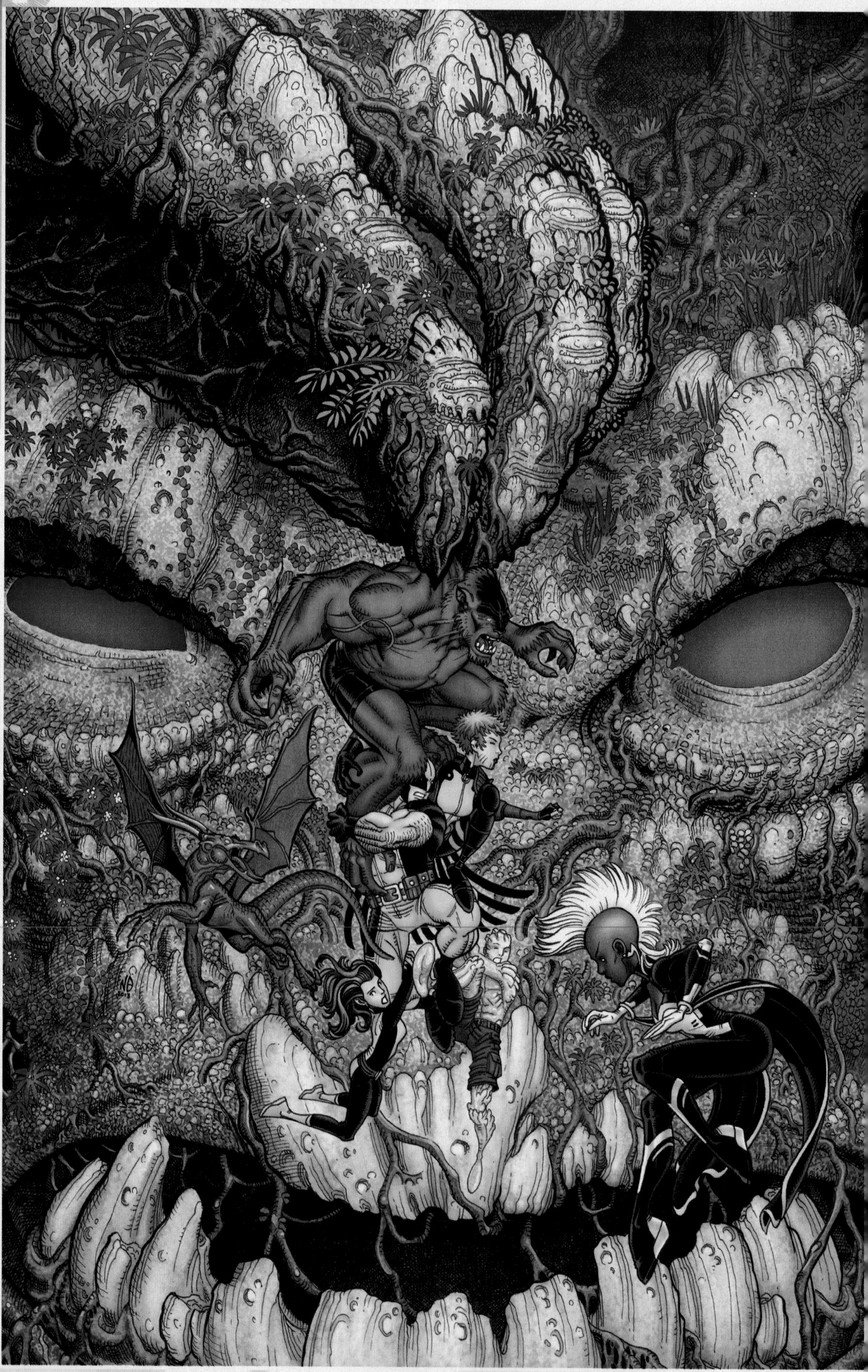

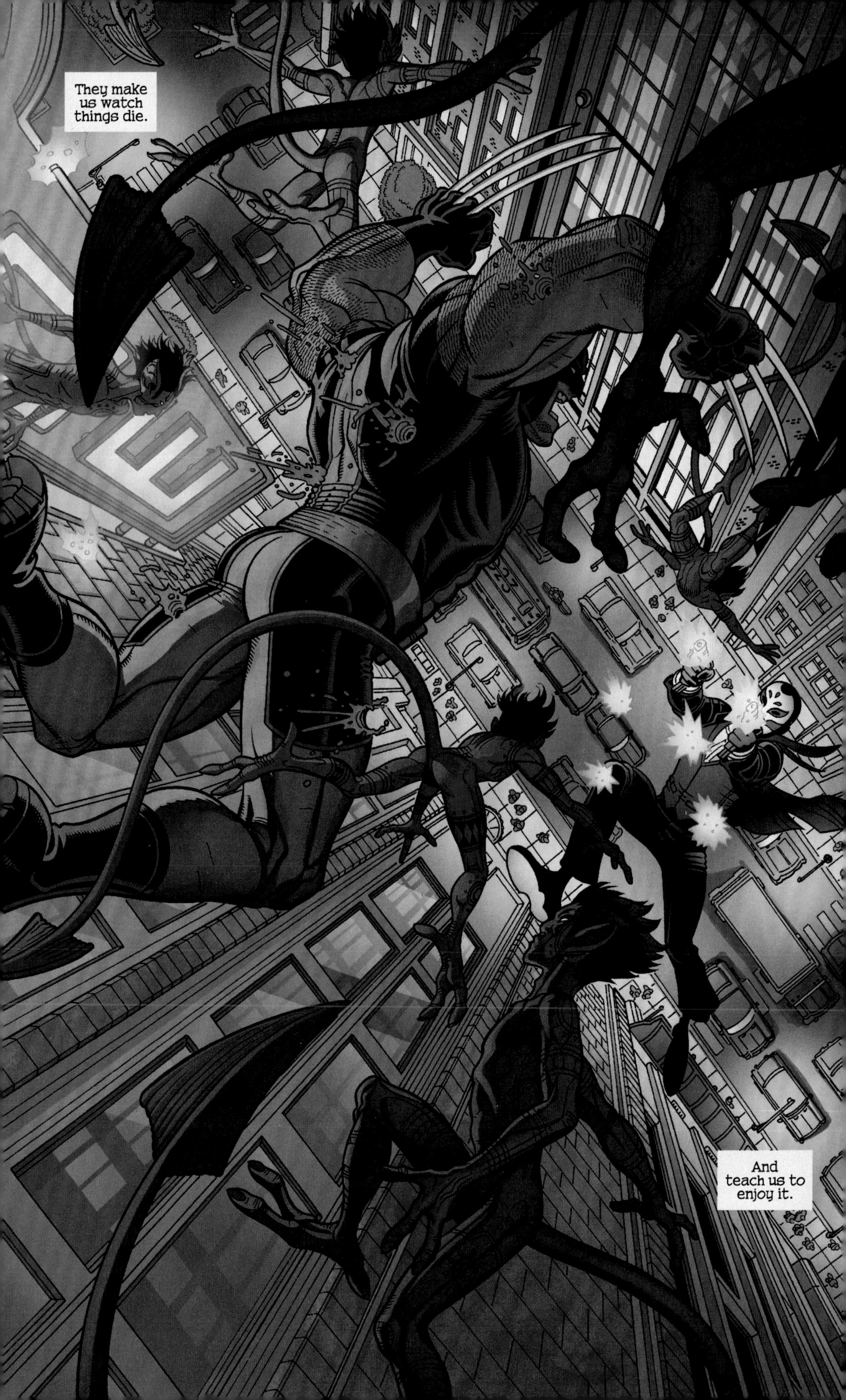
They make us watch things die.
And teach us to enjoy it.

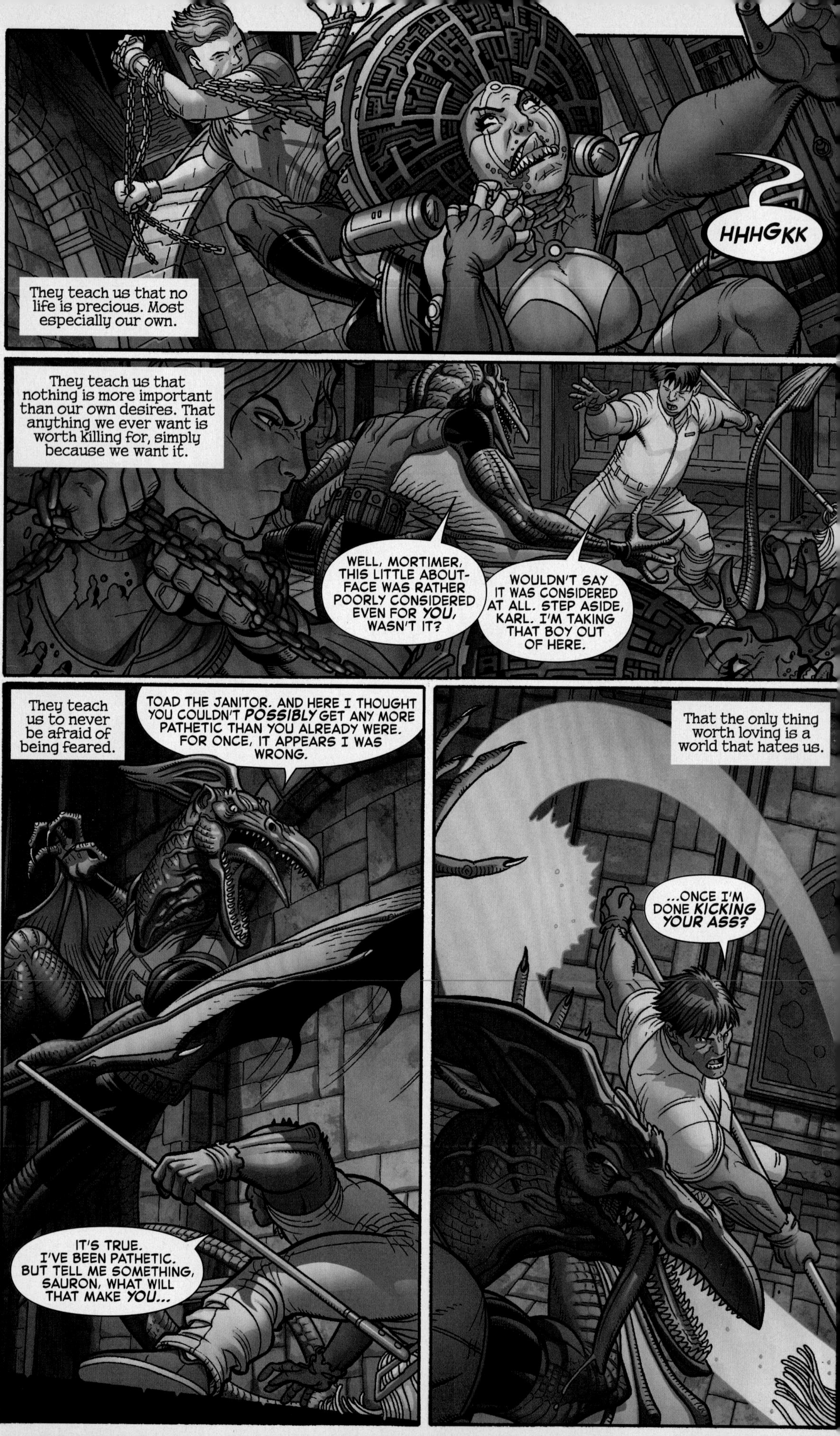
HHHGKK
They teach us that no life is precious. Most especially our own.
They teach us that nothing is more important than our own desires. That anything we ever want is worth killing for, simply because we want it.
WELL, MORTIMER, THIS LITTLE ABOUT-FACE WAS RATHER POORLY CONSIDERED EVEN FOR YOU, WASN'T IT?
WOULDN'T SAY IT WAS CONSIDERED AT ALL. STEP ASIDE, KARL. I'M TAKING THAT BOY OUT OF HERE.
They teach us to never be afraid of being feared.
TOAD THE JANITOR. AND HERE I THOUGHT YOU COULDN'T POSSIBLY GET ANY MORE PATHETIC THAN YOU ALREADY WERE. FOR ONCE, IT APPEARS I WAS WRONG.
IT'S TRUE. I'VE BEEN PATHETIC. BUT TELL ME SOMETHING, SAURON, WHAT WILL THAT MAKE YOU...
That the only thing worth loving is a world that hates us.
...ONCE I'M DONE KICKING YOUR ASS?

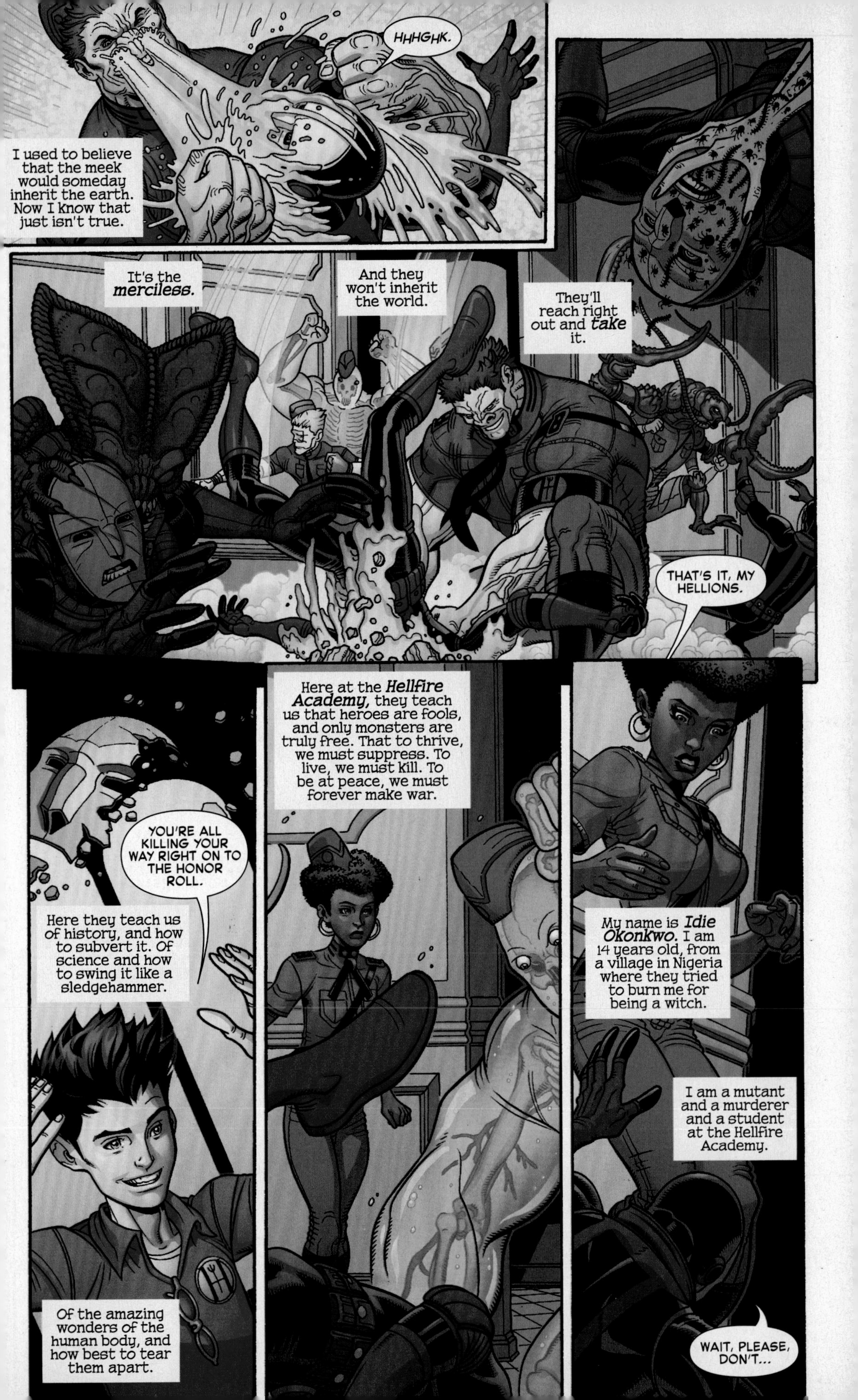
HHHGHK.
I used to believe that the meek would someday inherit the earth. Now I know that just isn't true.
It's the *merciless.*
And they won't inherit the world.
They'll reach right out and *take* it.
THAT'S IT, MY HELLIONS.
YOU'RE ALL KILLING YOUR WAY RIGHT ON TO THE HONOR ROLL.
Here they teach us of history, and how to subvert it. Of science and how to swing it like a sledgehammer.
Of the amazing wonders of the human body, and how best to tear them apart.
Here at the *Hellfire Academy,* they teach us that heroes are fools, and only monsters are truly free. That to thrive, we must suppress. To live, we must kill. To be at peace, we must forever make war.
My name is *Idie Okonkwo.* I am 14 years old, from a village in Nigeria where they tried to burn me for being a witch.
I am a mutant and a murderer and a student at the Hellfire Academy.
WAIT, PLEASE, DON'T...

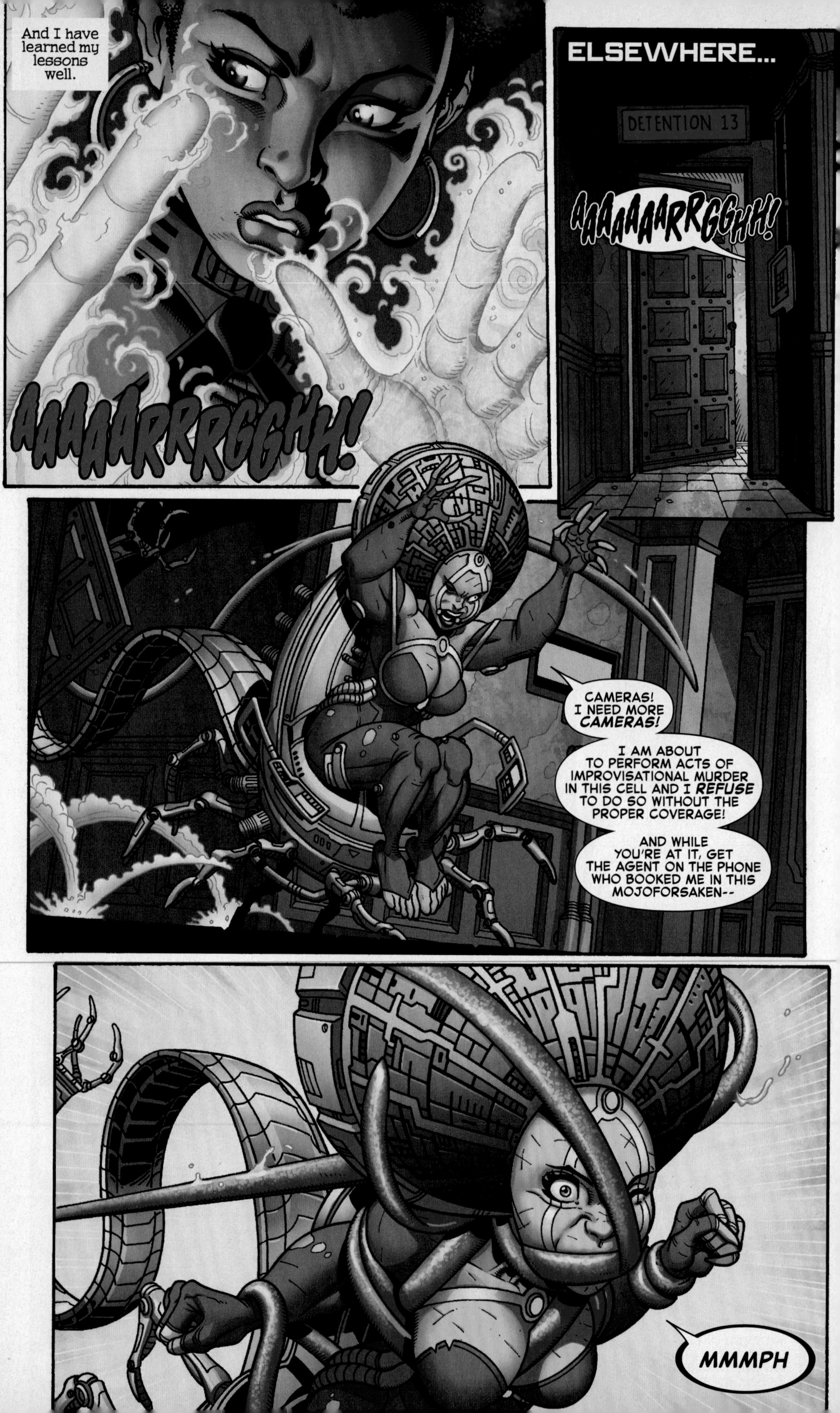
And I have learned my lessons well.
AAAAARRRGGHH!
ELSEWHERE...
DETENTION 13
AAAAAAARRGGHH!
CAMERAS! I NEED MORE CAMERAS!
I AM ABOUT TO PERFORM ACTS OF IMPROVISATIONAL MURDER IN THIS CELL AND I REFUSE TO DO SO WITHOUT THE PROPER COVERAGE!
AND WHILE YOU'RE AT IT, GET THE AGENT ON THE PHONE WHO BOOKED ME IN THIS MOJOFORSAKEN--
MMMPH

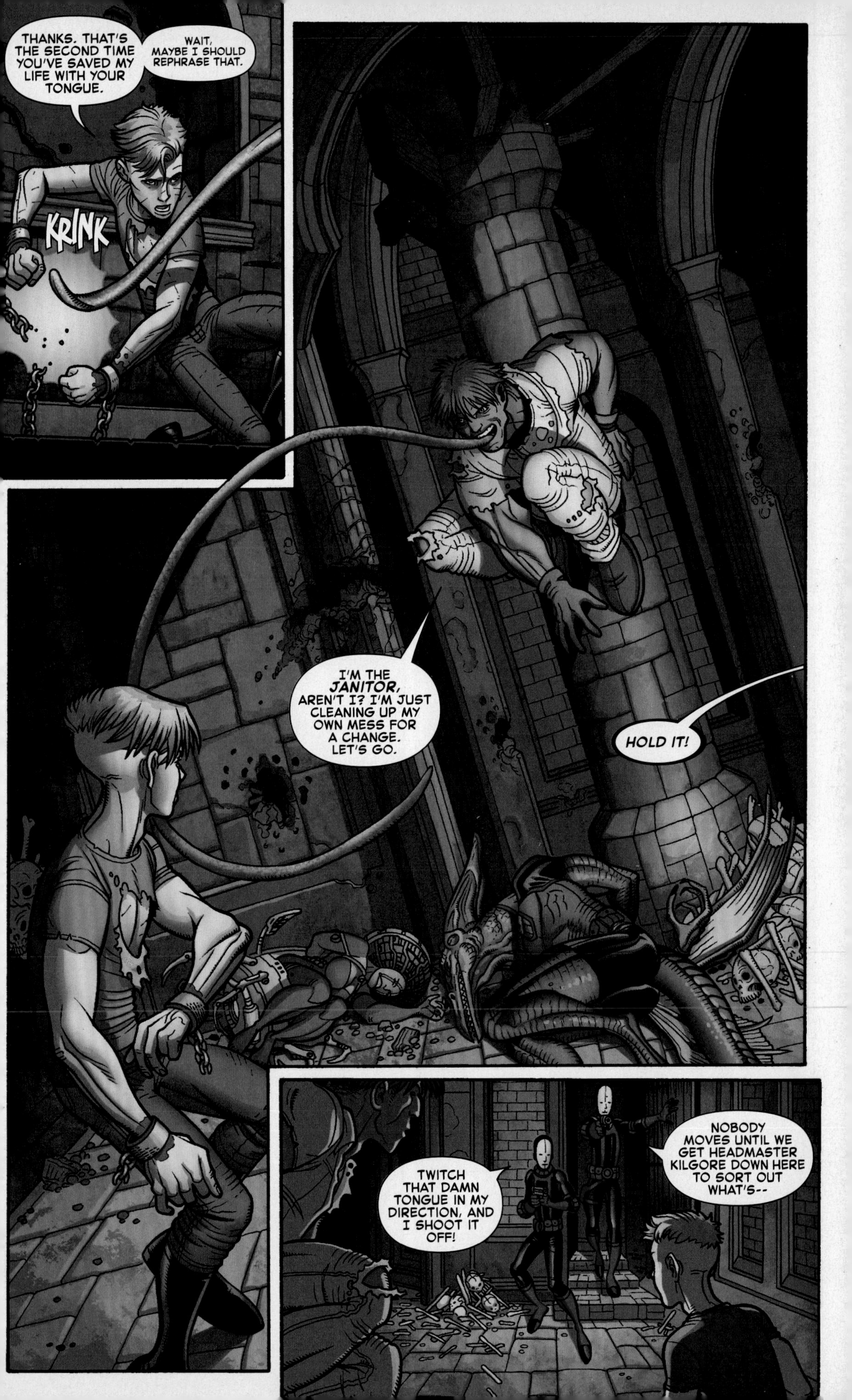
THANKS. THAT'S THE SECOND TIME YOU'VE SAVED MY LIFE WITH YOUR TONGUE.
WAIT, MAYBE I SHOULD REPHRASE THAT.
KRINK
I'M THE *JANITOR*, AREN'T I? I'M JUST CLEANING UP MY OWN MESS FOR A CHANGE. LET'S GO.
HOLD IT!
TWITCH THAT DAMN TONGUE IN MY DIRECTION, AND I SHOOT IT OFF!
NOBODY MOVES UNTIL WE GET HEADMASTER KILGORE DOWN HERE TO SORT OUT WHAT'S--

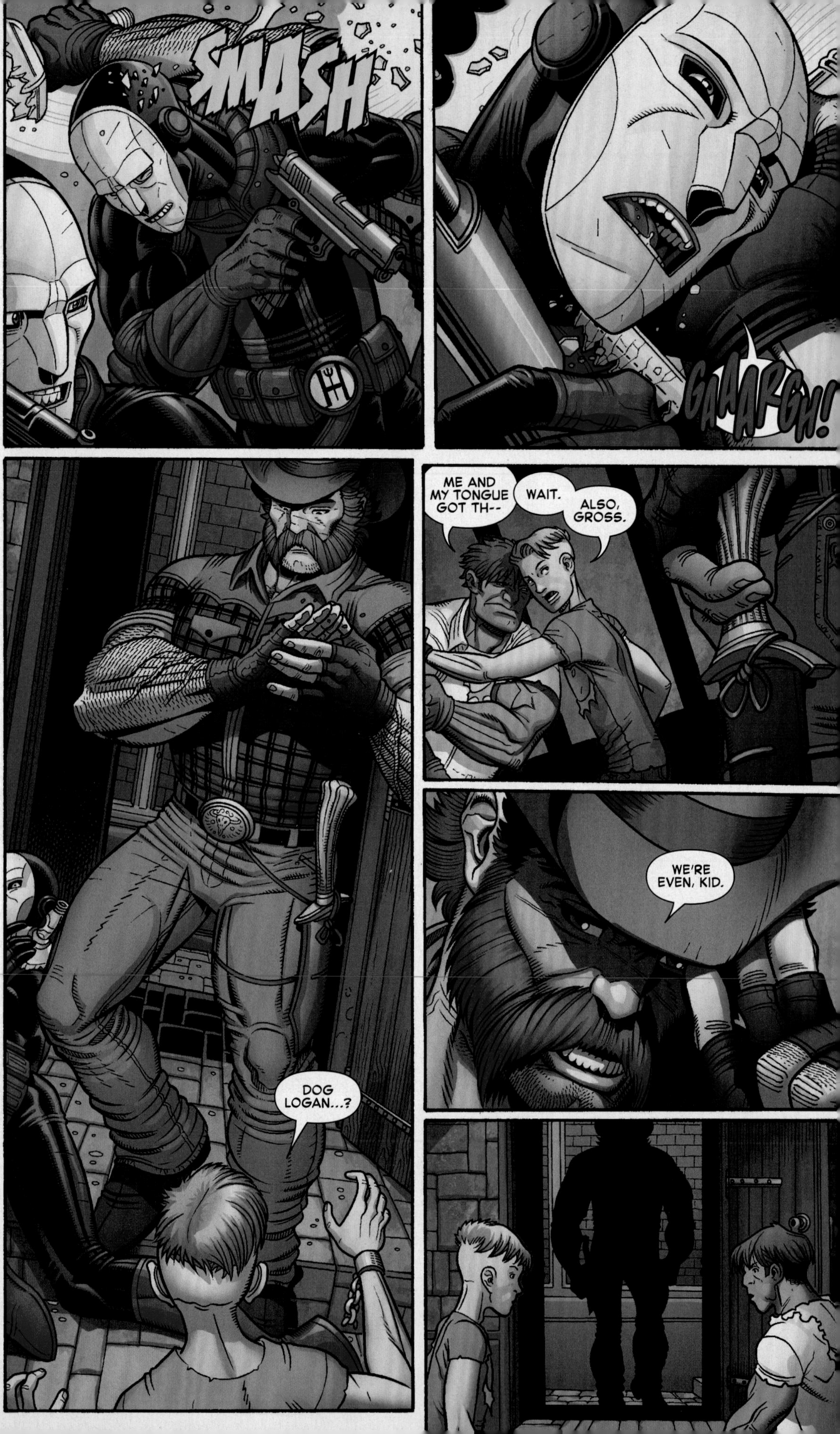
SMASH
GAAARGH!
DOG LOGAN...?
ME AND MY TONGUE GOT TH--
WAIT.
ALSO, GROSS.
WE'RE EVEN, KID.

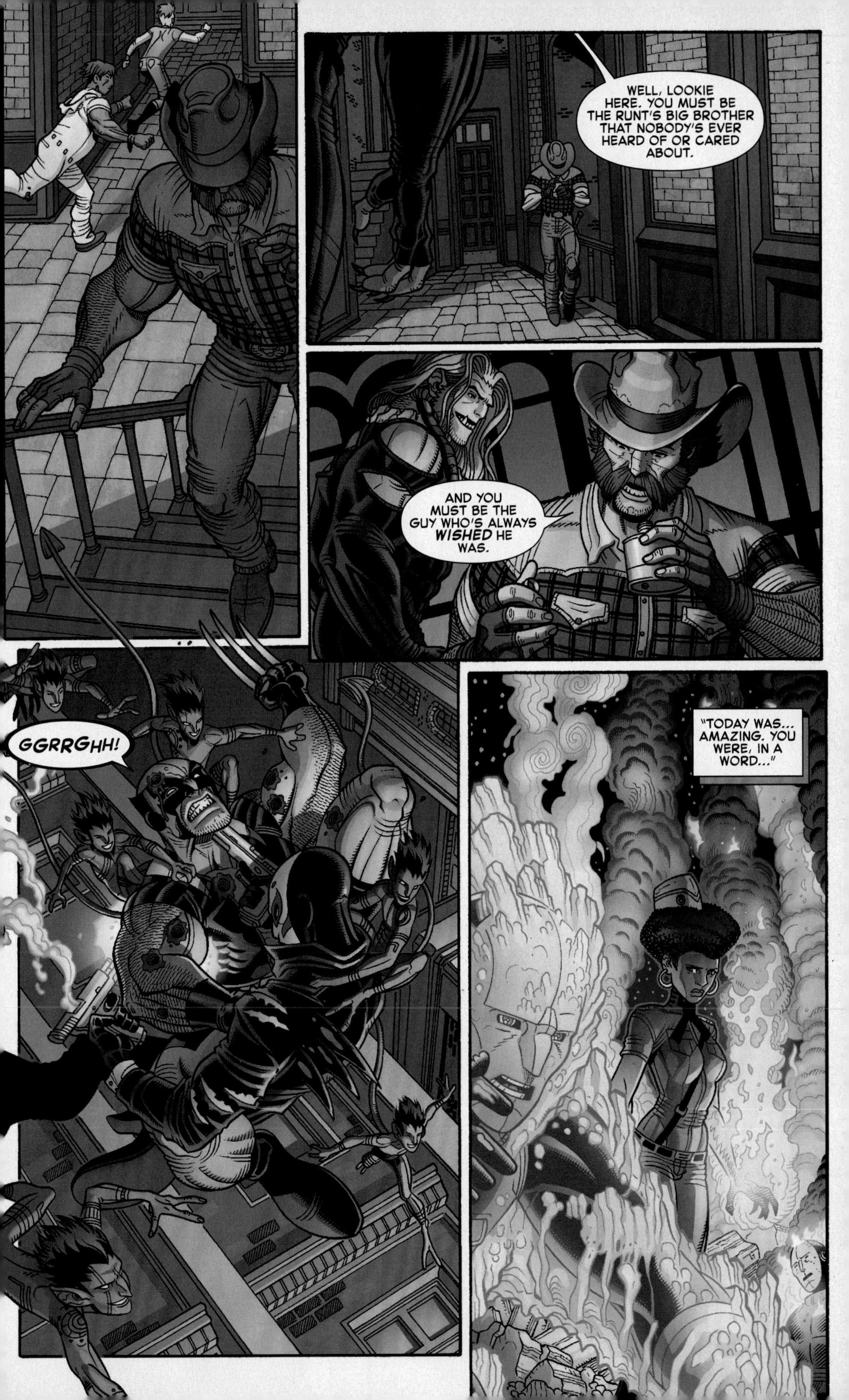
WELL, LOOKIE HERE. YOU MUST BE THE RUNT'S BIG BROTHER THAT NOBODY'S EVER HEARD OF OR CARED ABOUT.
AND YOU MUST BE THE GUY WHO'S ALWAYS WISHED HE WAS.
GGRRGHH!
"TODAY WAS... AMAZING. YOU WERE, IN A WORD..."

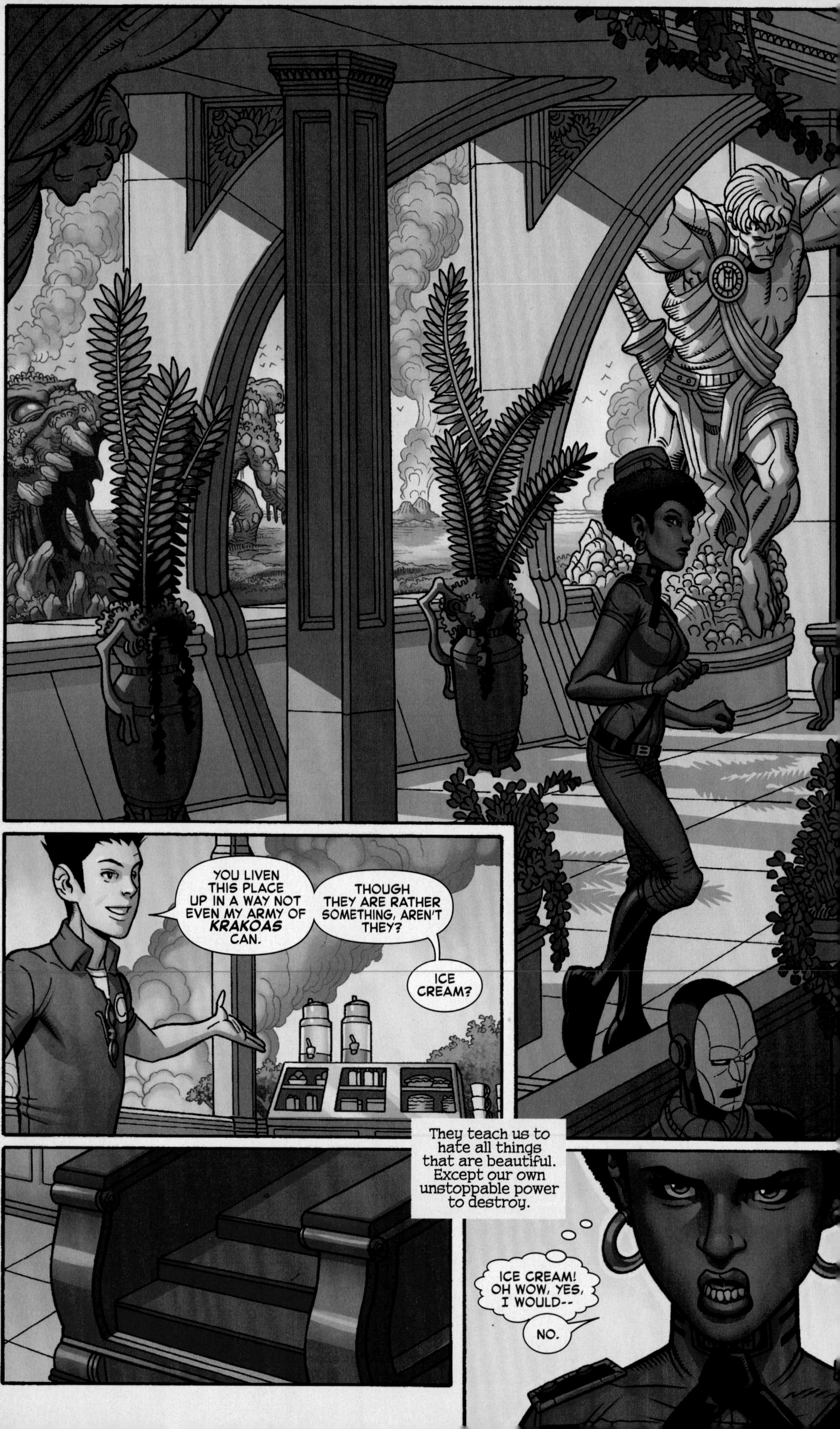
YOU LIVEN THIS PLACE UP IN A WAY NOT EVEN MY ARMY OF KRAKOAS CAN.
THOUGH THEY ARE RATHER SOMETHING, AREN'T THEY?
ICE CREAM?
They teach us to hate all things that are beautiful. Except our own unstoppable power to destroy.
ICE CREAM! OH WOW, YES, I WOULD--
NO.

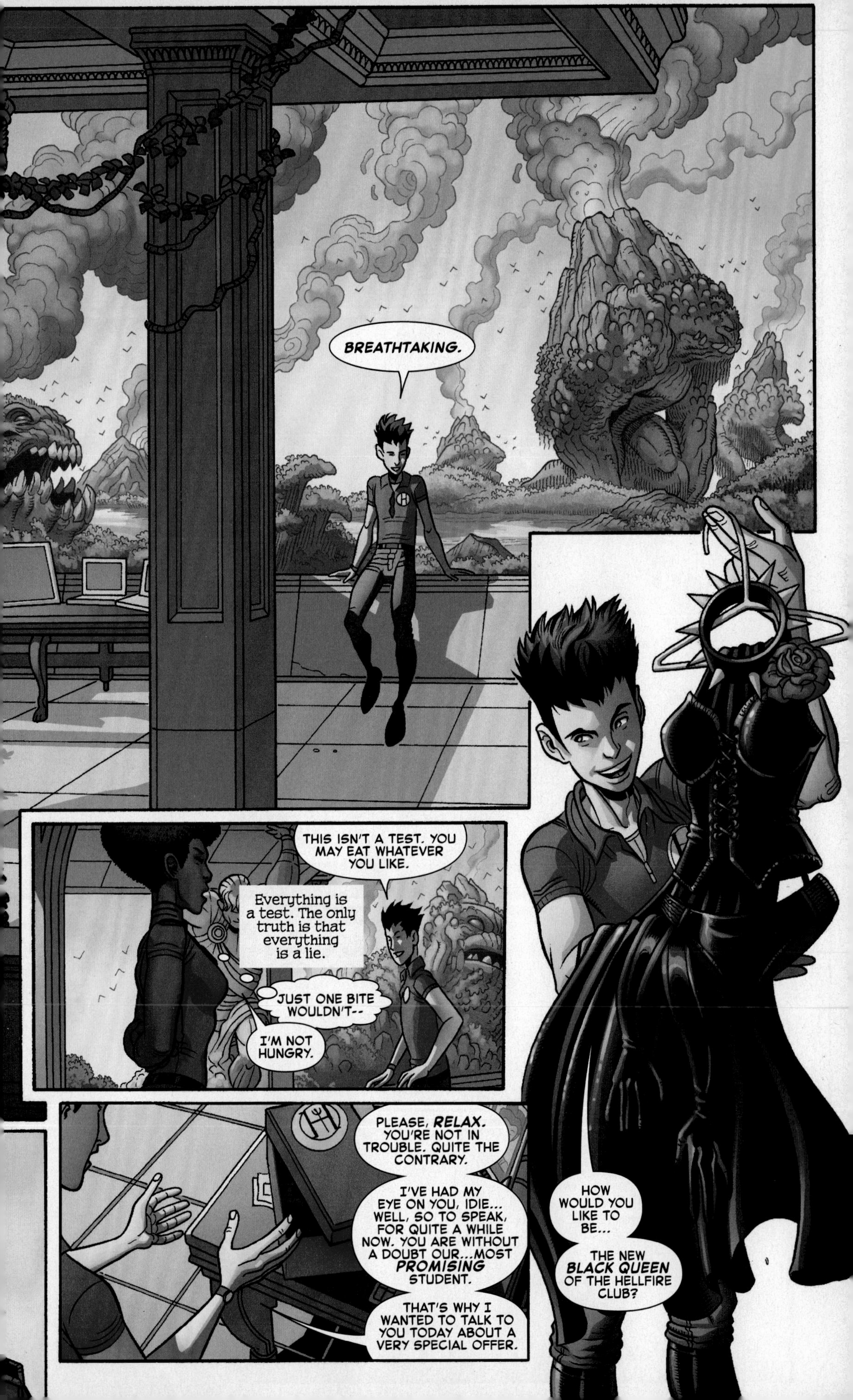
BREATHTAKING.
THIS ISN'T A TEST. YOU MAY EAT WHATEVER YOU LIKE.
Everything is a test. The only truth is that everything is a lie.
JUST ONE BITE WOULDN'T--
I'M NOT HUNGRY.
PLEASE, RELAX. YOU'RE NOT IN TROUBLE. QUITE THE CONTRARY.
I'VE HAD MY EYE ON YOU, IDIE... WELL, SO TO SPEAK, FOR QUITE A WHILE NOW. YOU ARE WITHOUT A DOUBT OUR...MOST PROMISING STUDENT.
THAT'S WHY I WANTED TO TALK TO YOU TODAY ABOUT A VERY SPECIAL OFFER.
HOW WOULD YOU LIKE TO BE...
THE NEW BLACK QUEEN OF THE HELLFIRE CLUB?

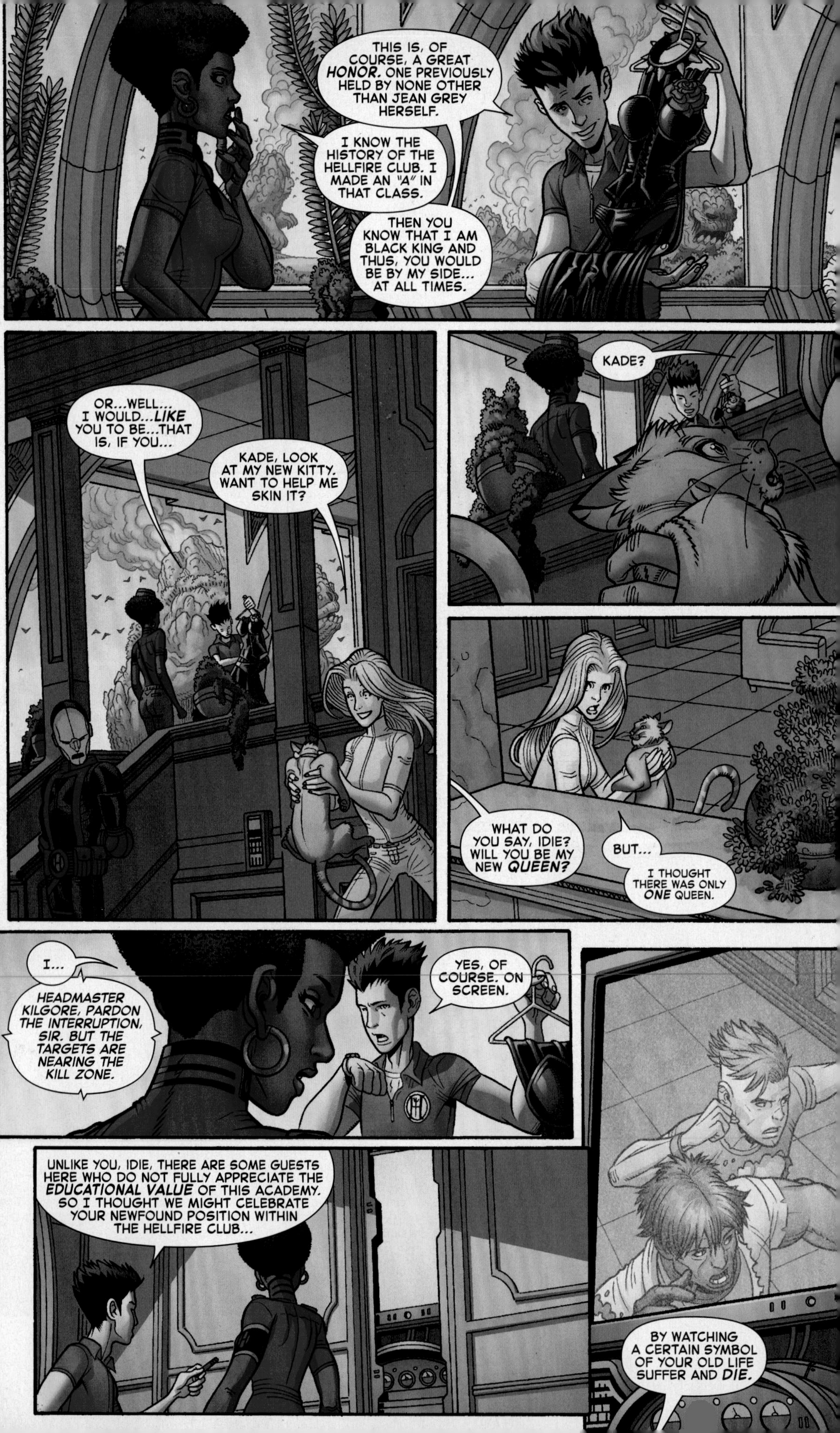
THIS IS, OF COURSE, A GREAT HONOR. ONE PREVIOUSLY HELD BY NONE OTHER THAN JEAN GREY HERSELF.
I KNOW THE HISTORY OF THE HELLFIRE CLUB. I MADE AN "A" IN THAT CLASS.
THEN YOU KNOW THAT I AM BLACK KING AND THUS, YOU WOULD BE BY MY SIDE... AT ALL TIMES.
OR...WELL... I WOULD...LIKE YOU TO BE...THAT IS, IF YOU...
KADE, LOOK AT MY NEW KITTY. WANT TO HELP ME SKIN IT?
KADE?
WHAT DO YOU SAY, IDIE? WILL YOU BE MY NEW QUEEN?
BUT...
I THOUGHT THERE WAS ONLY ONE QUEEN.
I...
HEADMASTER KILGORE, PARDON THE INTERRUPTION, SIR. BUT THE TARGETS ARE NEARING THE KILL ZONE.
YES, OF COURSE. ON SCREEN.
UNLIKE YOU, IDIE, THERE ARE SOME GUESTS HERE WHO DO NOT FULLY APPRECIATE THE EDUCATIONAL VALUE OF THIS ACADEMY. SO I THOUGHT WE MIGHT CELEBRATE YOUR NEWFOUND POSITION WITHIN THE HELLFIRE CLUB...
BY WATCHING A CERTAIN SYMBOL OF YOUR OLD LIFE SUFFER AND DIE.

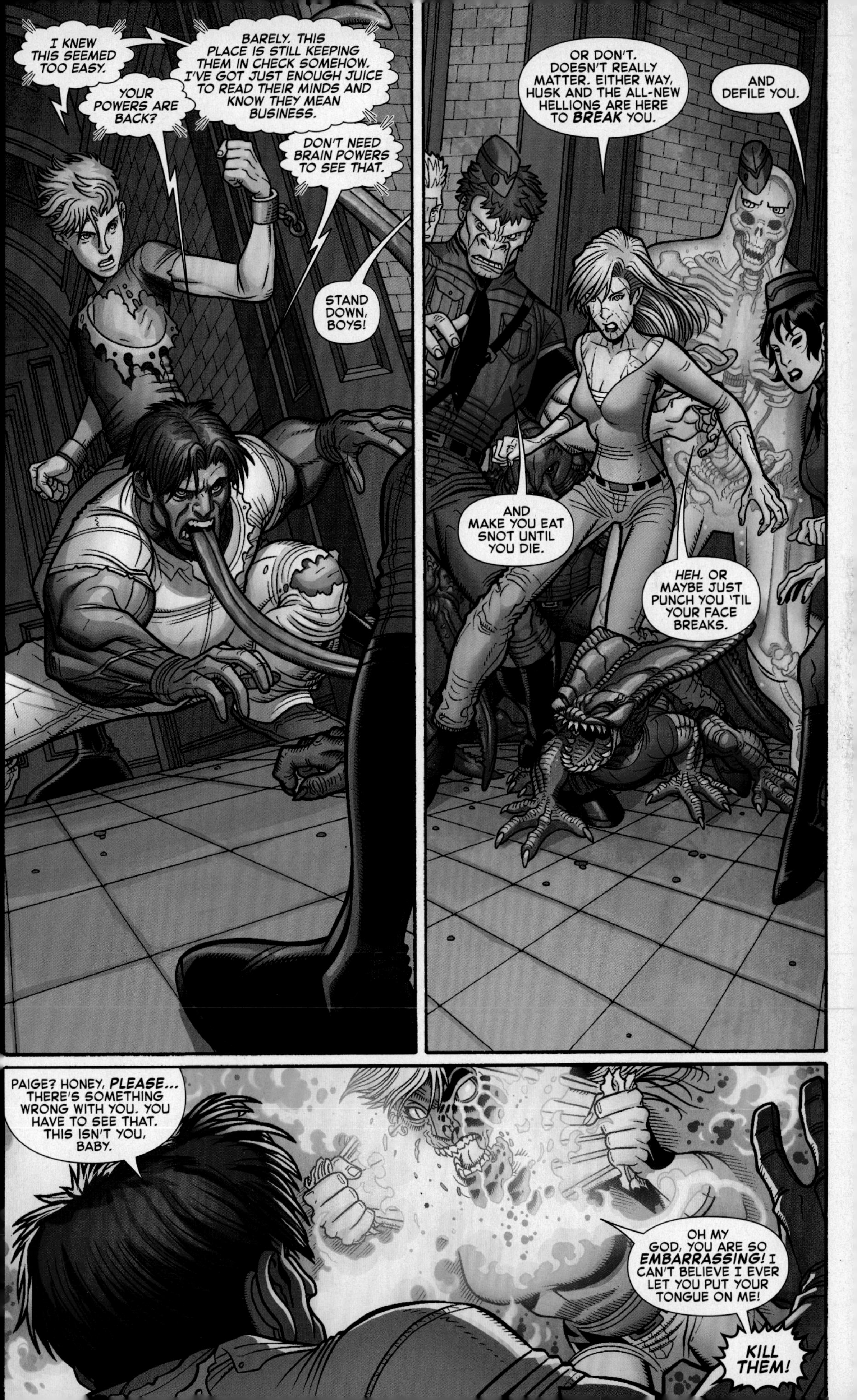
I KNEW THIS SEEMED TOO EASY.
YOUR POWERS ARE BACK?
BARELY. THIS PLACE IS STILL KEEPING THEM IN CHECK SOMEHOW. I'VE GOT JUST ENOUGH JUICE TO READ THEIR MINDS AND KNOW THEY MEAN BUSINESS.
DON'T NEED BRAIN POWERS TO SEE THAT.
STAND DOWN, BOYS!
OR DON'T. DOESN'T REALLY MATTER. EITHER WAY, HUSK AND THE ALL-NEW HELLIONS ARE HERE TO BREAK YOU.
AND DEFILE YOU.
AND MAKE YOU EAT SNOT UNTIL YOU DIE.
HEH. OR MAYBE JUST PUNCH YOU 'TIL YOUR FACE BREAKS.
PAIGE? HONEY, PLEASE... THERE'S SOMETHING WRONG WITH YOU. YOU HAVE TO SEE THAT. THIS ISN'T YOU, BABY.
OH MY GOD, YOU ARE SO EMBARRASSING! I CAN'T BELIEVE I EVER LET YOU PUT YOUR TONGUE ON ME!
KILL THEM!

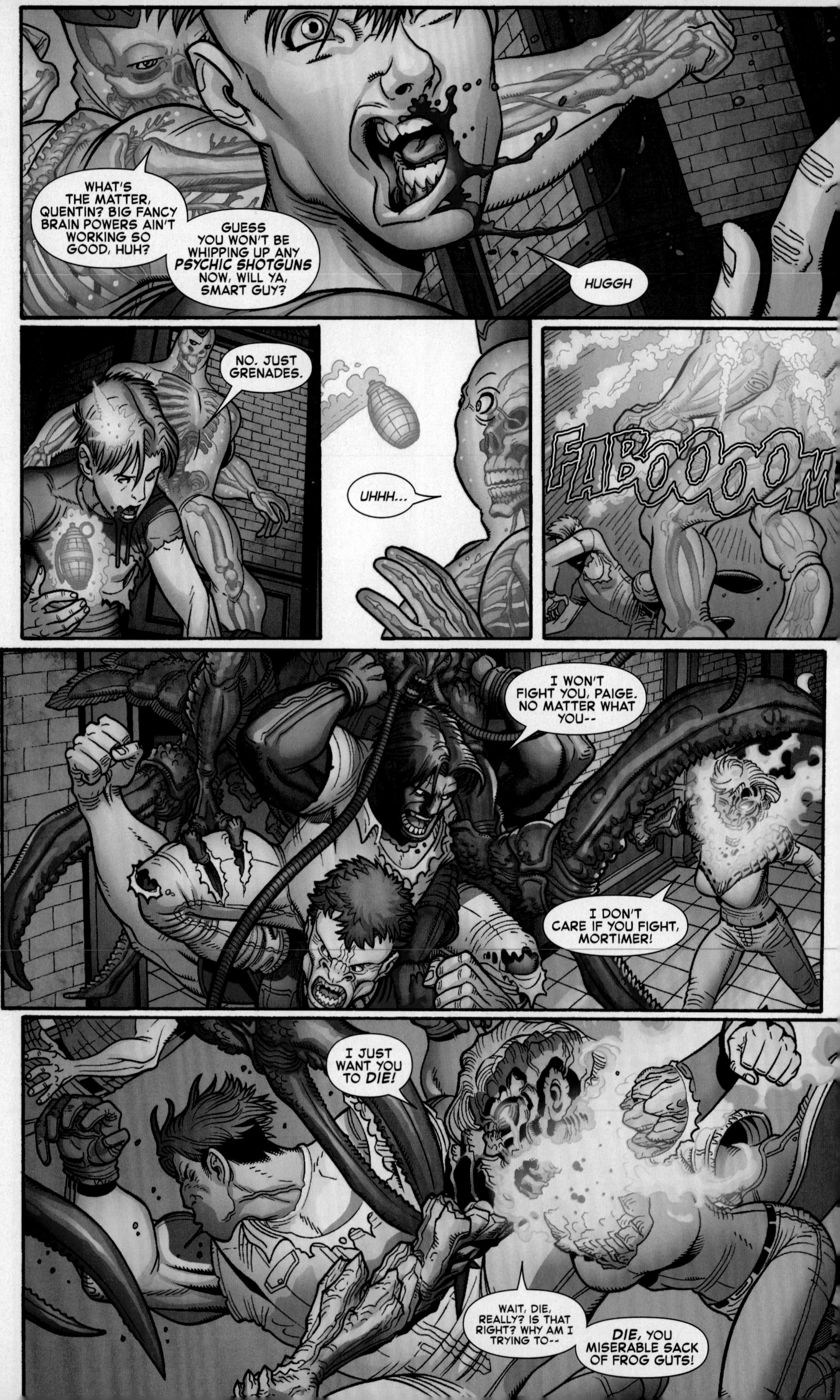
WHAT'S THE MATTER, QUENTIN? BIG FANCY BRAIN POWERS AIN'T WORKING SO GOOD, HUH?
GUESS YOU WON'T BE WHIPPING UP ANY *PSYCHIC SHOTGUNS* NOW, WILL YA, SMART GUY?
HUGGH
NO. JUST GRENADES.
UHHH...
FABOOOOOM
I WON'T FIGHT YOU, PAIGE. NO MATTER WHAT YOU--
I DON'T CARE IF YOU FIGHT, MORTIMER!
I JUST WANT YOU TO *DIE!*
WAIT, DIE, REALLY? IS THAT RIGHT? WHY AM I TRYING TO--
DIE, YOU MISERABLE SACK OF FROG GUTS!

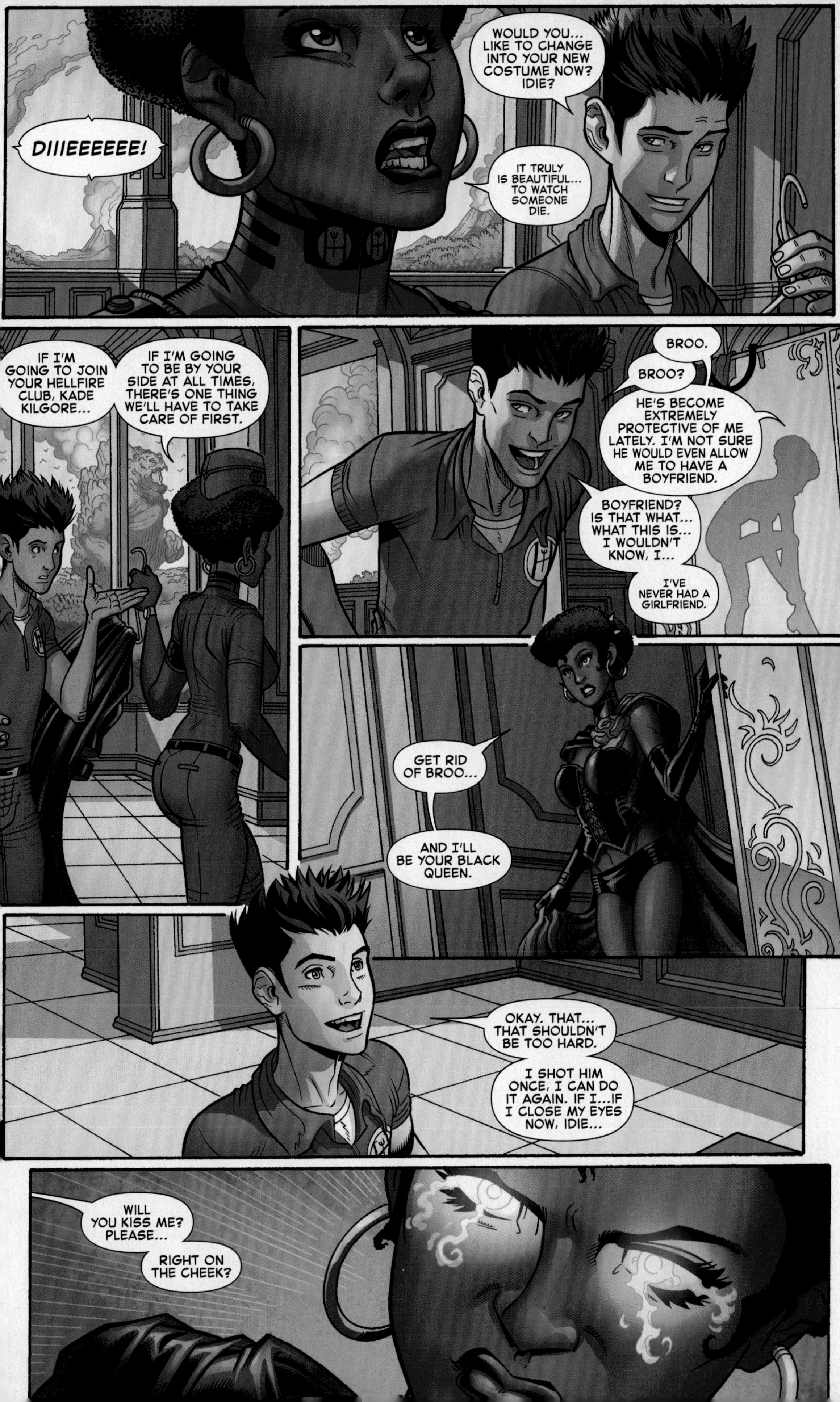
WOULD YOU... LIKE TO CHANGE INTO YOUR NEW COSTUME NOW? IDIE?
DIIIEEEEEE!
IT TRULY IS BEAUTIFUL... TO WATCH SOMEONE DIE.
IF I'M GOING TO JOIN YOUR HELLFIRE CLUB, KADE KILGORE...
IF I'M GOING TO BE BY YOUR SIDE AT ALL TIMES, THERE'S ONE THING WE'LL HAVE TO TAKE CARE OF FIRST.
BROO.
BROO?
HE'S BECOME EXTREMELY PROTECTIVE OF ME LATELY. I'M NOT SURE HE WOULD EVEN ALLOW ME TO HAVE A BOYFRIEND.
BOYFRIEND? IS THAT WHAT... WHAT THIS IS... I WOULDN'T KNOW, I...
I'VE NEVER HAD A GIRLFRIEND.
GET RID OF BROO...
AND I'LL BE YOUR BLACK QUEEN.
OKAY. THAT... THAT SHOULDN'T BE TOO HARD.
I SHOT HIM ONCE, I CAN DO IT AGAIN. IF I...IF I CLOSE MY EYES NOW, IDIE...
WILL YOU KISS ME? PLEASE...
RIGHT ON THE CHEEK?

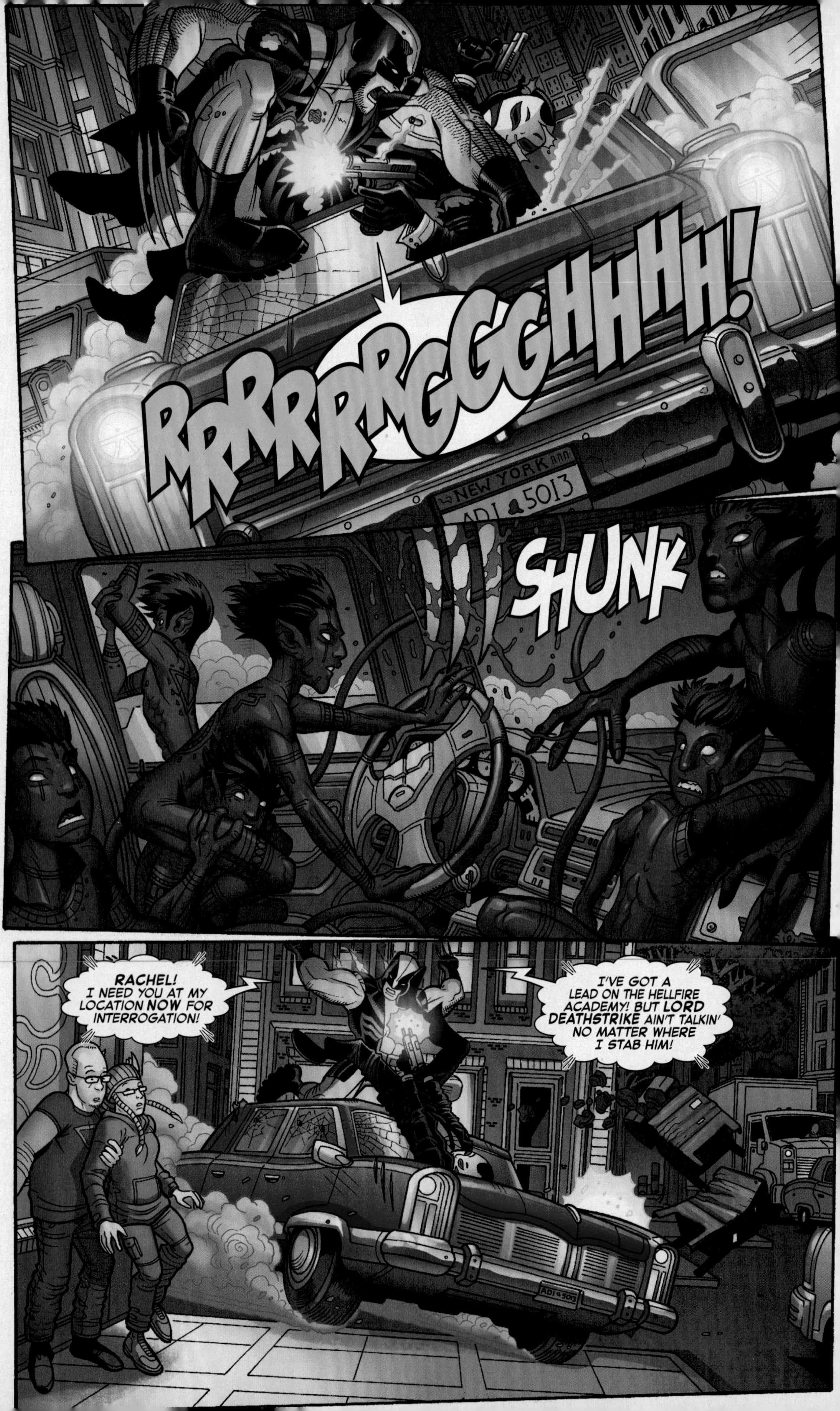
RRRRRRGGGHHHH!
NEW YORK
ADI 5013
SHUNK
RACHEL! I NEED YOU AT MY LOCATION NOW FOR INTERROGATION!
I'VE GOT A LEAD ON THE HELLFIRE ACADEMY! BUT LORD DEATHSTRIKE AIN'T TALKIN' NO MATTER WHERE I STAB HIM!

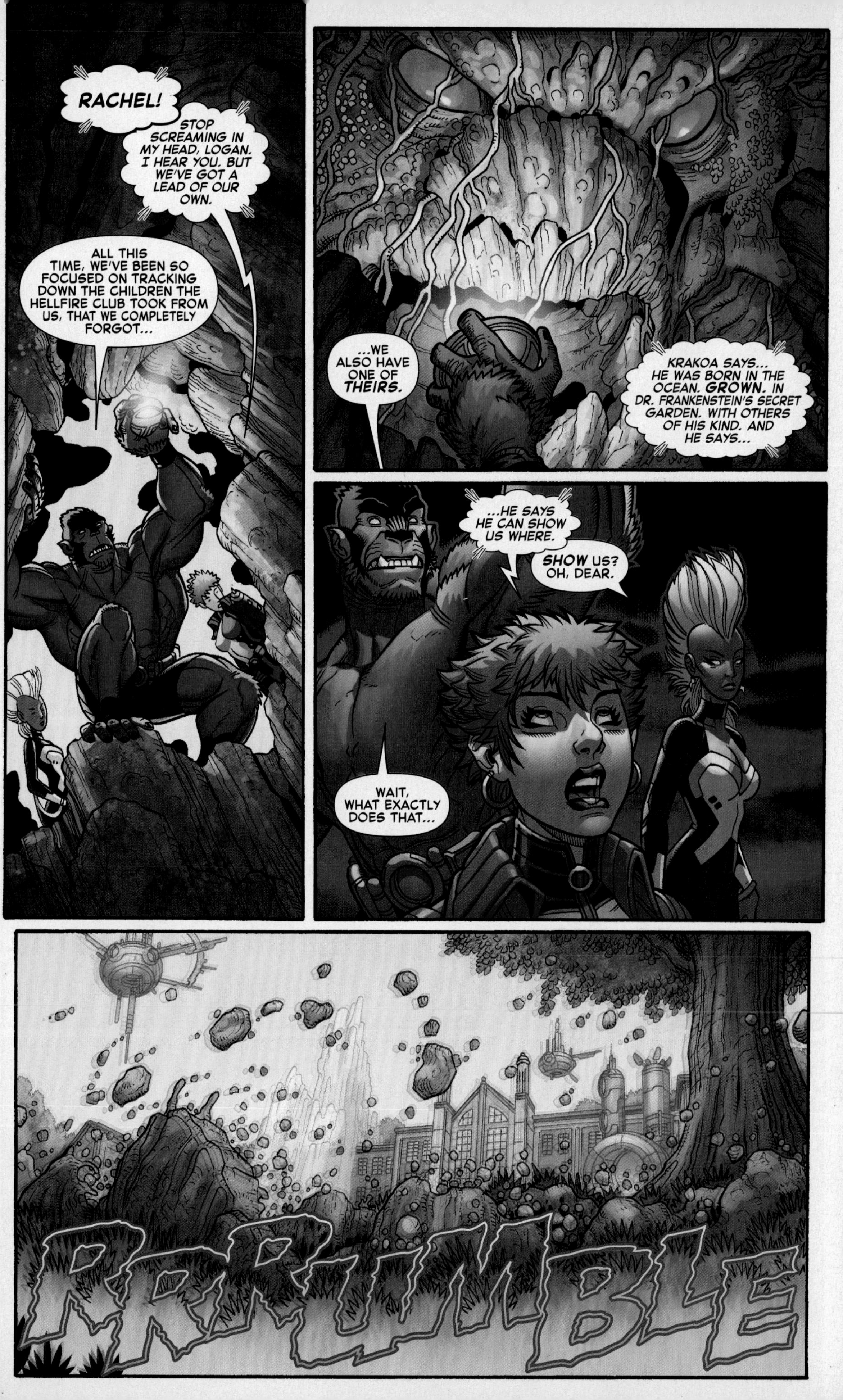
RACHEL!
STOP SCREAMING IN MY HEAD, LOGAN. I HEAR YOU. BUT WE'VE GOT A LEAD OF OUR OWN.
ALL THIS TIME, WE'VE BEEN SO FOCUSED ON TRACKING DOWN THE CHILDREN THE HELLFIRE CLUB TOOK FROM US, THAT WE COMPLETELY FORGOT...
...WE ALSO HAVE ONE OF THEIRS.
KRAKOA SAYS... HE WAS BORN IN THE OCEAN. GROWN. IN DR. FRANKENSTEIN'S SECRET GARDEN. WITH OTHERS OF HIS KIND. AND HE SAYS...
...HE SAYS HE CAN SHOW US WHERE.
SHOW US? OH, DEAR.
WAIT, WHAT EXACTLY DOES THAT...
RRRUMBLE

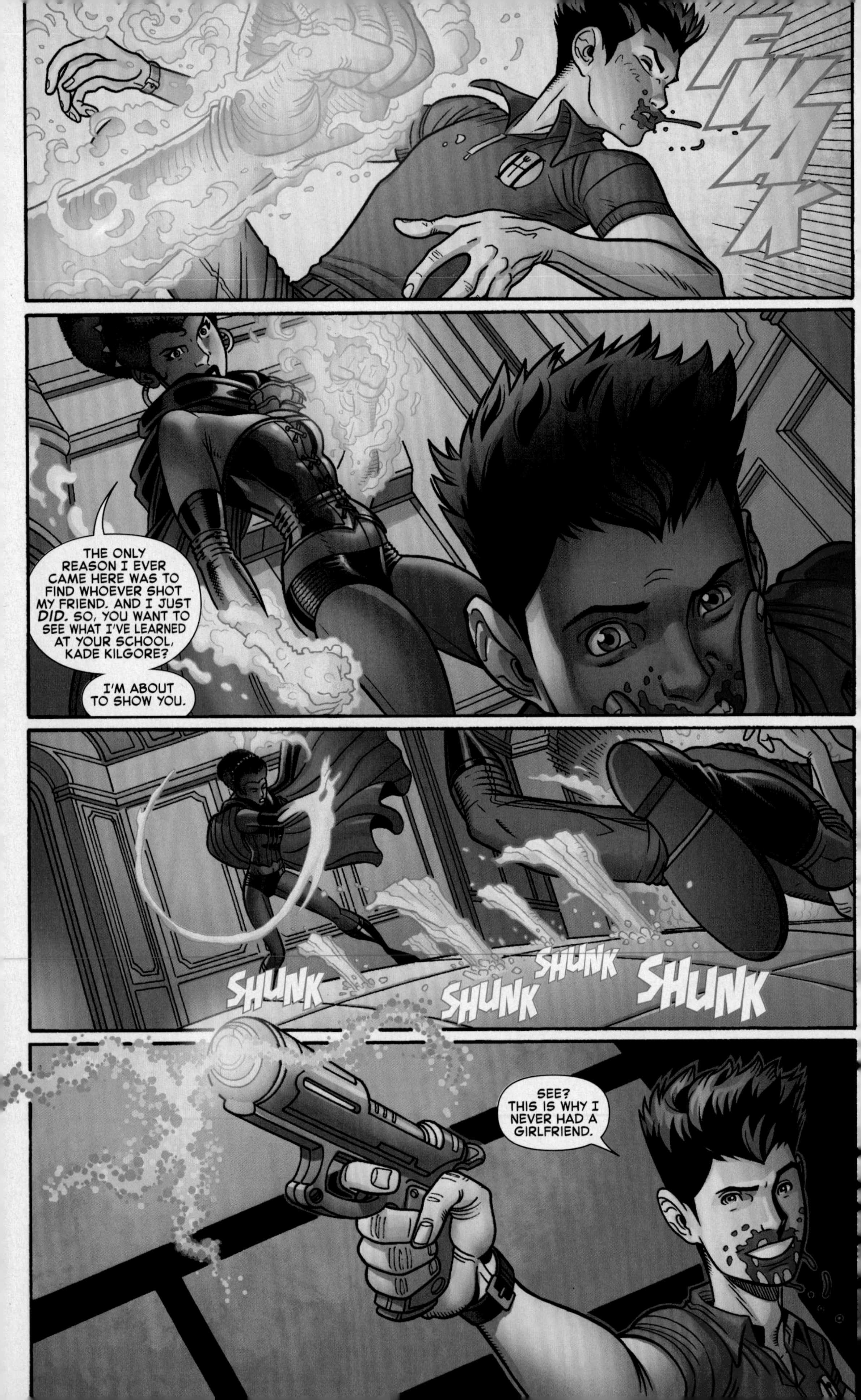
FWAK
THE ONLY REASON I EVER CAME HERE WAS TO FIND WHOEVER SHOT MY FRIEND. AND I JUST *DID.* SO, YOU WANT TO SEE WHAT I'VE LEARNED AT YOUR SCHOOL, KADE KILGORE?
I'M ABOUT TO SHOW YOU.
SHUNK
SHUNK
SHUNK
SHUNK
SEE? THIS IS WHY I NEVER HAD A GIRLFRIEND.

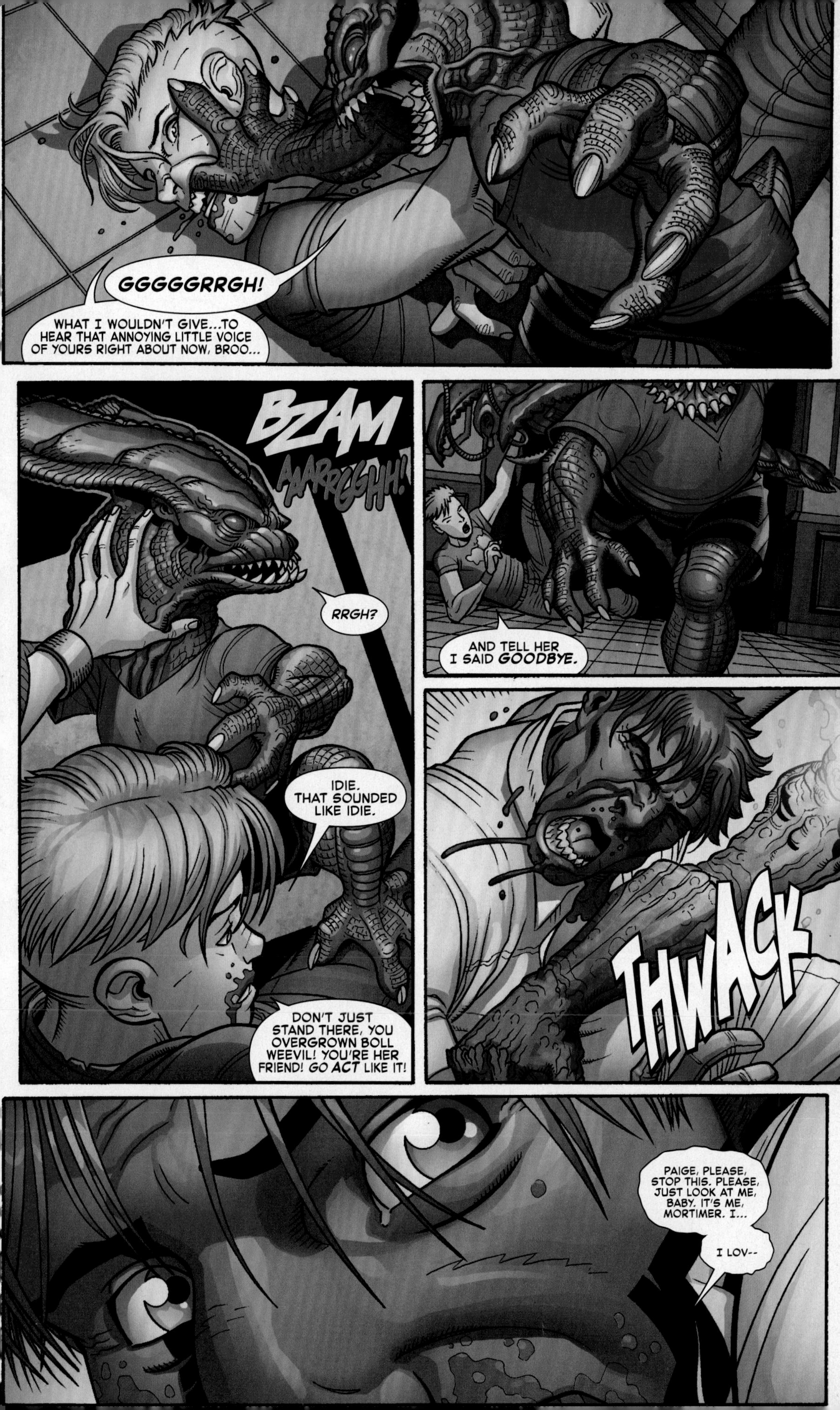
GGGGGRRGH!
WHAT I WOULDN'T GIVE...TO HEAR THAT ANNOYING LITTLE VOICE OF YOURS RIGHT ABOUT NOW, BROO...
BZAM
AAARRGGHH!
RRGH?
IDIE. THAT SOUNDED LIKE IDIE.
DON'T JUST STAND THERE, YOU OVERGROWN BOLL WEEVIL! YOU'RE HER FRIEND! GO ACT LIKE IT!
AND TELL HER I SAID GOODBYE.
THWACK
PAIGE, PLEASE, STOP THIS. PLEASE, JUST LOOK AT ME, BABY. IT'S ME, MORTIMER. I...
I LOV--

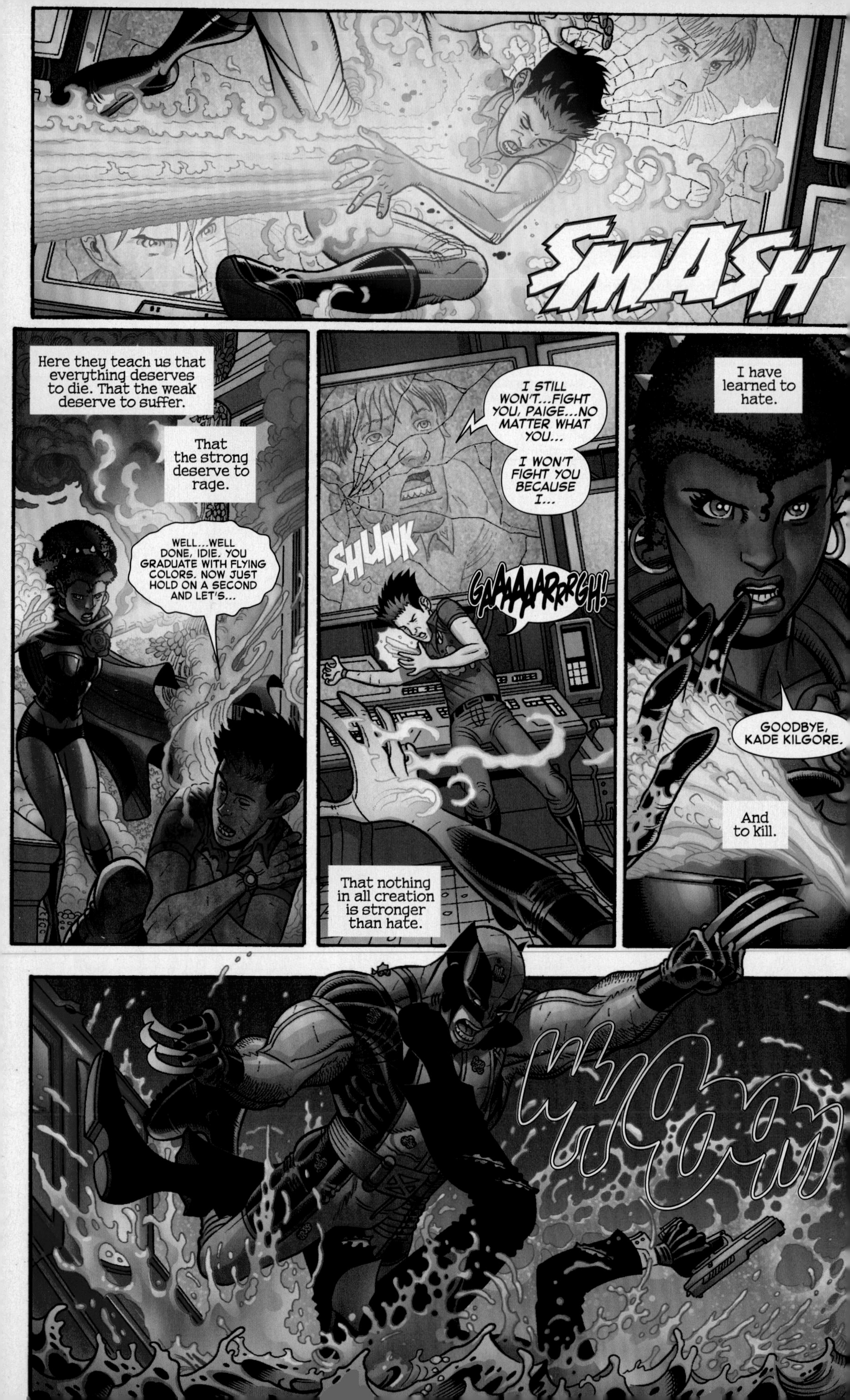
SMASH
Here they teach us that everything deserves to die. That the weak deserve to suffer.
That the strong deserve to rage.
WELL...WELL DONE, IDIE. YOU GRADUATE WITH FLYING COLORS. NOW JUST HOLD ON A SECOND AND LET'S...
I STILL WON'T...FIGHT YOU, PAIGE...NO MATTER WHAT YOU...
I WON'T FIGHT YOU BECAUSE I...
SHUNK
GAAAAAARRRGH!
That nothing in all creation is stronger than hate.
I have learned to hate.
GOODBYE, KADE KILGORE.
And to kill.

I have learned to fight without mercy.

PAIGE, I...LOVE YOU.

To not flinch at the sight of blood.

To ignore screams.

To never hesitate at the moment of murder.

I have learned to kill and feel nothing.

EVEN IF YOU KILL ME... I STILL LOVE YOU...

I have learned to kill and feel nothing.

...I STILL LOVE YOU.

Feel nothing.

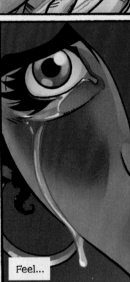

Feel...

So many lessons. So much learning.

And yet I still get the feeling...

That I have so much left to learn.

HUH?

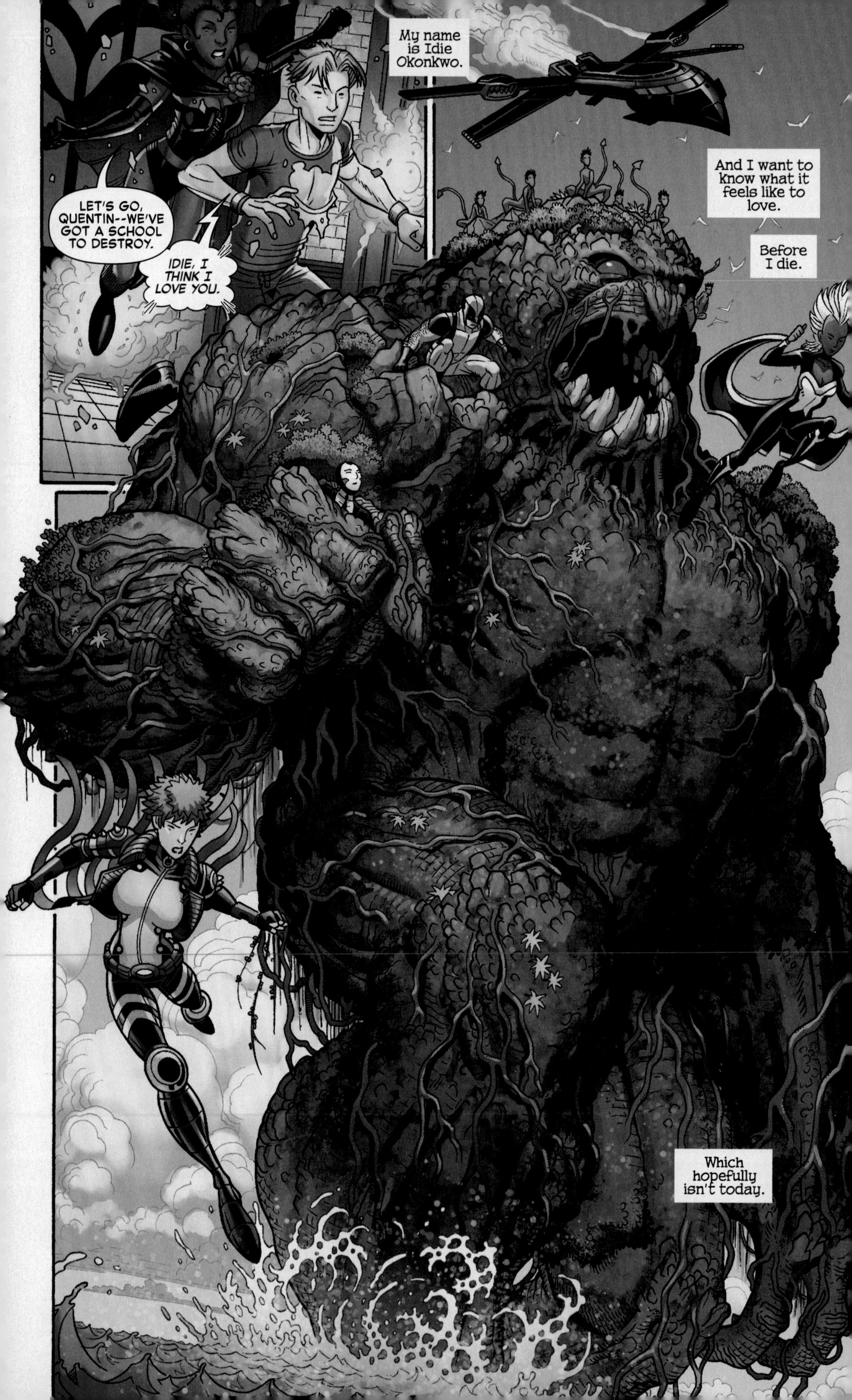

My name is Idie Okonkwo.
LET'S GO, QUENTIN--WE'VE GOT A SCHOOL TO DESTROY.
IDIE, I THINK I LOVE YOU.
And I want to know what it feels like to love.
Before I die.
Which hopefully isn't today.

WOULD YOU RATHER
DREAM ABOUT THE FUTURE OR
BE THE FUTURE?

HELLFIRE ACADEMY

"FAIS CE QUE TU VOUDRAS."

The Hellfire Academy is the only superhuman school in the world where mutant children are trained to realize their full potential. Let our staff of qualified experts teach you to master the awesome power at your fingertips, so that nothing will ever stand in the way of the destiny you deserve.

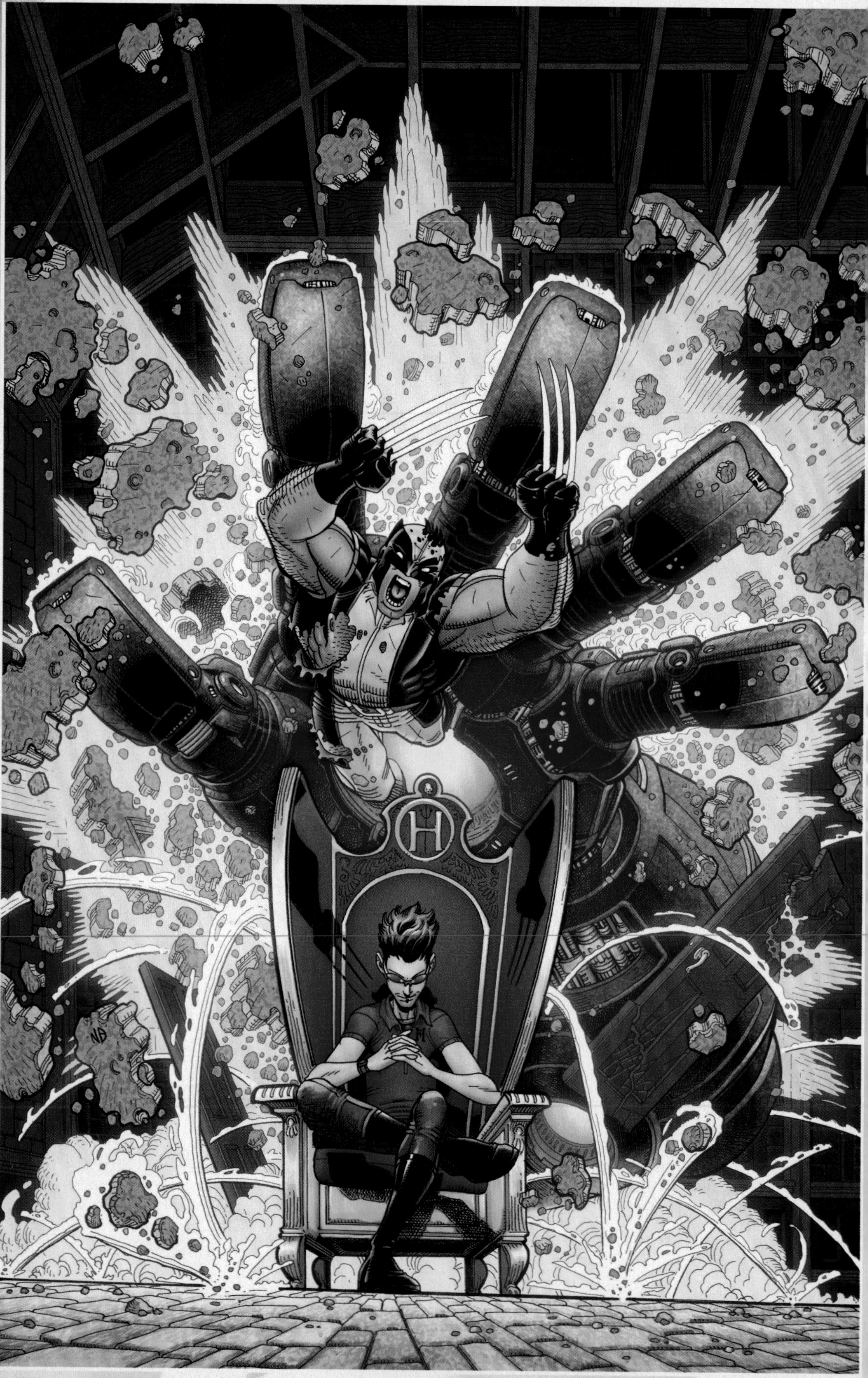

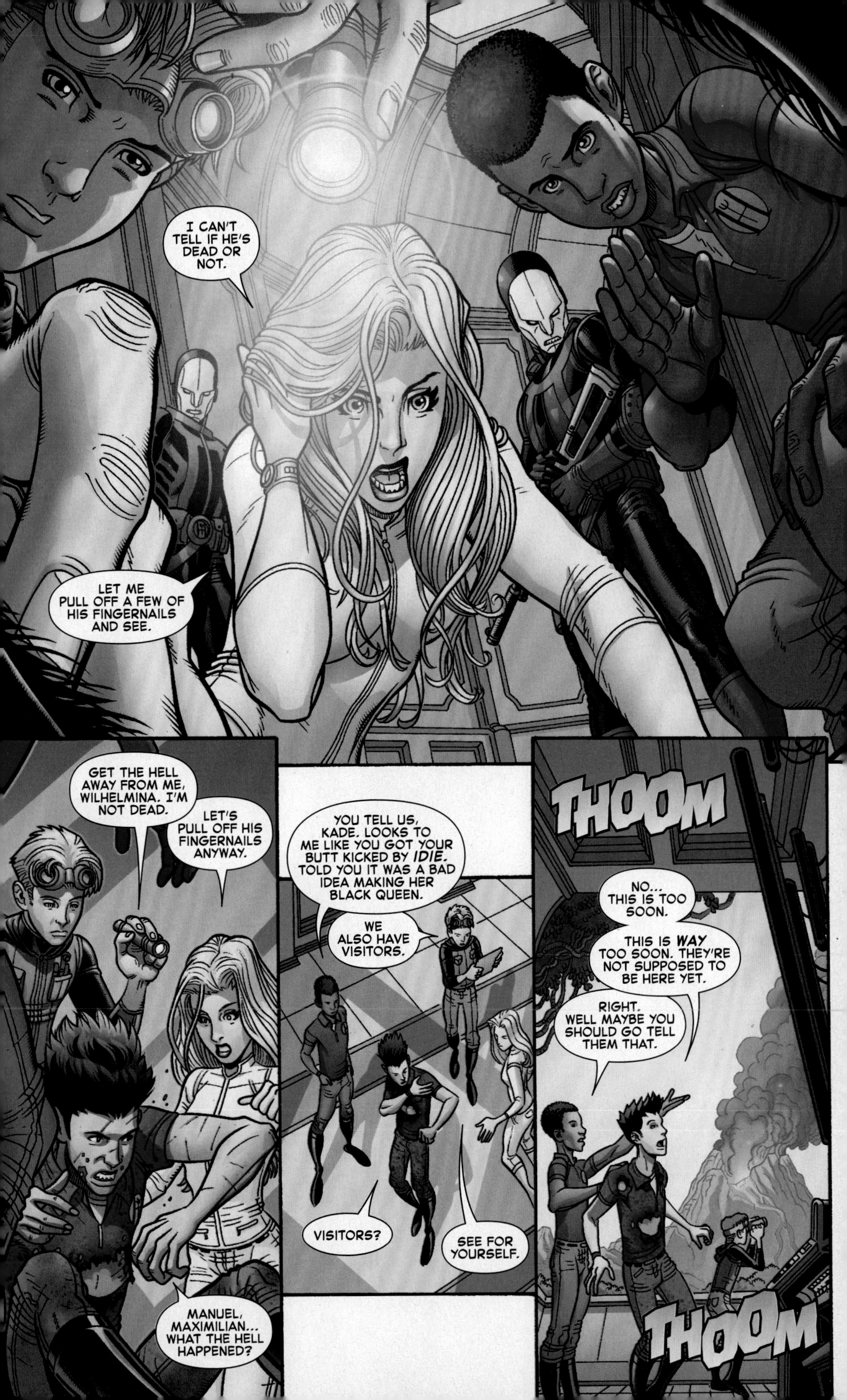
I CAN'T TELL IF HE'S DEAD OR NOT.
LET ME PULL OFF A FEW OF HIS FINGERNAILS AND SEE.
GET THE HELL AWAY FROM ME, WILHELMINA. I'M NOT DEAD.
LET'S PULL OFF HIS FINGERNAILS ANYWAY.
MANUEL, MAXIMILIAN... WHAT THE HELL HAPPENED?
YOU TELL US, KADE. LOOKS TO ME LIKE YOU GOT YOUR BUTT KICKED BY *IDIE*. TOLD YOU IT WAS A BAD IDEA MAKING HER BLACK QUEEN.
WE ALSO HAVE VISITORS.
VISITORS?
SEE FOR YOURSELF.
THOOM
NO... THIS IS TOO SOON.
THIS IS *WAY* TOO SOON. THEY'RE NOT SUPPOSED TO BE HERE YET.
RIGHT. WELL MAYBE YOU SHOULD GO TELL THEM THAT.
THOOM

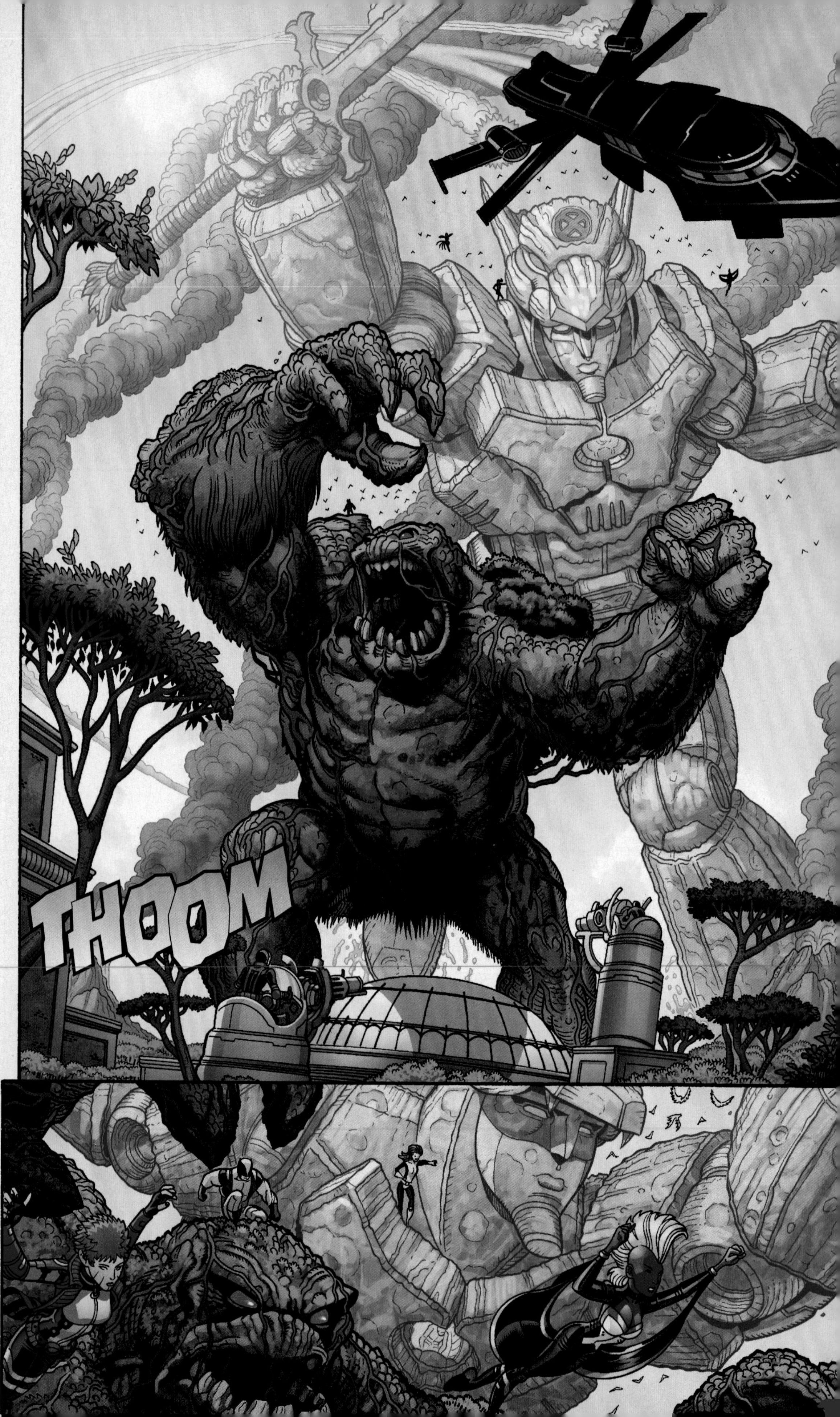
THOOM

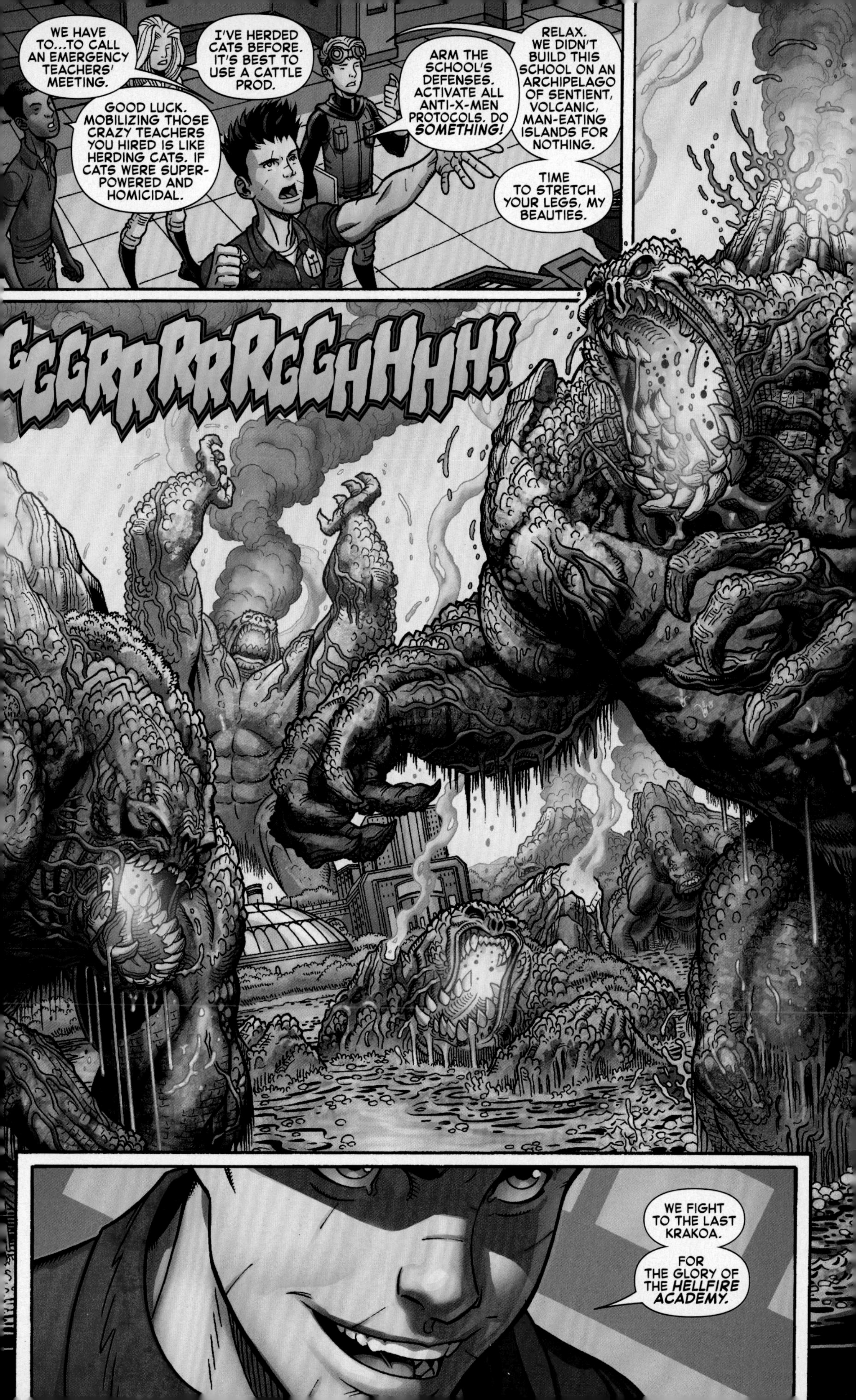
WE HAVE TO...TO CALL AN EMERGENCY TEACHERS' MEETING.
I'VE HERDED CATS BEFORE. IT'S BEST TO USE A CATTLE PROD.
GOOD LUCK. MOBILIZING THOSE CRAZY TEACHERS YOU HIRED IS LIKE HERDING CATS. IF CATS WERE SUPER-POWERED AND HOMICIDAL.
ARM THE SCHOOL'S DEFENSES. ACTIVATE ALL ANTI-X-MEN PROTOCOLS. DO *SOMETHING!*
RELAX. WE DIDN'T BUILD THIS SCHOOL ON AN ARCHIPELAGO OF SENTIENT, VOLCANIC, MAN-EATING ISLANDS FOR NOTHING.
TIME TO STRETCH YOUR LEGS, MY BEAUTIES.
GGRRRRRGHHHH!
WE FIGHT TO THE LAST KRAKOA.
FOR THE GLORY OF THE *HELLFIRE ACADEMY.*

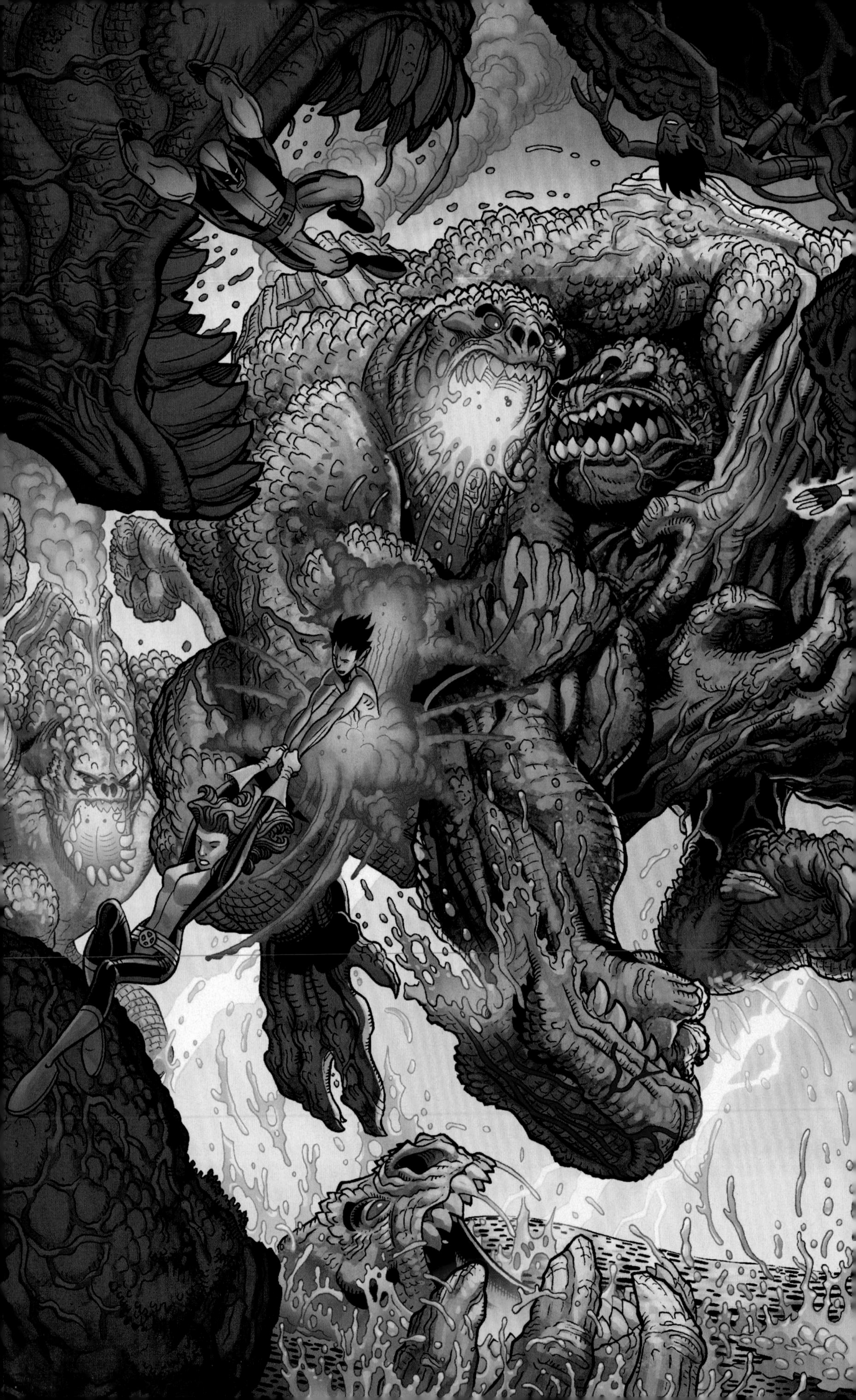

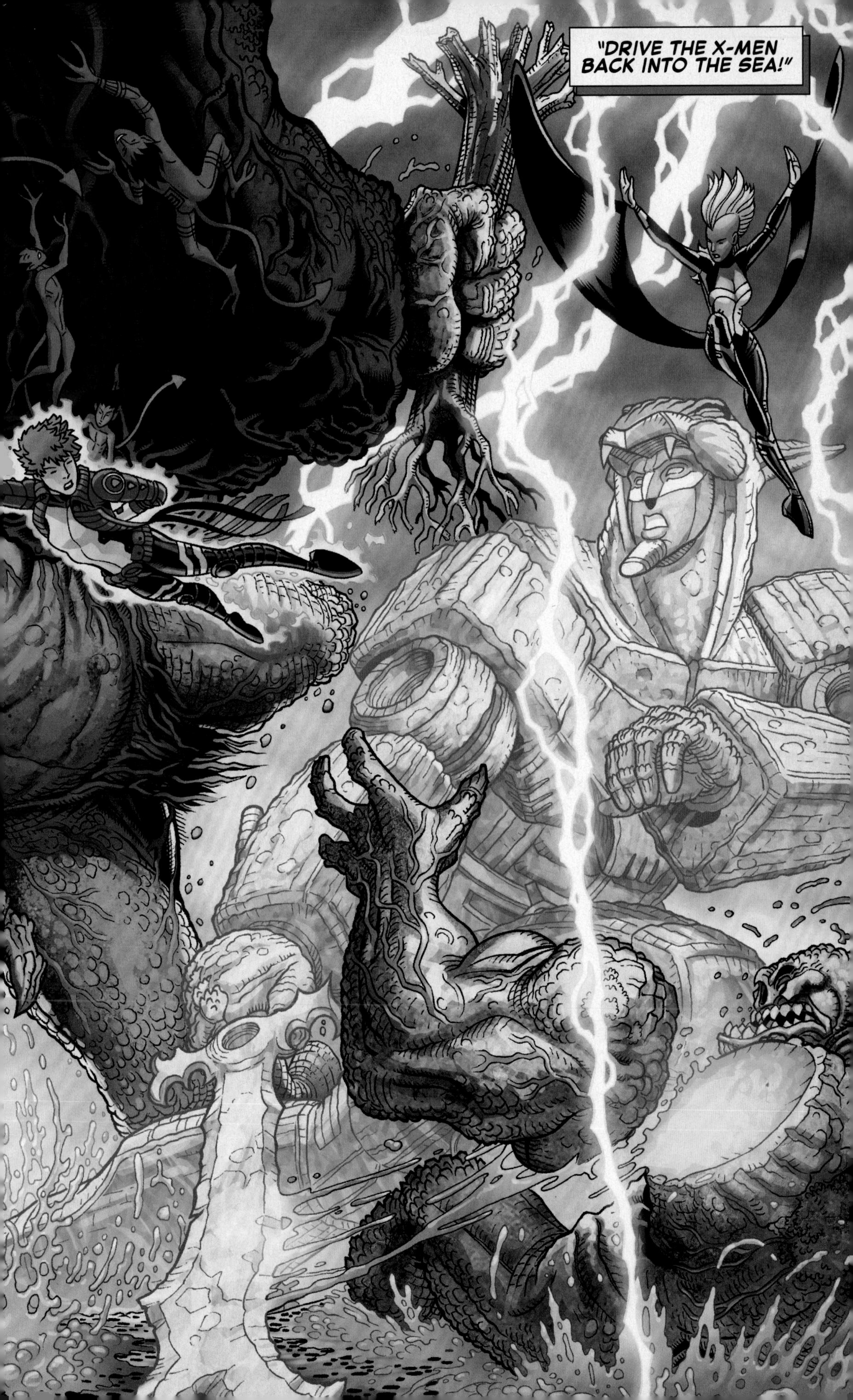
"DRIVE THE X-MEN BACK INTO THE SEA!"

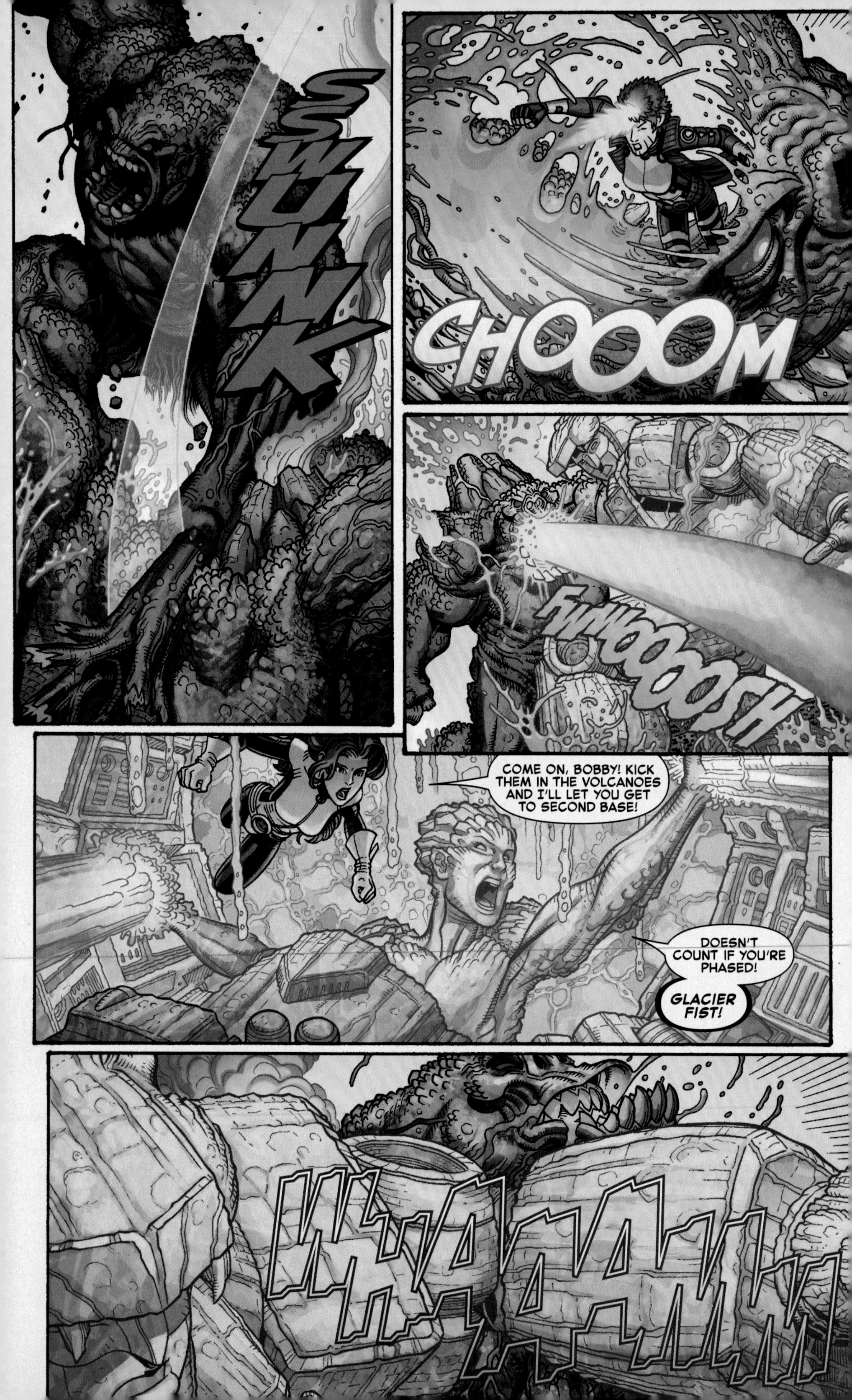
SSWUNK
CHOOOM
FWOOOOSH
COME ON, BOBBY! KICK THEM IN THE VOLCANOES AND I'LL LET YOU GET TO SECOND BASE!
DOESN'T COUNT IF YOU'RE PHASED!
GLACIER FIST!

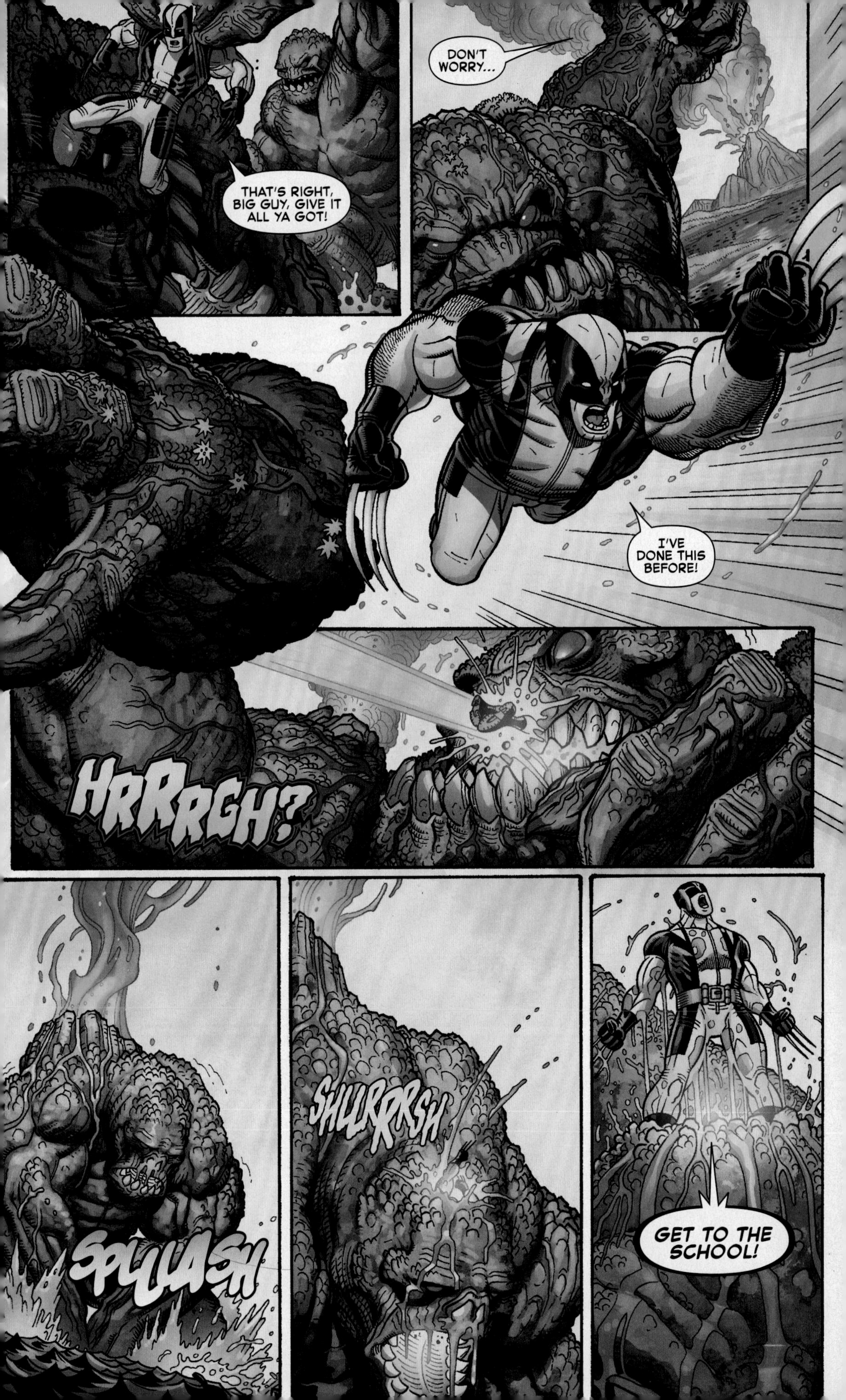
THAT'S RIGHT, BIG GUY, GIVE IT ALL YA GOT!
DON'T WORRY...
I'VE DONE THIS BEFORE!
HRRRGH?
SPLLLASH
SHLLRRRSH
GET TO THE SCHOOL!

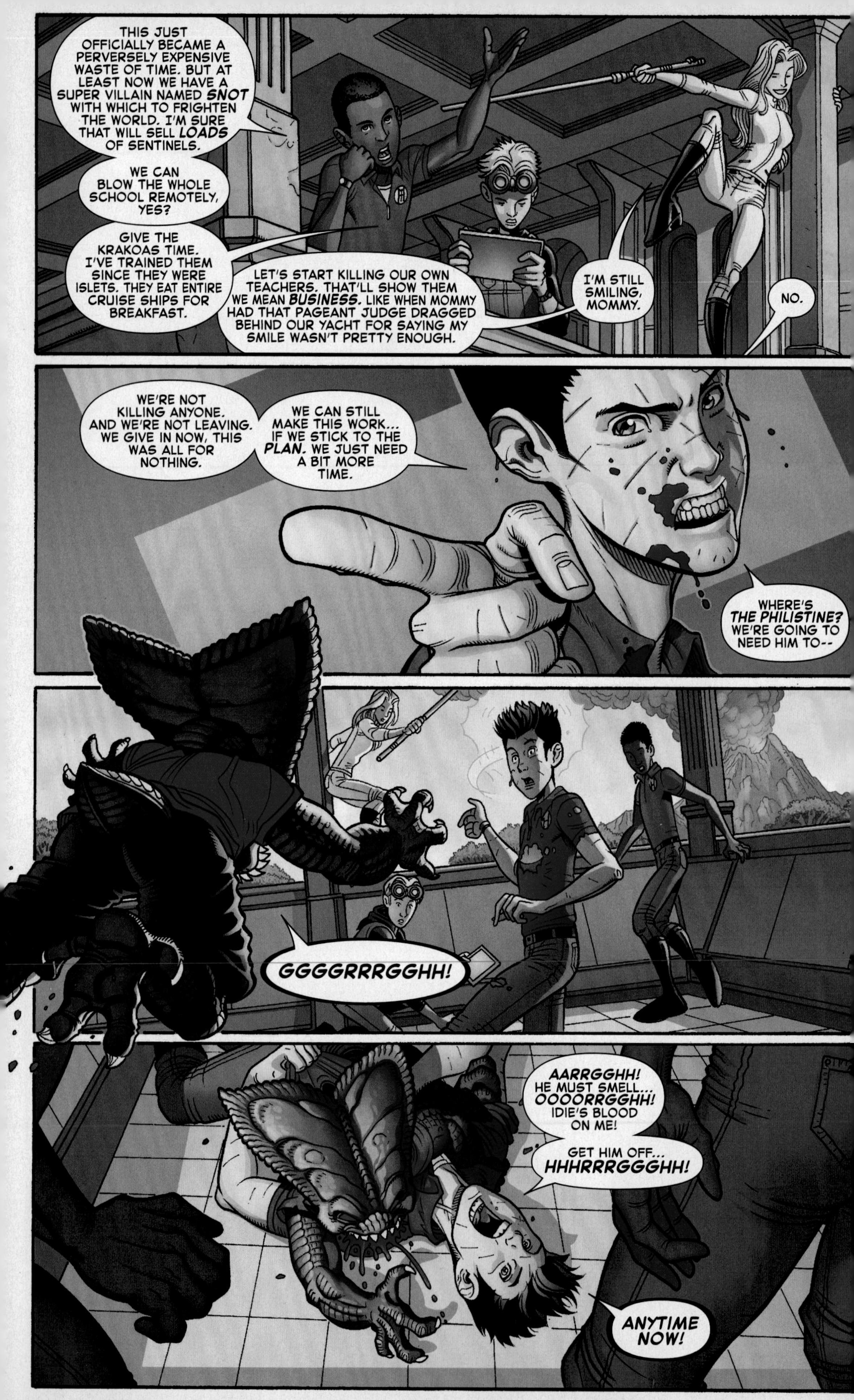
THIS JUST OFFICIALLY BECAME A PERVERSELY EXPENSIVE WASTE OF TIME. BUT AT LEAST NOW WE HAVE A SUPER VILLAIN NAMED SNOT WITH WHICH TO FRIGHTEN THE WORLD. I'M SURE THAT WILL SELL LOADS OF SENTINELS.
WE CAN BLOW THE WHOLE SCHOOL REMOTELY, YES?
GIVE THE KRAKOAS TIME. I'VE TRAINED THEM SINCE THEY WERE ISLETS. THEY EAT ENTIRE CRUISE SHIPS FOR BREAKFAST.
LET'S START KILLING OUR OWN TEACHERS. THAT'LL SHOW THEM WE MEAN BUSINESS. LIKE WHEN MOMMY HAD THAT PAGEANT JUDGE DRAGGED BEHIND OUR YACHT FOR SAYING MY SMILE WASN'T PRETTY ENOUGH.
I'M STILL SMILING, MOMMY.
NO.
WE'RE NOT KILLING ANYONE. AND WE'RE NOT LEAVING. WE GIVE IN NOW, THIS WAS ALL FOR NOTHING.
WE CAN STILL MAKE THIS WORK... IF WE STICK TO THE PLAN. WE JUST NEED A BIT MORE TIME.
WHERE'S THE PHILISTINE? WE'RE GOING TO NEED HIM TO--
GGGGRRRGGHH!
AARRGGHH! HE MUST SMELL... OOOORRGGHH! IDIE'S BLOOD ON ME!
GET HIM OFF... HHHRRRGGGHH!
ANYTIME NOW!

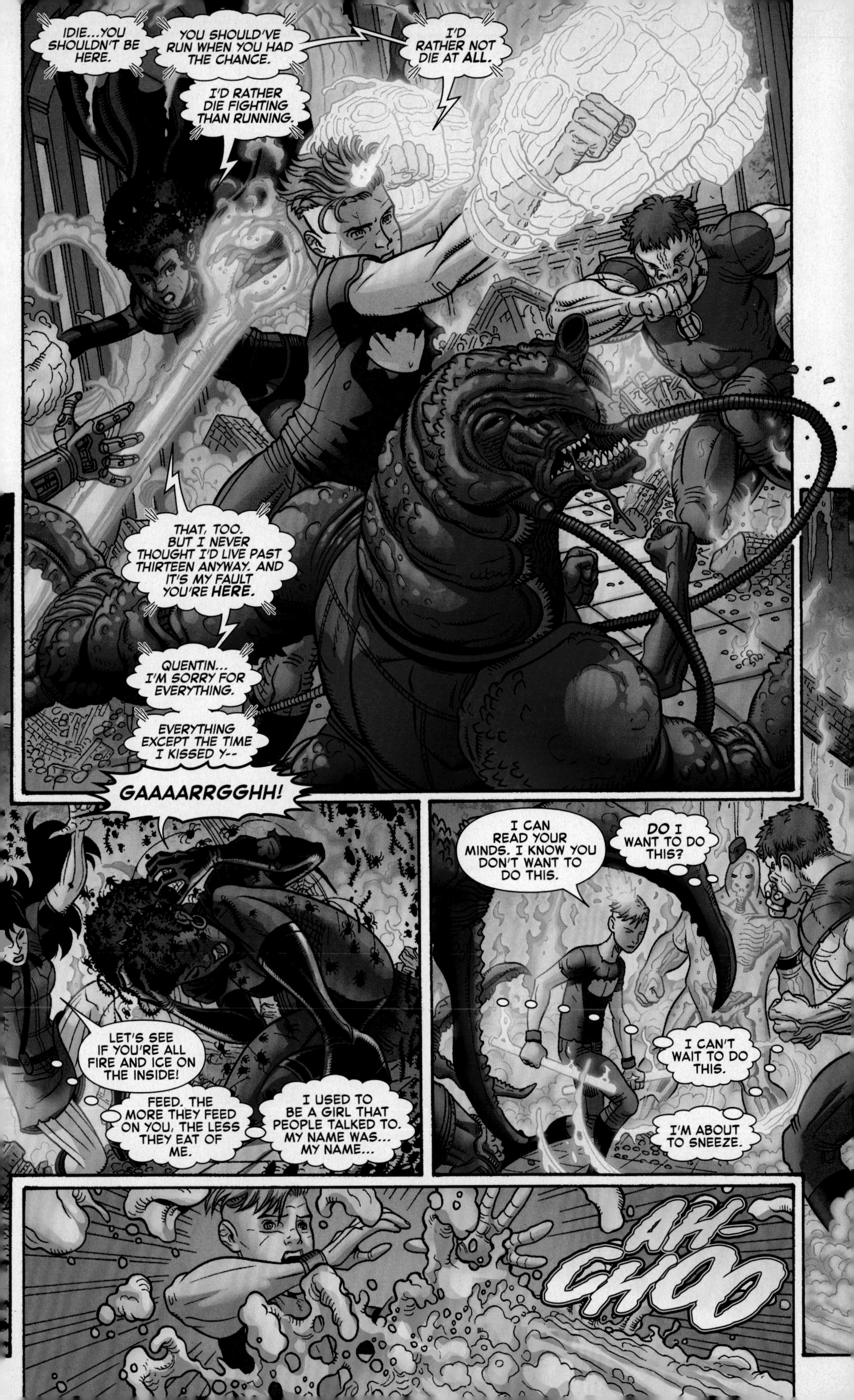
IDIE...YOU SHOULDN'T BE HERE.
YOU SHOULD'VE RUN WHEN YOU HAD THE CHANCE.
I'D RATHER NOT DIE AT ALL.
I'D RATHER DIE FIGHTING THAN RUNNING.
THAT, TOO. BUT I NEVER THOUGHT I'D LIVE PAST THIRTEEN ANYWAY. AND IT'S MY FAULT YOU'RE HERE.
QUENTIN... I'M SORRY FOR EVERYTHING.
EVERYTHING EXCEPT THE TIME I KISSED Y--
GAAAARRGGHH!
LET'S SEE IF YOU'RE ALL FIRE AND ICE ON THE INSIDE!
FEED. THE MORE THEY FEED ON YOU, THE LESS THEY EAT OF ME.
I USED TO BE A GIRL THAT PEOPLE TALKED TO. MY NAME WAS... MY NAME...
I CAN READ YOUR MINDS. I KNOW YOU DON'T WANT TO DO THIS.
DO I WANT TO DO THIS?
I CAN'T WAIT TO DO THIS.
I'M ABOUT TO SNEEZE.
AH-CHOO

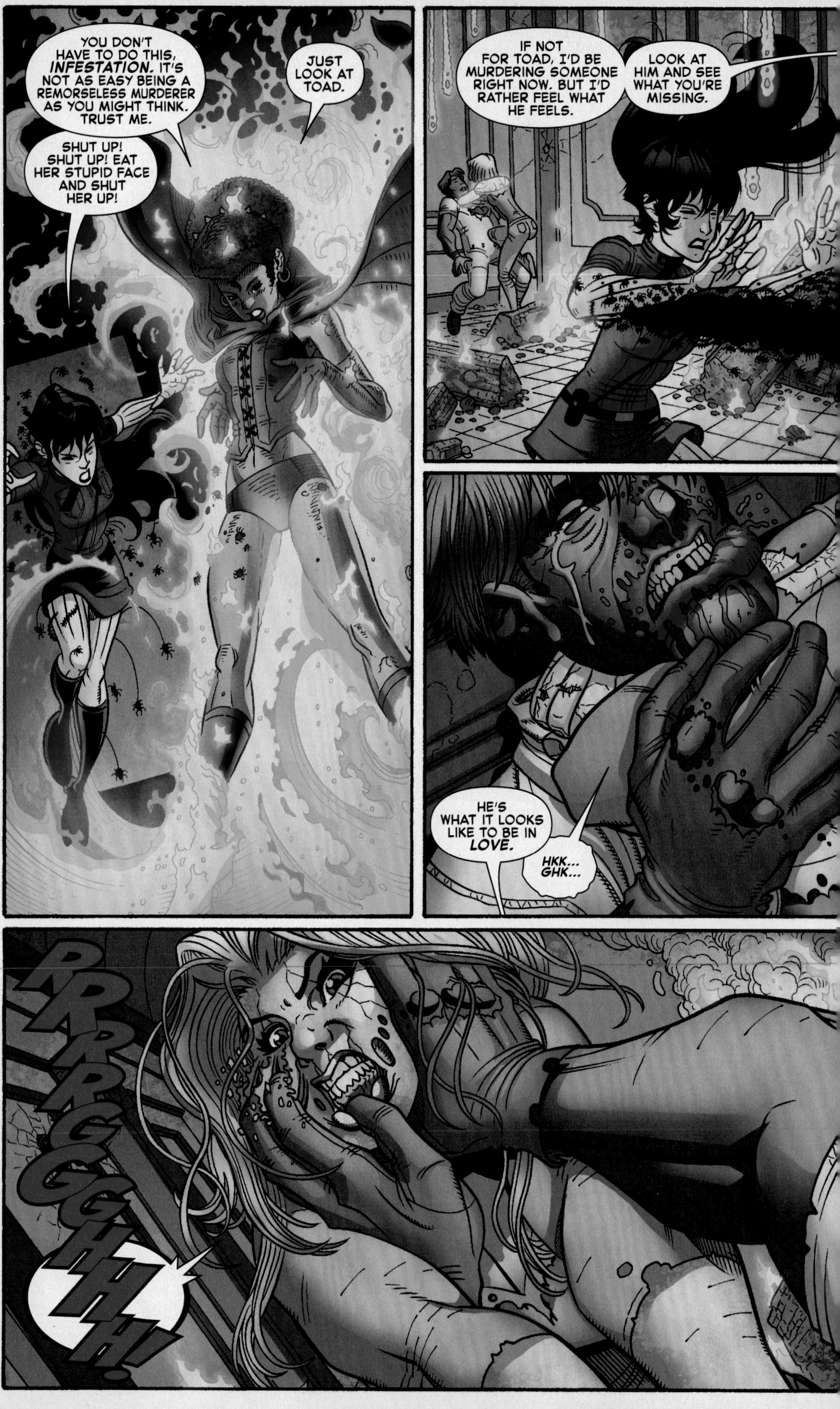
YOU DON'T HAVE TO DO THIS, *INFESTATION.* IT'S NOT AS EASY BEING A REMORSELESS MURDERER AS YOU MIGHT THINK. TRUST ME.
JUST LOOK AT TOAD.
SHUT UP! SHUT UP! EAT HER STUPID FACE AND SHUT HER UP!
IF NOT FOR TOAD, I'D BE MURDERING SOMEONE RIGHT NOW. BUT I'D RATHER FEEL WHAT HE FEELS.
LOOK AT HIM AND SEE WHAT YOU'RE MISSING.
HE'S WHAT IT LOOKS LIKE TO BE IN *LOVE.*
HKK... GHK...
RRRRGGGHHH!

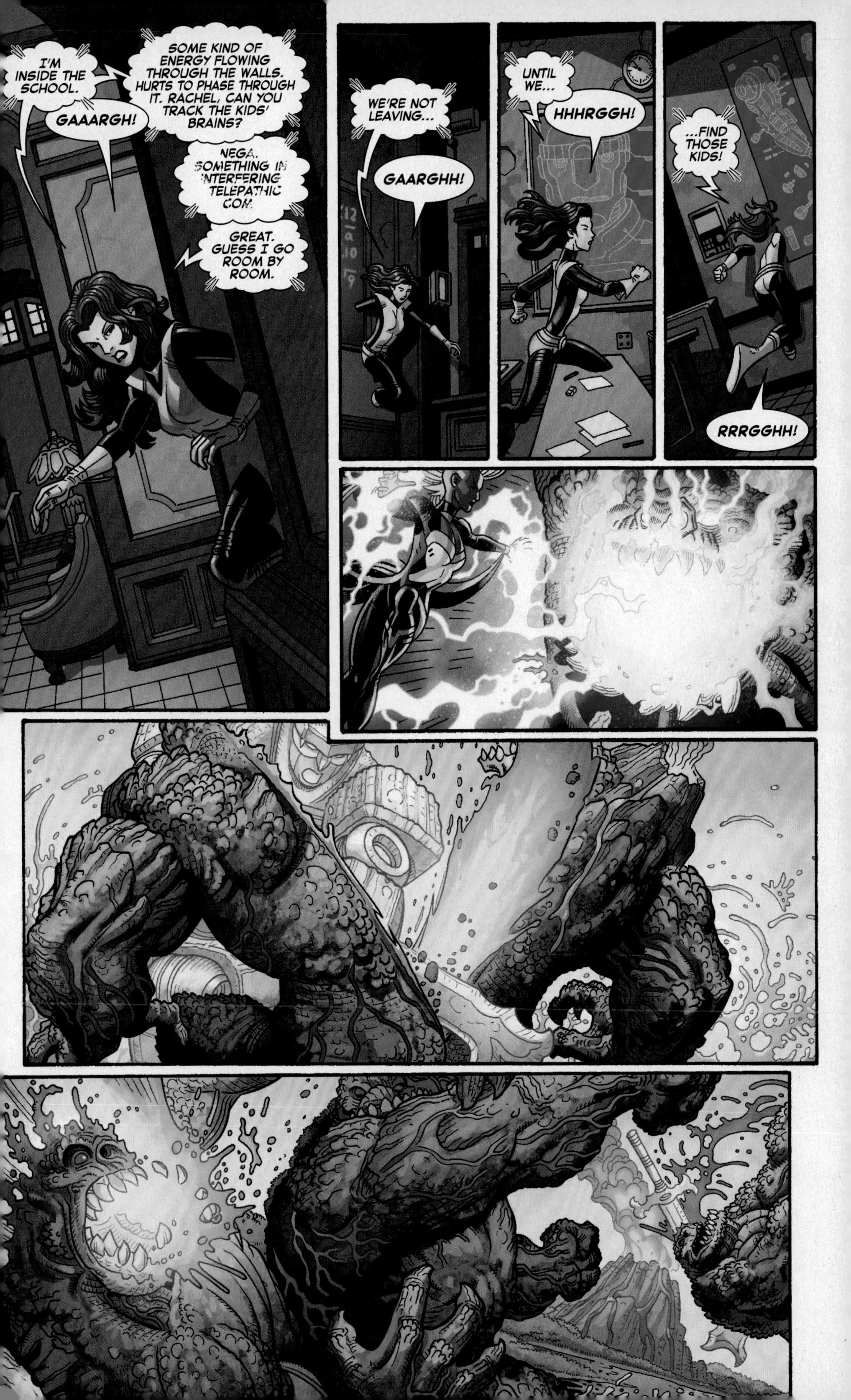
I'M INSIDE THE SCHOOL.
GAAARGH!
SOME KIND OF ENERGY FLOWING THROUGH THE WALLS. HURTS TO PHASE THROUGH IT. RACHEL, CAN YOU TRACK THE KIDS' BRAINS?
NEGA. SOMETHING IN 'NTERFERING TELEPATHIC COM.
GREAT. GUESS I GO ROOM BY ROOM.
WE'RE NOT LEAVING...
GAARGHH!
UNTIL WE...
HHHRGGH!
...FIND THOSE KIDS!
RRRGGHH!

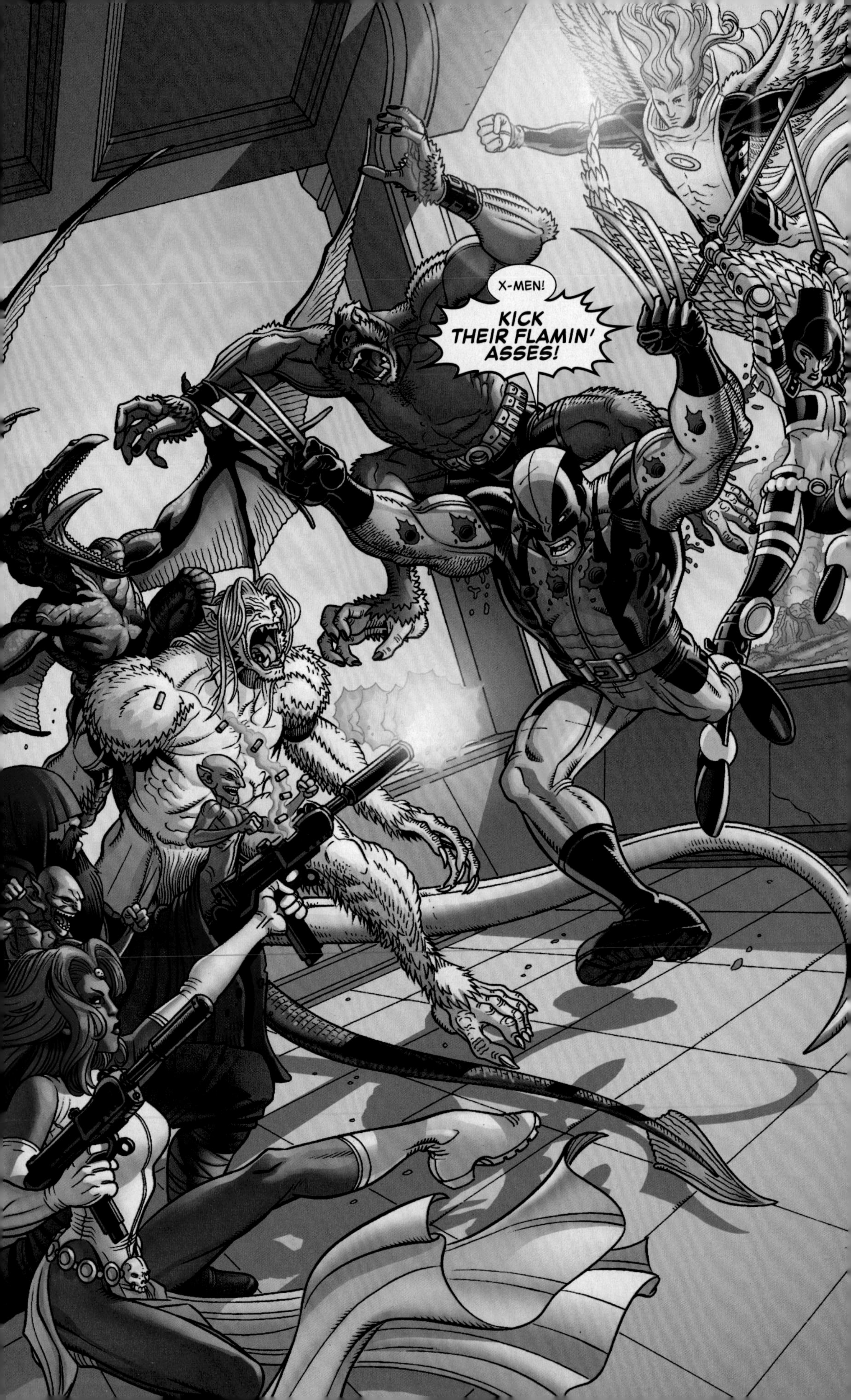
X-MEN!
KICK THEIR FLAMIN' ASSES!

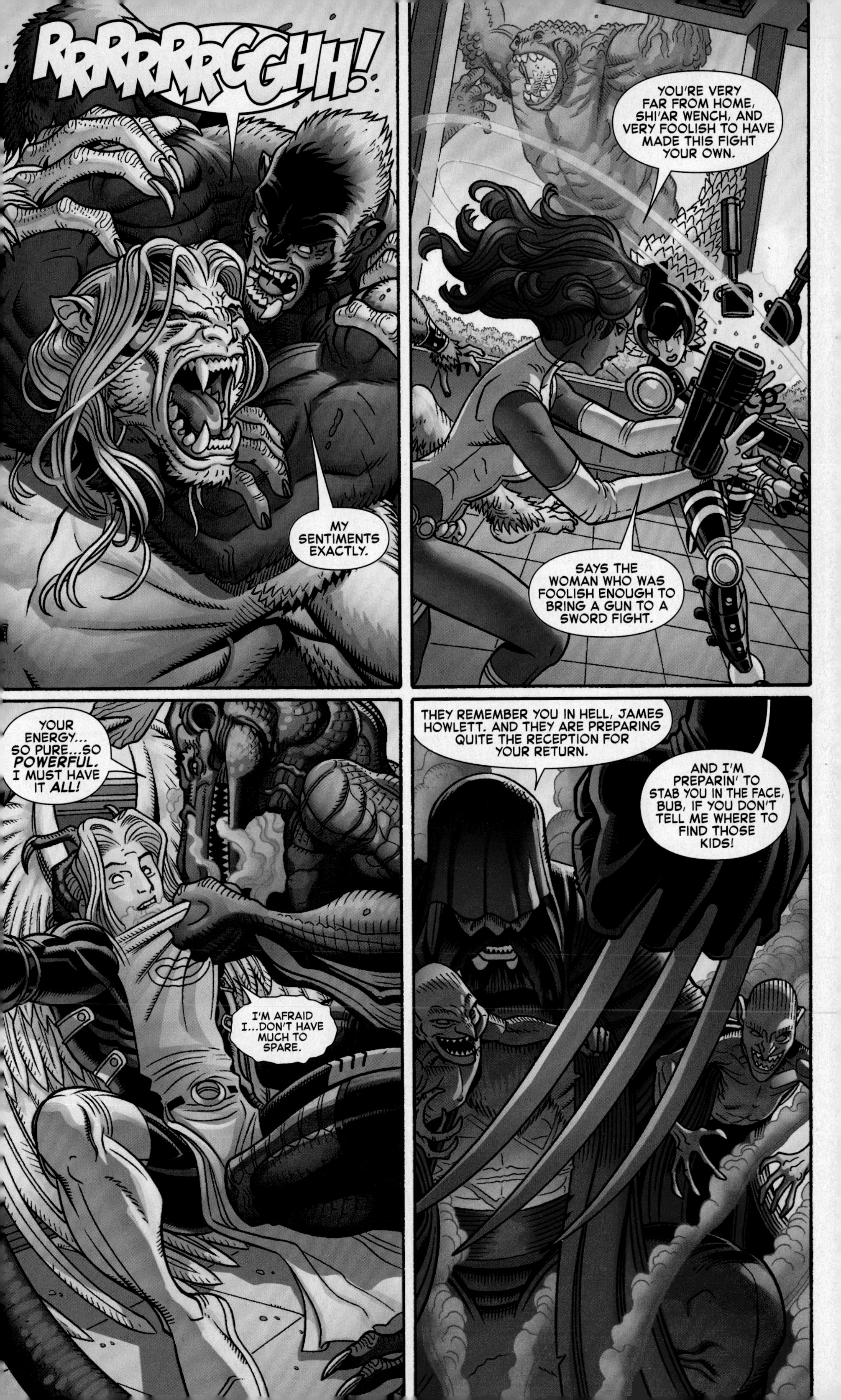
RRRRRRRGGHH!
MY SENTIMENTS EXACTLY.
YOU'RE VERY FAR FROM HOME, SHI'AR WENCH, AND VERY FOOLISH TO HAVE MADE THIS FIGHT YOUR OWN.
SAYS THE WOMAN WHO WAS FOOLISH ENOUGH TO BRING A GUN TO A SWORD FIGHT.
YOUR ENERGY... SO PURE...SO POWERFUL. I MUST HAVE IT ALL!
I'M AFRAID I...DON'T HAVE MUCH TO SPARE.
THEY REMEMBER YOU IN HELL, JAMES HOWLETT. AND THEY ARE PREPARING QUITE THE RECEPTION FOR YOUR RETURN.
AND I'M PREPARIN' TO STAB YOU IN THE FACE, BUB, IF YOU DON'T TELL ME WHERE TO FIND THOSE KIDS!

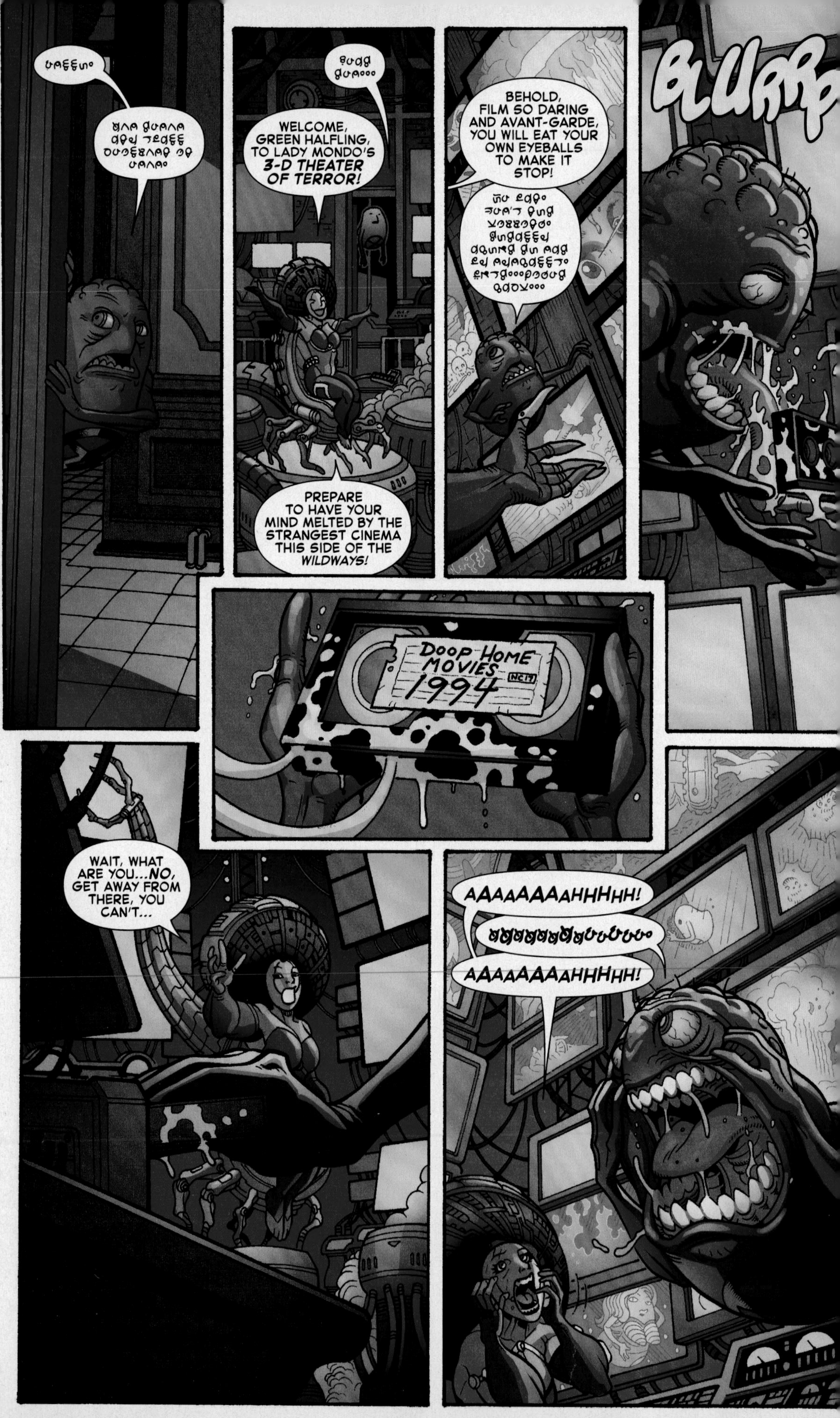
WELCOME, GREEN HALFLING, TO LADY MONDO'S *3-D THEATER OF TERROR!*
PREPARE TO HAVE YOUR MIND MELTED BY THE STRANGEST CINEMA THIS SIDE OF THE *WILDWAYS!*
BEHOLD, FILM SO DARING AND AVANT-GARDE, YOU WILL EAT YOUR OWN EYEBALLS TO MAKE IT STOP!
BLURP
DOOP HOME MOVIES
NC17
1994
WAIT, WHAT ARE YOU...*NO*, GET AWAY FROM THERE, YOU CAN'T...
AAAAAAAAHHHHH!
AAAAAAAAHHHHH!

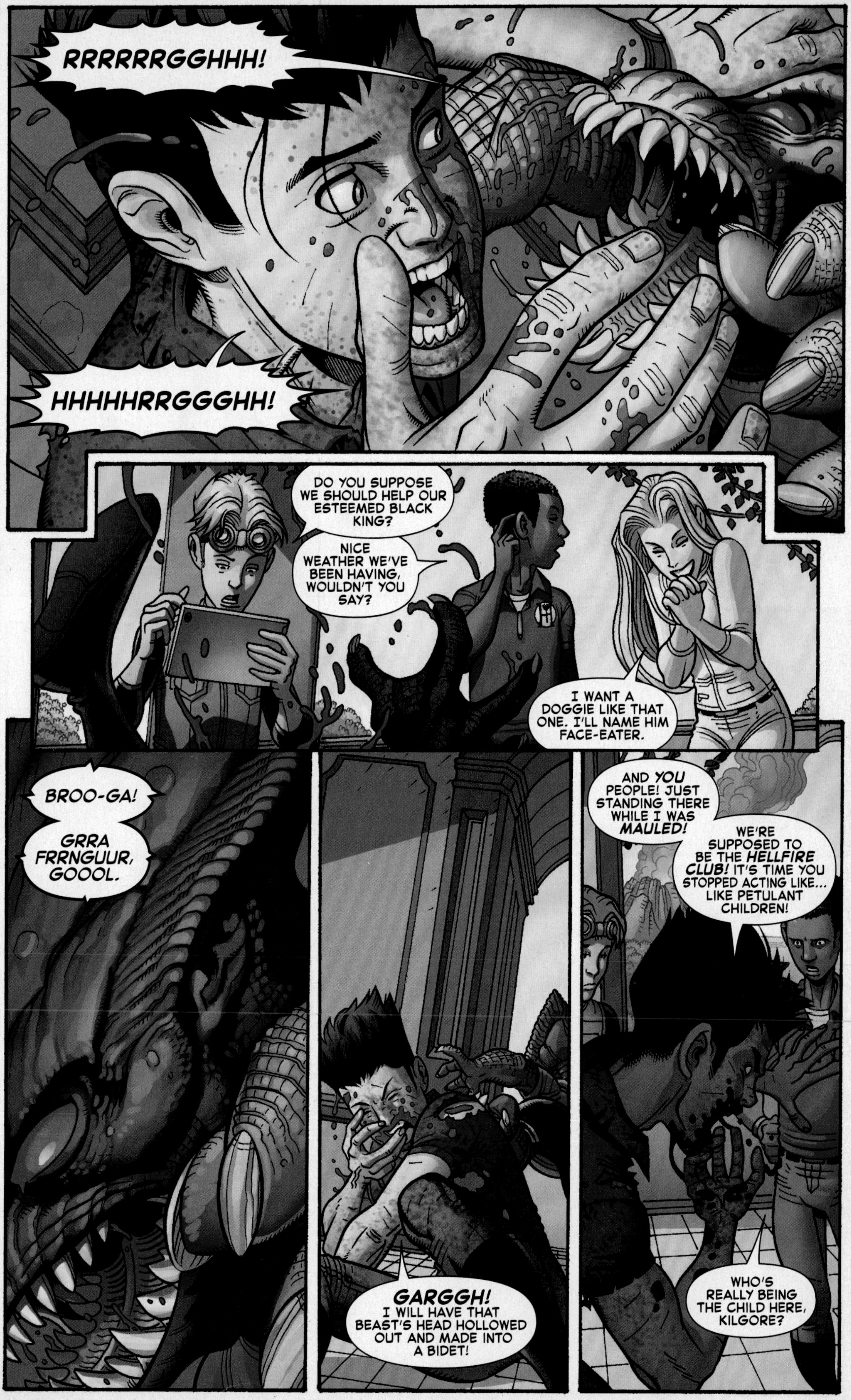
RRRRRRGGHHH!
HHHHHRRGGGHH!
DO YOU SUPPOSE WE SHOULD HELP OUR ESTEEMED BLACK KING?
NICE WEATHER WE'VE BEEN HAVING, WOULDN'T YOU SAY?
I WANT A DOGGIE LIKE THAT ONE. I'LL NAME HIM FACE-EATER.
BROO-GA!
GRRA FRRNGUUR, GOOOL.
GARGGH! I WILL HAVE THAT BEAST'S HEAD HOLLOWED OUT AND MADE INTO A BIDET!
AND YOU PEOPLE! JUST STANDING THERE WHILE I WAS MAULED!
WE'RE SUPPOSED TO BE THE HELLFIRE CLUB! IT'S TIME YOU STOPPED ACTING LIKE... LIKE PETULANT CHILDREN!
WHO'S REALLY BEING THE CHILD HERE, KILGORE?

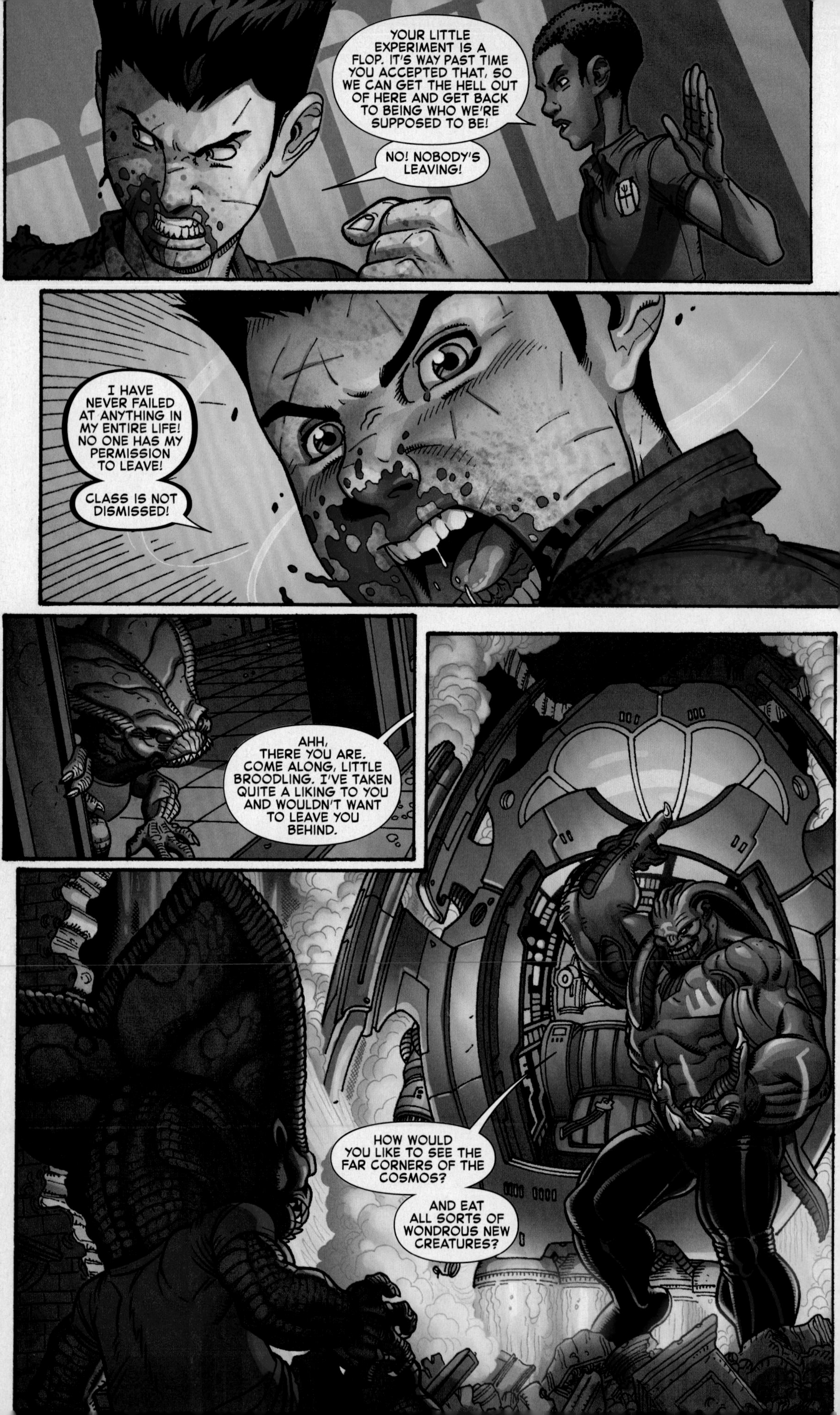
YOUR LITTLE EXPERIMENT IS A FLOP. IT'S WAY PAST TIME YOU ACCEPTED THAT, SO WE CAN GET THE HELL OUT OF HERE AND GET BACK TO BEING WHO WE'RE SUPPOSED TO BE!
NO! NOBODY'S LEAVING!
I HAVE NEVER FAILED AT ANYTHING IN MY ENTIRE LIFE! NO ONE HAS MY PERMISSION TO LEAVE!
CLASS IS NOT DISMISSED!
AHH, THERE YOU ARE. COME ALONG, LITTLE BROODLING. I'VE TAKEN QUITE A LIKING TO YOU AND WOULDN'T WANT TO LEAVE YOU BEHIND.
HOW WOULD YOU LIKE TO SEE THE FAR CORNERS OF THE COSMOS?
AND EAT ALL SORTS OF WONDROUS NEW CREATURES?

PAIGE...
PLEASE...DON'T
MAKE ME...

...HURT
YOU...

RRR
RRIPP

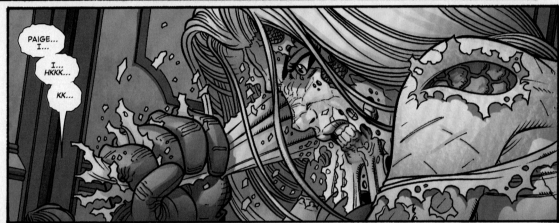

PAIGE...
I...

I....
HKKK...

KK...

GLUG

YEAH! LOOK
AT *HIM!* QUENTIN
QUIRE'S DYING!

GOOD
RIDDANCE, KID
OMEGA!

QUENTIN?
QUENTIN, CAN YOU
HEAR ME?

THIS WASN'T MY,
YOU KNOW...I MEAN,
I NEVER WANTED TO...
NOT LIKE...BUT I *GOT* TO
OR...THAT SNOT GUY, HE
CAN BE REALLY SCARY,
YOU KNOW?

IT'S
ALL RIGHT,
GLOB...

I'M
SORRY,
TOO.

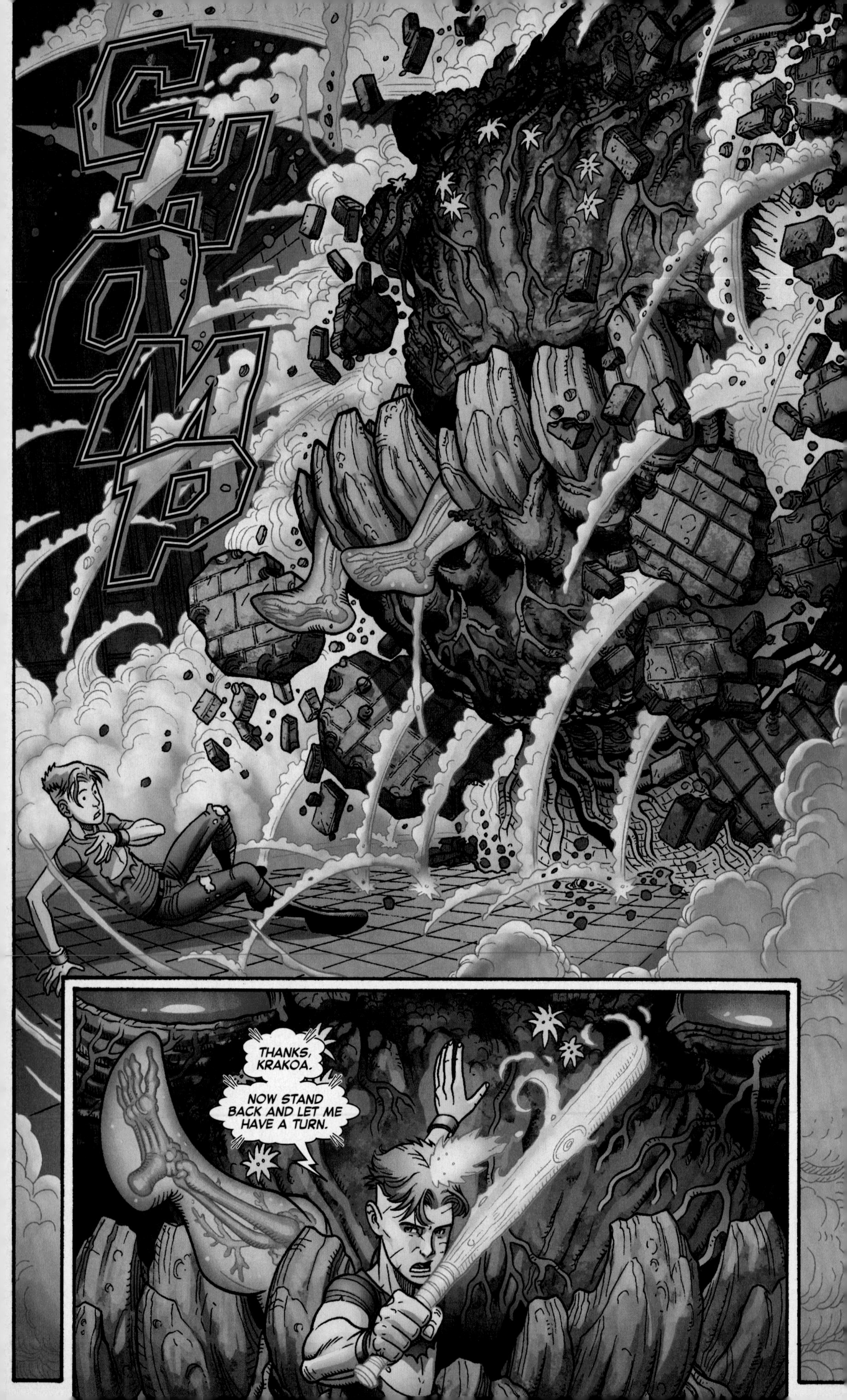
CHOMP
THANKS, KRAKOA.
NOW STAND BACK AND LET ME HAVE A TURN.

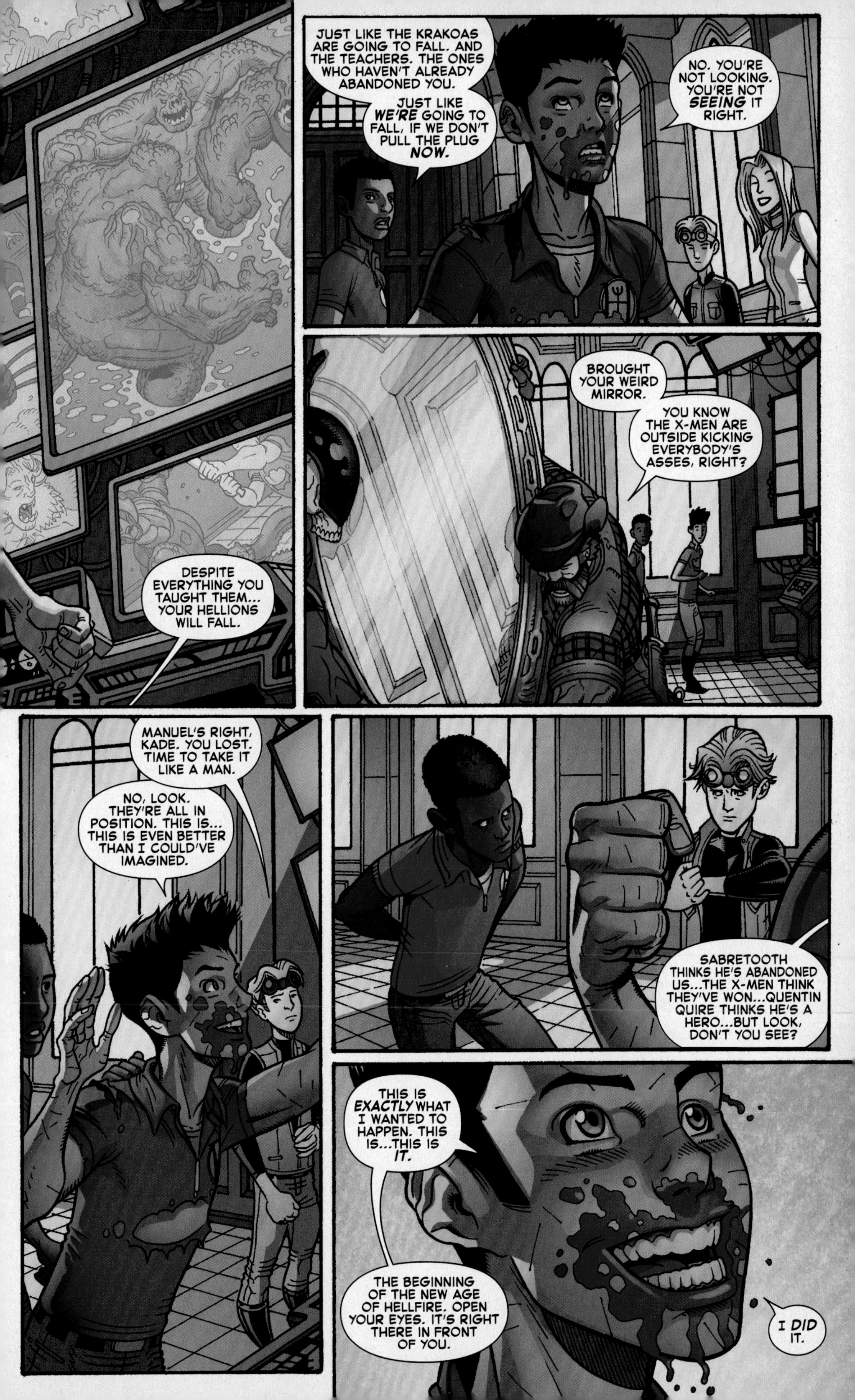
JUST LIKE THE KRAKOAS ARE GOING TO FALL. AND THE TEACHERS. THE ONES WHO HAVEN'T ALREADY ABANDONED YOU.
JUST LIKE WE'RE GOING TO FALL, IF WE DON'T PULL THE PLUG NOW.
NO. YOU'RE NOT LOOKING. YOU'RE NOT SEEING IT RIGHT.
DESPITE EVERYTHING YOU TAUGHT THEM... YOUR HELLIONS WILL FALL.
BROUGHT YOUR WEIRD MIRROR.
YOU KNOW THE X-MEN ARE OUTSIDE KICKING EVERYBODY'S ASSES, RIGHT?
MANUEL'S RIGHT, KADE. YOU LOST. TIME TO TAKE IT LIKE A MAN.
NO, LOOK. THEY'RE ALL IN POSITION. THIS IS... THIS IS EVEN BETTER THAN I COULD'VE IMAGINED.
SABRETOOTH THINKS HE'S ABANDONED US...THE X-MEN THINK THEY'VE WON...QUENTIN QUIRE THINKS HE'S A HERO...BUT LOOK, DON'T YOU SEE?
THIS IS EXACTLY WHAT I WANTED TO HAPPEN. THIS IS...THIS IS IT.
THE BEGINNING OF THE NEW AGE OF HELLFIRE. OPEN YOUR EYES. IT'S RIGHT THERE IN FRONT OF YOU.
I DID IT.

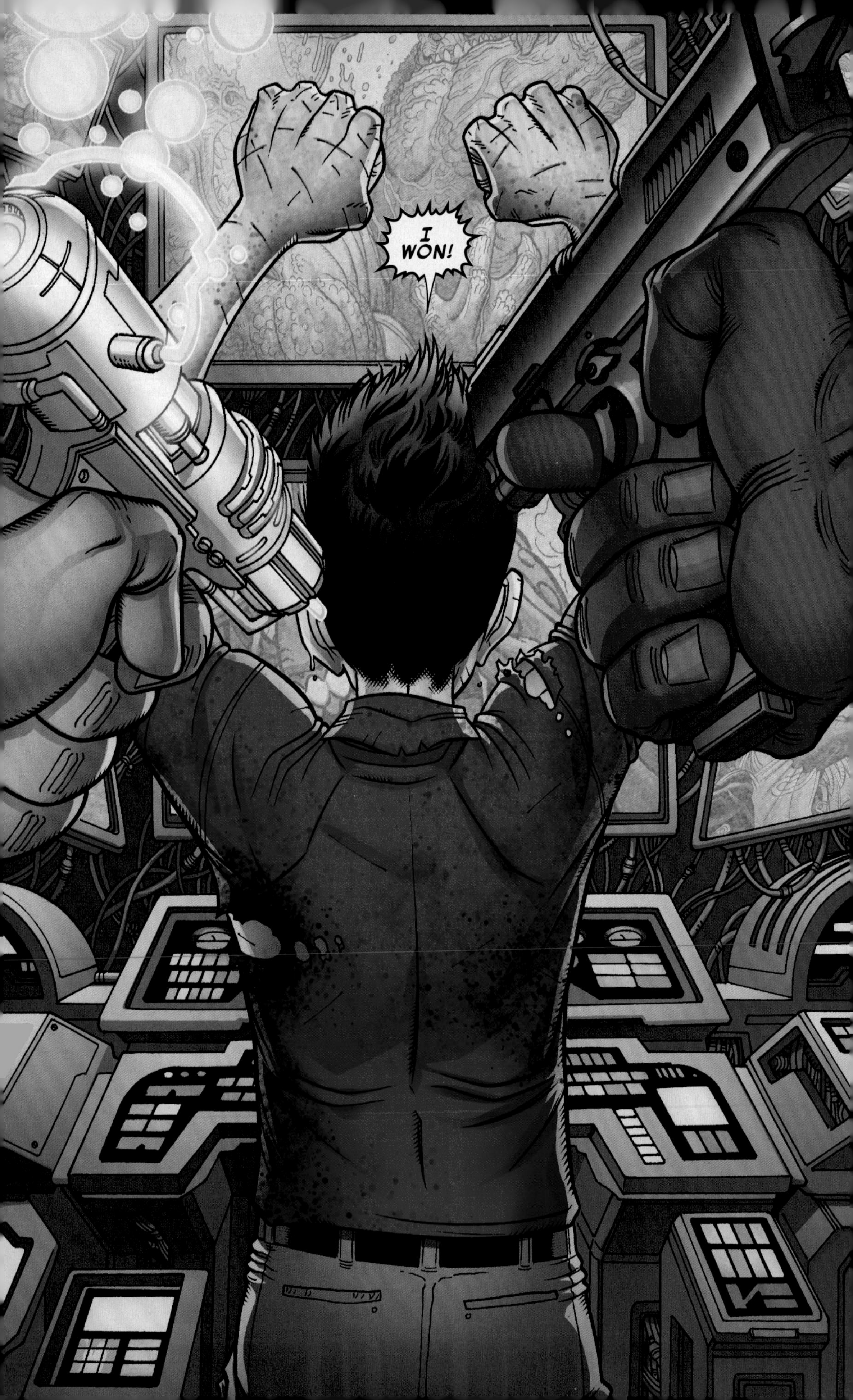
I WON!

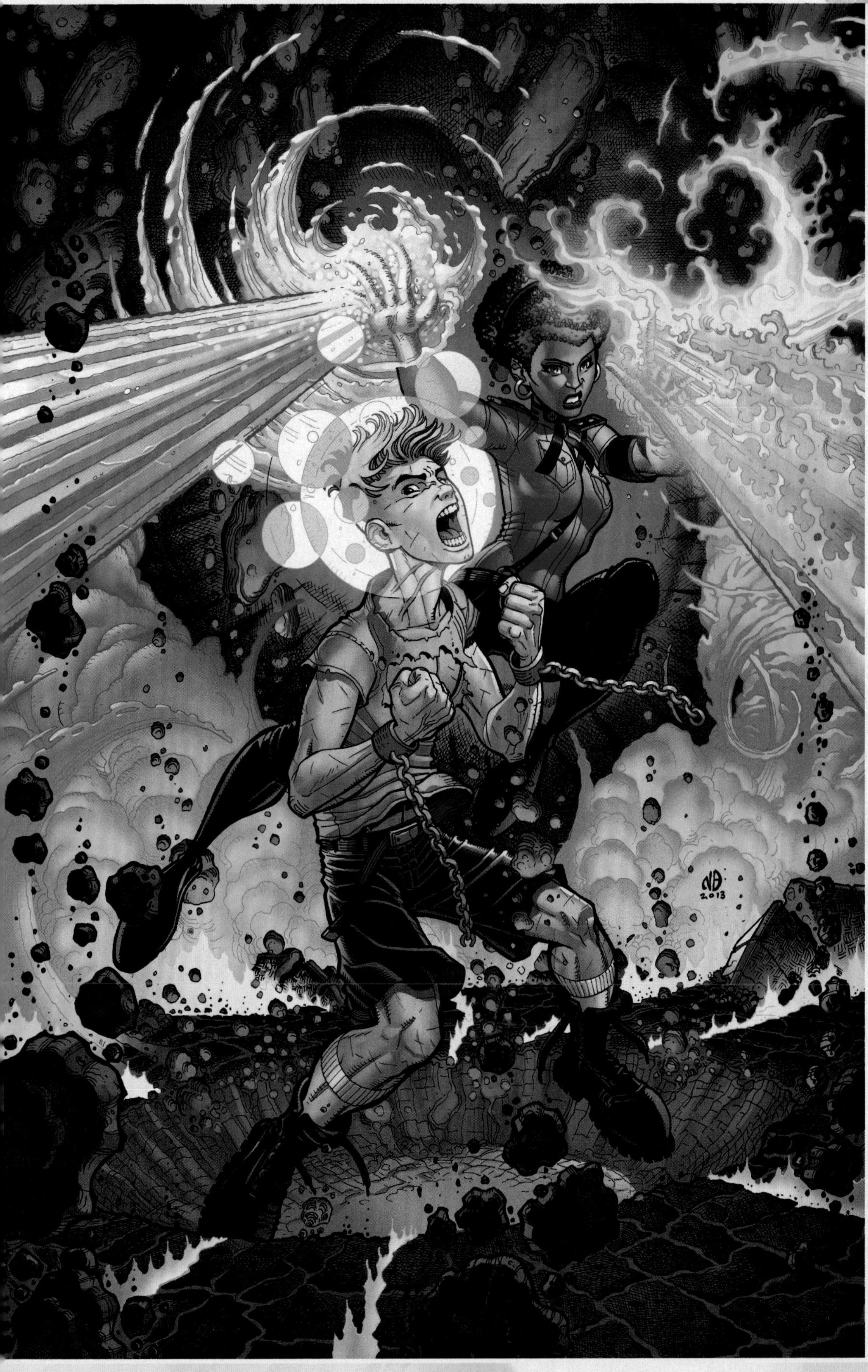

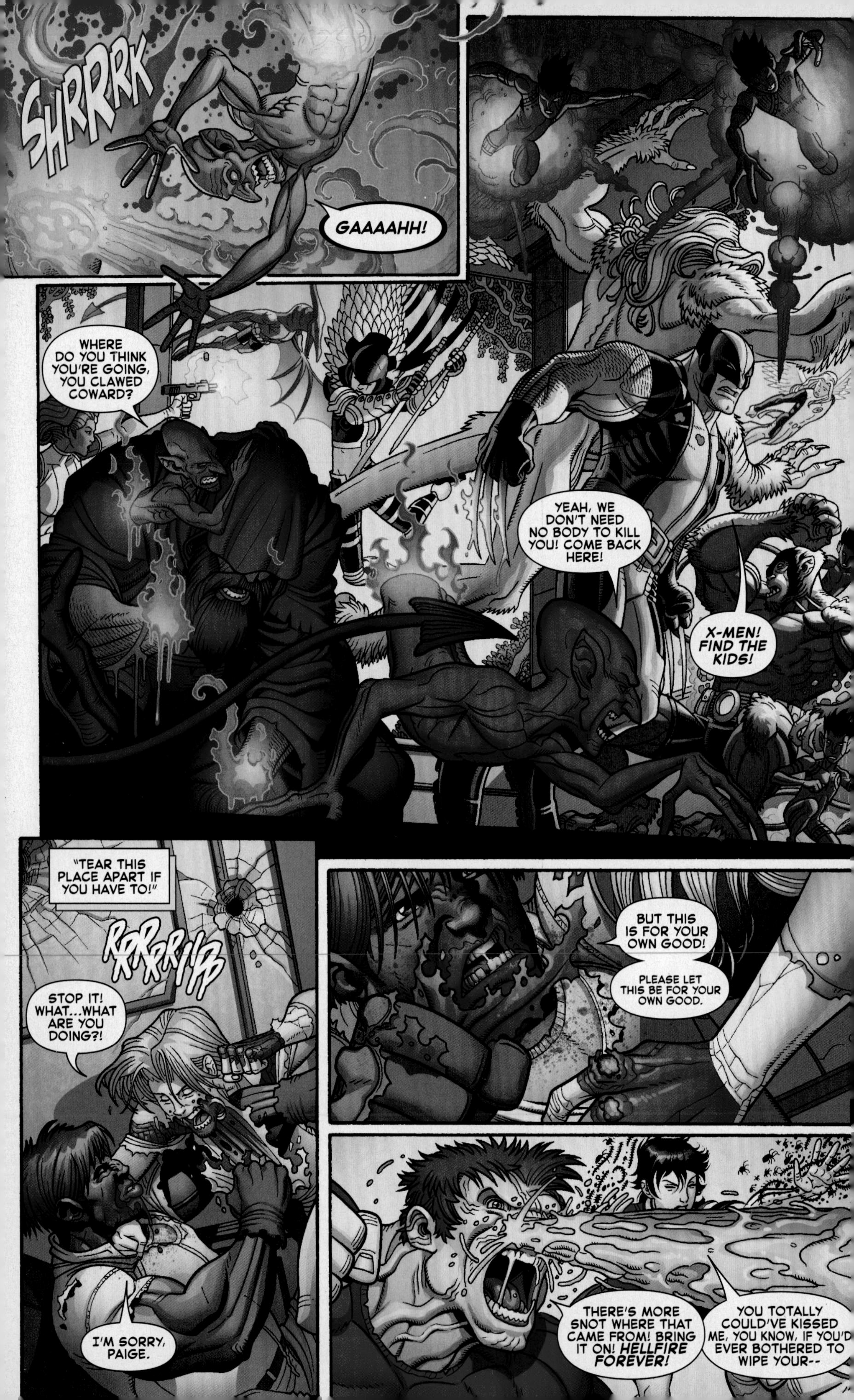
SHRRRK
GAAAAHH!
WHERE DO YOU THINK YOU'RE GOING, YOU CLAWED COWARD?
YEAH, WE DON'T NEED NO BODY TO KILL YOU! COME BACK HERE!
X-MEN! FIND THE KIDS!
"TEAR THIS PLACE APART IF YOU HAVE TO!"
RRRRRIPP
STOP IT! WHAT...WHAT ARE YOU DOING?!
I'M SORRY, PAIGE.
BUT THIS IS FOR YOUR OWN GOOD!
PLEASE LET THIS BE FOR YOUR OWN GOOD.
THERE'S MORE SNOT WHERE THAT CAME FROM! BRING IT ON! HELLFIRE FOREVER!
YOU TOTALLY COULD'VE KISSED ME, YOU KNOW, IF YOU'D EVER BOTHERED TO WIPE YOUR--

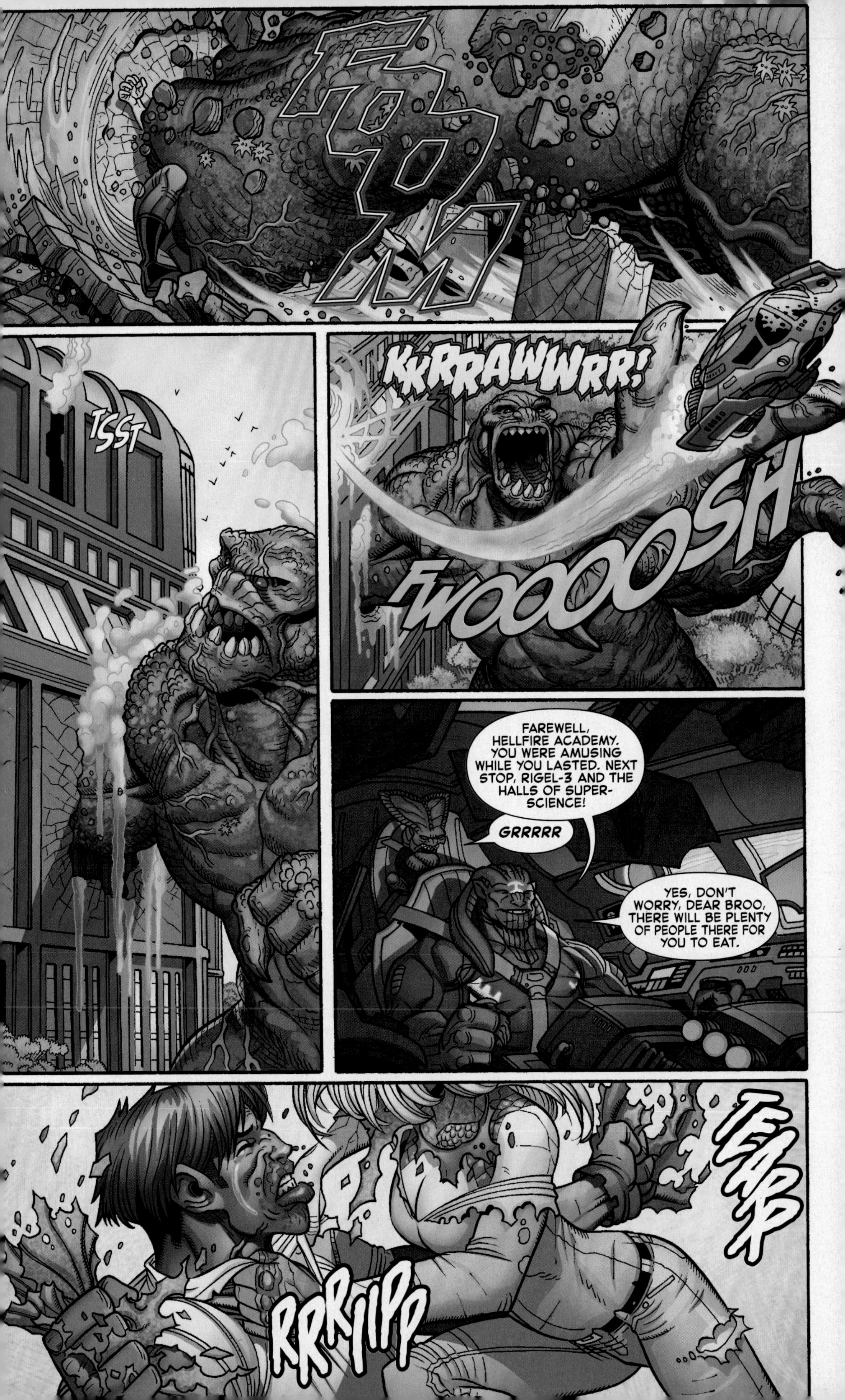
TSST
KKRRAWWRR!
FWOOOOOSH
FAREWELL, HELLFIRE ACADEMY. YOU WERE AMUSING WHILE YOU LASTED. NEXT STOP, RIGEL-3 AND THE HALLS OF SUPER-SCIENCE!
GRRRRR
YES, DON'T WORRY, DEAR BROO, THERE WILL BE PLENTY OF PEOPLE THERE FOR YOU TO EAT.
TEAR
RRRIIPP

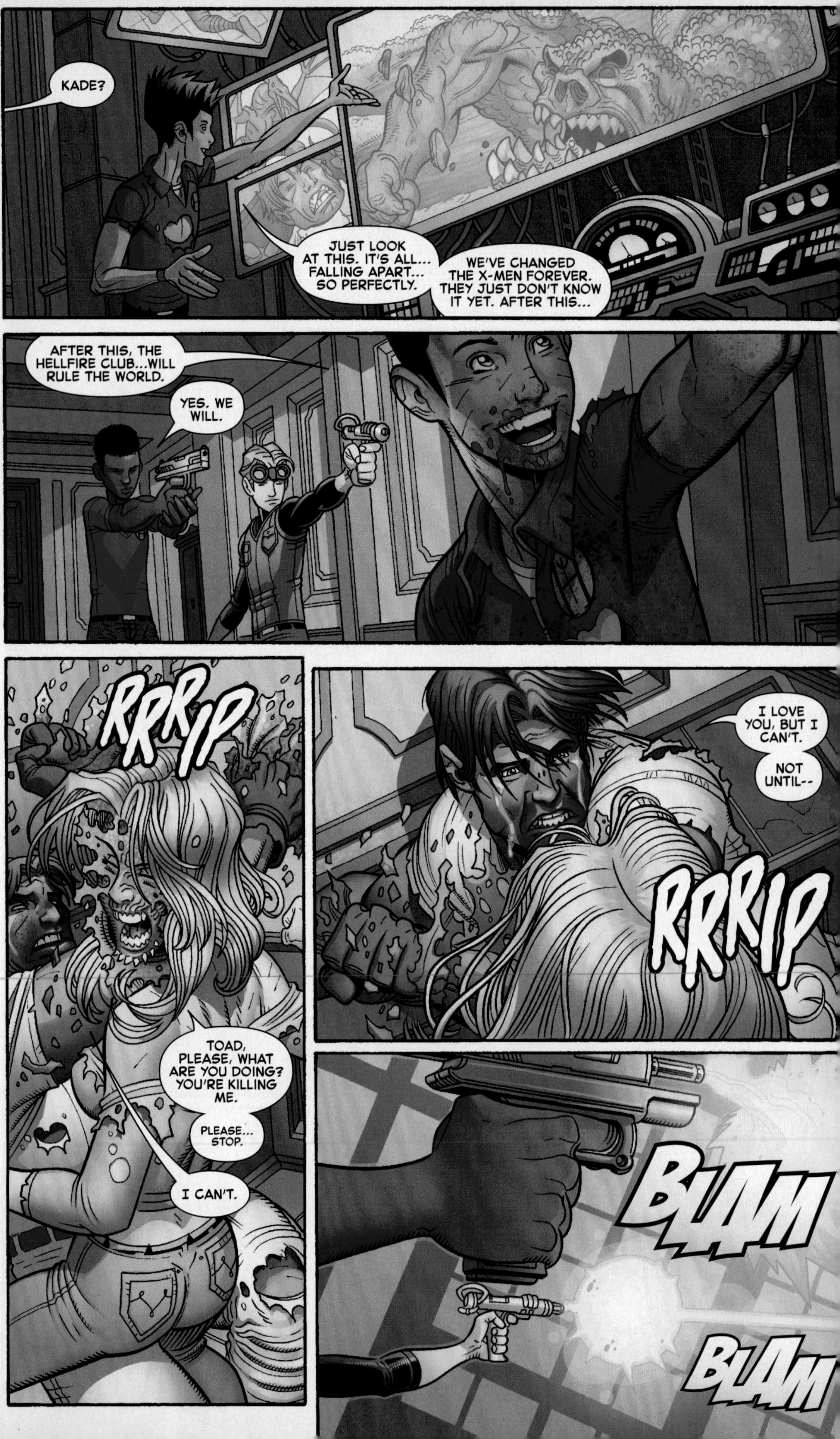
KADE?
JUST LOOK AT THIS. IT'S ALL... FALLING APART... SO PERFECTLY.
WE'VE CHANGED THE X-MEN FOREVER. THEY JUST DON'T KNOW IT YET. AFTER THIS...
AFTER THIS, THE HELLFIRE CLUB...WILL RULE THE WORLD.
YES. WE WILL.
RRRIP
TOAD, PLEASE, WHAT ARE YOU DOING? YOU'RE KILLING ME.
PLEASE... STOP.
I CAN'T.
I LOVE YOU, BUT I CAN'T.
NOT UNTIL--
RRRIP
BLAM
BLAM

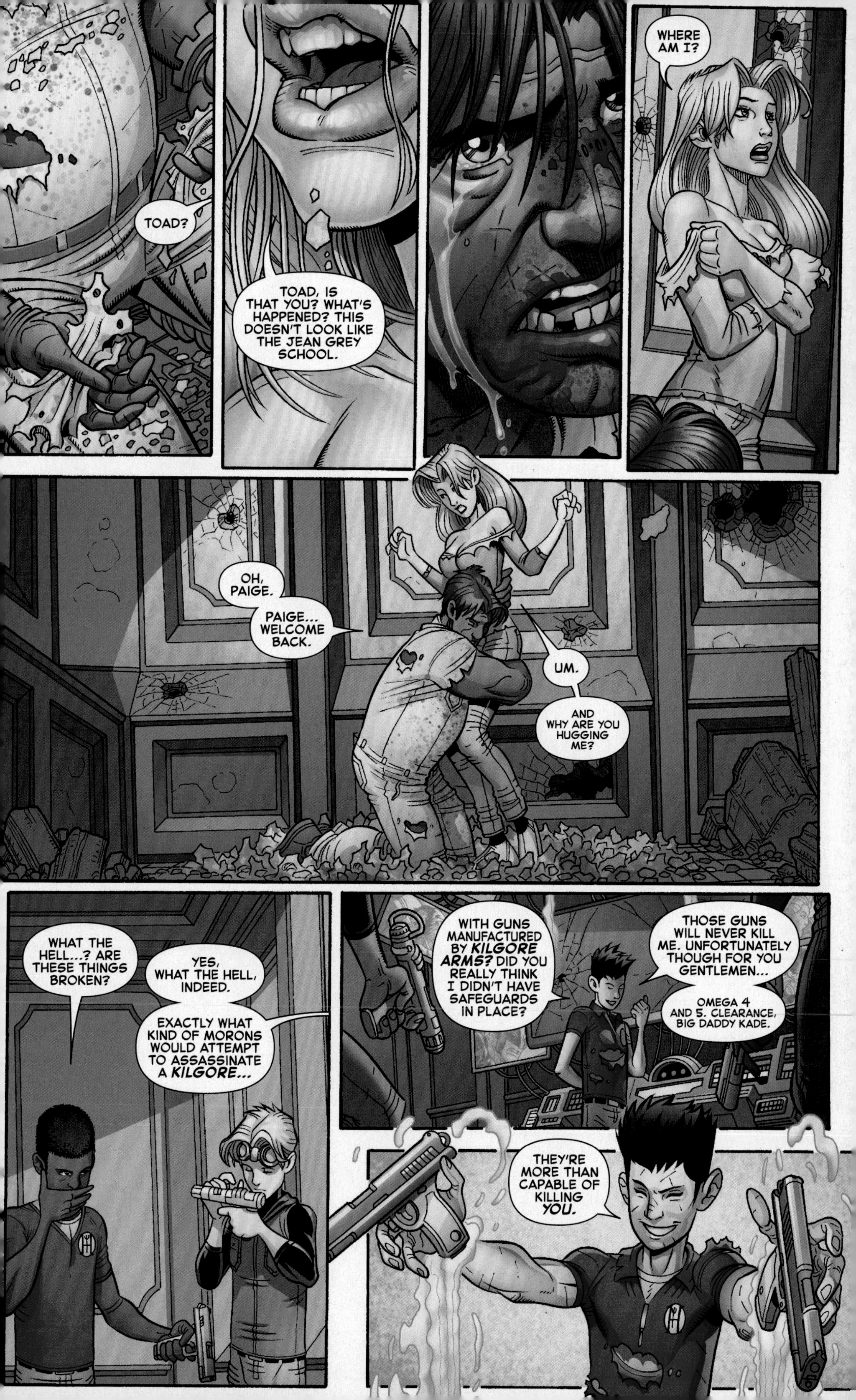
TOAD?
TOAD, IS THAT YOU? WHAT'S HAPPENED? THIS DOESN'T LOOK LIKE THE JEAN GREY SCHOOL.
WHERE AM I?
OH, PAIGE.
PAIGE... WELCOME BACK.
UM.
AND WHY ARE YOU HUGGING ME?
WHAT THE HELL...? ARE THESE THINGS BROKEN?
YES, WHAT THE HELL, INDEED.
EXACTLY WHAT KIND OF MORONS WOULD ATTEMPT TO ASSASSINATE A *KILGORE*...
WITH GUNS MANUFACTURED BY *KILGORE ARMS?* DID YOU REALLY THINK I DIDN'T HAVE SAFEGUARDS IN PLACE?
THOSE GUNS WILL NEVER KILL ME. UNFORTUNATELY THOUGH FOR YOU GENTLEMEN...
OMEGA 4 AND 5. CLEARANCE, BIG DADDY KADE.
THEY'RE MORE THAN CAPABLE OF KILLING *YOU.*

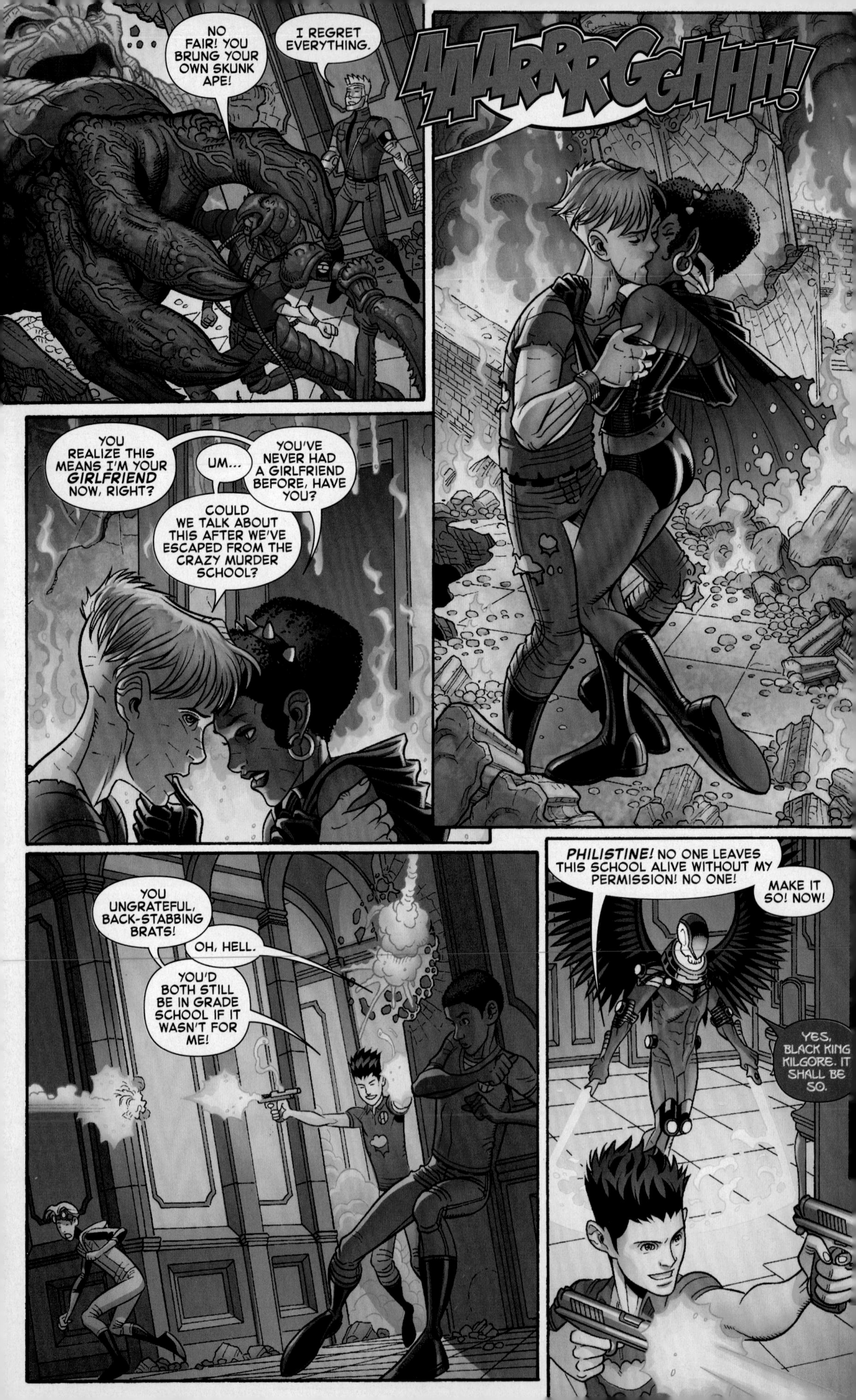
NO FAIR! YOU BRUNG YOUR OWN SKUNK APE!
I REGRET EVERYTHING.
AAARRRRGGHHH!
YOU REALIZE THIS MEANS I'M YOUR GIRLFRIEND NOW, RIGHT?
UM...
YOU'VE NEVER HAD A GIRLFRIEND BEFORE, HAVE YOU?
COULD WE TALK ABOUT THIS AFTER WE'VE ESCAPED FROM THE CRAZY MURDER SCHOOL?
YOU UNGRATEFUL, BACK-STABBING BRATS!
OH, HELL.
YOU'D BOTH STILL BE IN GRADE SCHOOL IF IT WASN'T FOR ME!
PHILISTINE! NO ONE LEAVES THIS SCHOOL ALIVE WITHOUT MY PERMISSION! NO ONE!
MAKE IT SO! NOW!
YES, BLACK KING KILGORE. IT SHALL BE SO.

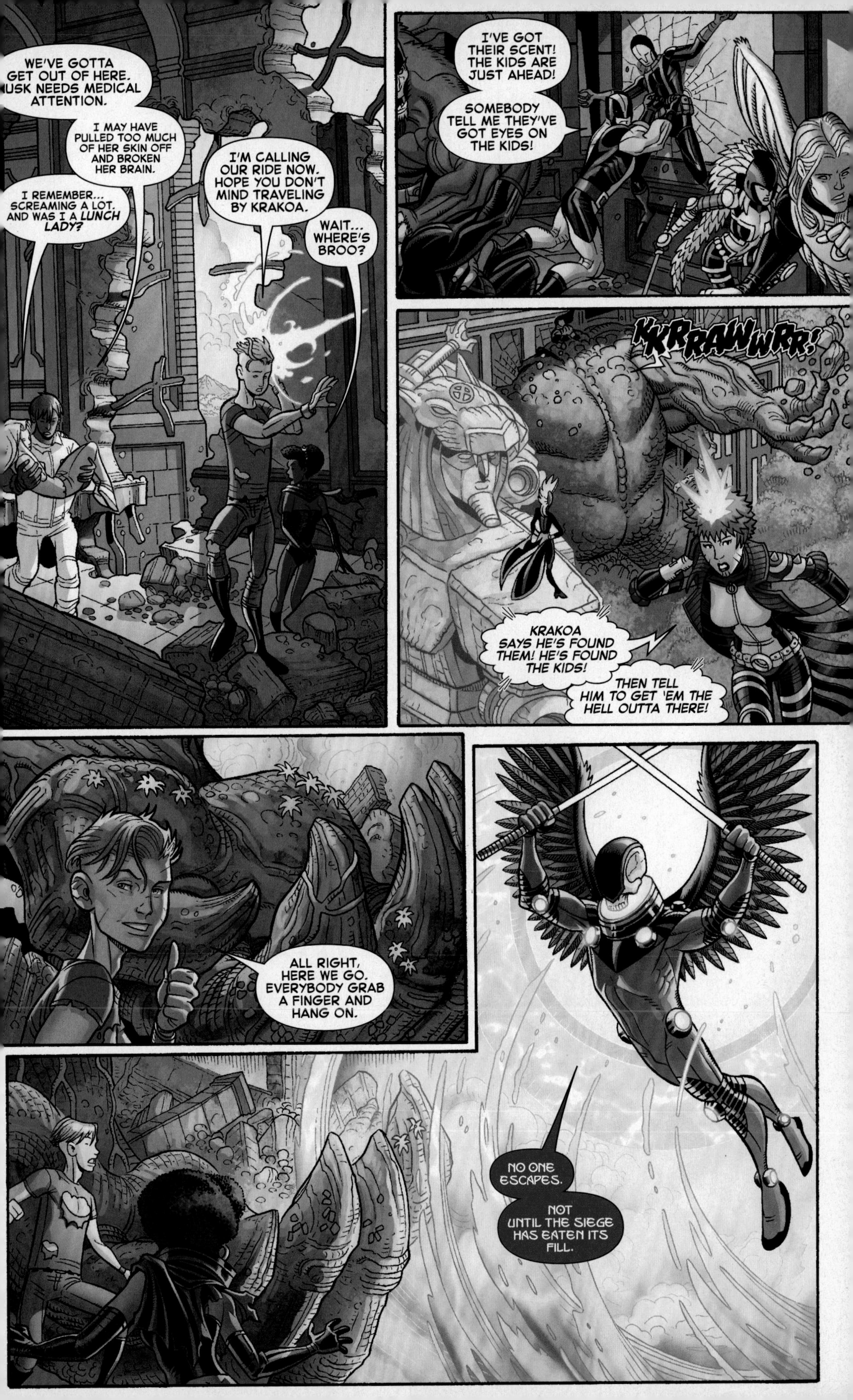
WE'VE GOTTA GET OUT OF HERE. HUSK NEEDS MEDICAL ATTENTION.
I MAY HAVE PULLED TOO MUCH OF HER SKIN OFF AND BROKEN HER BRAIN.
I REMEMBER... SCREAMING A LOT. AND WAS I A LUNCH LADY?
I'M CALLING OUR RIDE NOW. HOPE YOU DON'T MIND TRAVELING BY KRAKOA.
WAIT... WHERE'S BROO?
I'VE GOT THEIR SCENT! THE KIDS ARE JUST AHEAD!
SOMEBODY TELL ME THEY'VE GOT EYES ON THE KIDS!
KKRRAWWRR!
KRAKOA SAYS HE'S FOUND THEM! HE'S FOUND THE KIDS!
THEN TELL HIM TO GET 'EM THE HELL OUTTA THERE!
ALL RIGHT, HERE WE GO. EVERYBODY GRAB A FINGER AND HANG ON.
NO ONE ESCAPES.
NOT UNTIL THE SIEGE HAS EATEN ITS FILL.

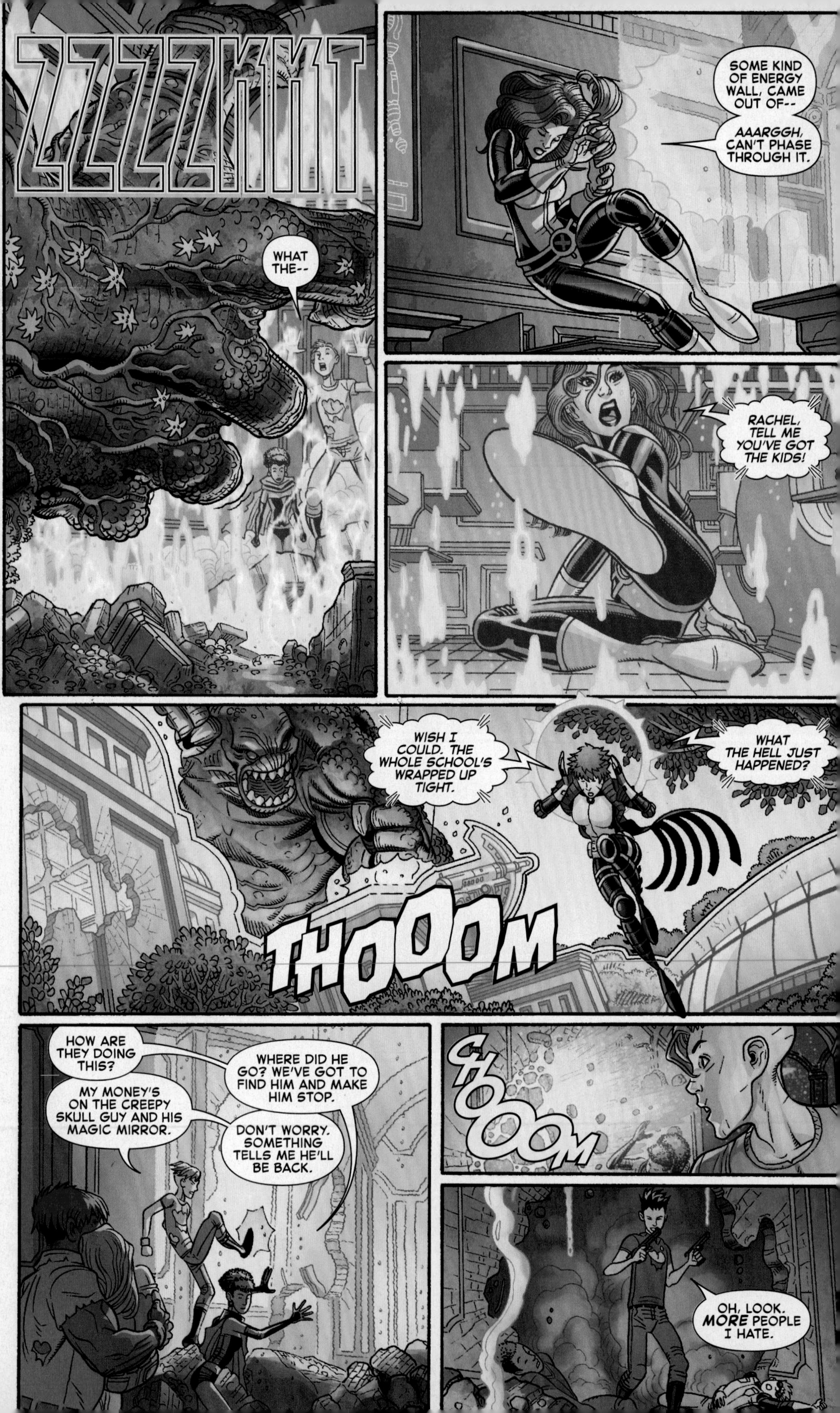
ZZZZZKKT
WHAT THE--
SOME KIND OF ENERGY WALL, CAME OUT OF--
AAARGGH, CAN'T PHASE THROUGH IT.
RACHEL, TELL ME YOU'VE GOT THE KIDS!
WISH I COULD. THE WHOLE SCHOOL'S WRAPPED UP TIGHT.
WHAT THE HELL JUST HAPPENED?
THOOOM
HOW ARE THEY DOING THIS?
MY MONEY'S ON THE CREEPY SKULL GUY AND HIS MAGIC MIRROR.
WHERE DID HE GO? WE'VE GOT TO FIND HIM AND MAKE HIM STOP.
DON'T WORRY. SOMETHING TELLS ME HE'LL BE BACK.
CHOOOM
OH, LOOK. MORE PEOPLE I HATE.

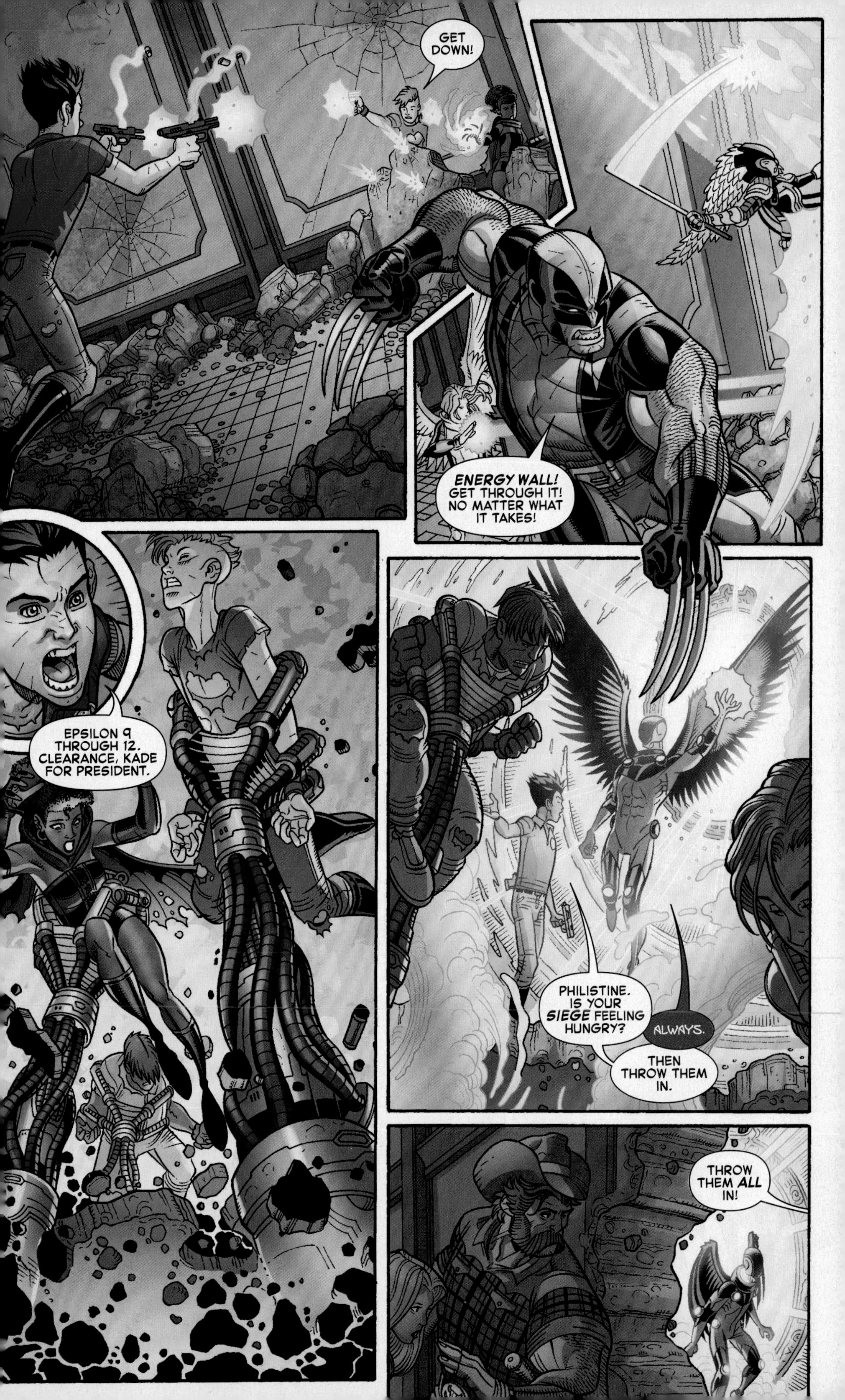
GET DOWN!
ENERGY WALL! GET THROUGH IT! NO MATTER WHAT IT TAKES!
EPSILON 9 THROUGH 12. CLEARANCE, KADE FOR PRESIDENT.
PHILISTINE. IS YOUR SIEGE FEELING HUNGRY?
ALWAYS.
THEN THROW THEM IN.
THROW THEM ALL IN!

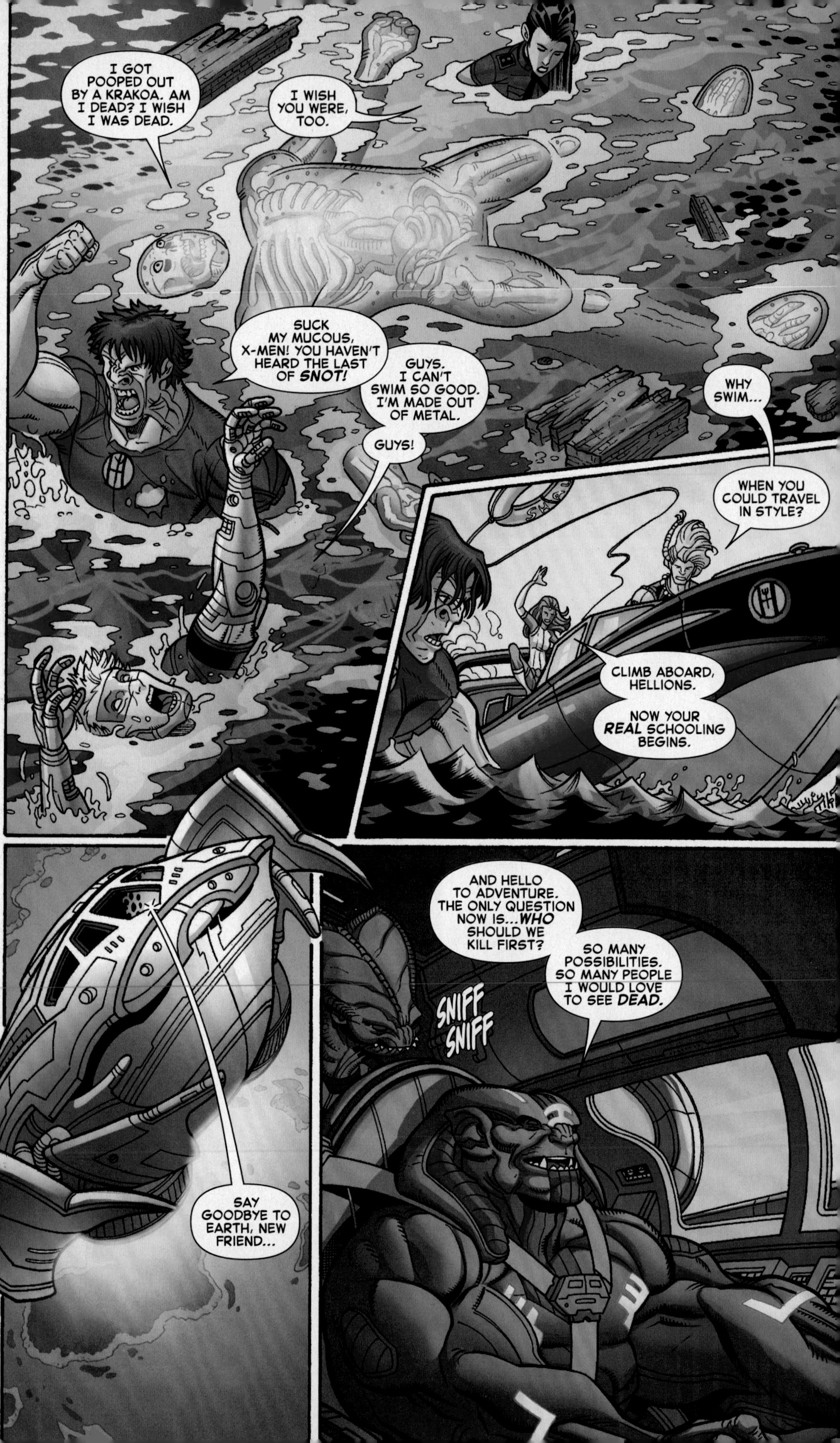
I GOT POOPED OUT BY A KRAKOA. AM I DEAD? I WISH I WAS DEAD.
I WISH YOU WERE, TOO.
SUCK MY MUCOUS, X-MEN! YOU HAVEN'T HEARD THE LAST OF **SNOT!**
GUYS. I CAN'T SWIM SO GOOD. I'M MADE OUT OF METAL.
GUYS!
WHY SWIM...
WHEN YOU COULD TRAVEL IN STYLE?
CLIMB ABOARD, HELLIONS.
NOW YOUR **REAL** SCHOOLING BEGINS.
SAY GOODBYE TO EARTH, NEW FRIEND...
AND HELLO TO ADVENTURE. THE ONLY QUESTION NOW IS...**WHO** SHOULD WE KILL FIRST?
SO MANY POSSIBILITIES. SO MANY PEOPLE I WOULD LOVE TO SEE **DEAD.**
SNIFF SNIFF

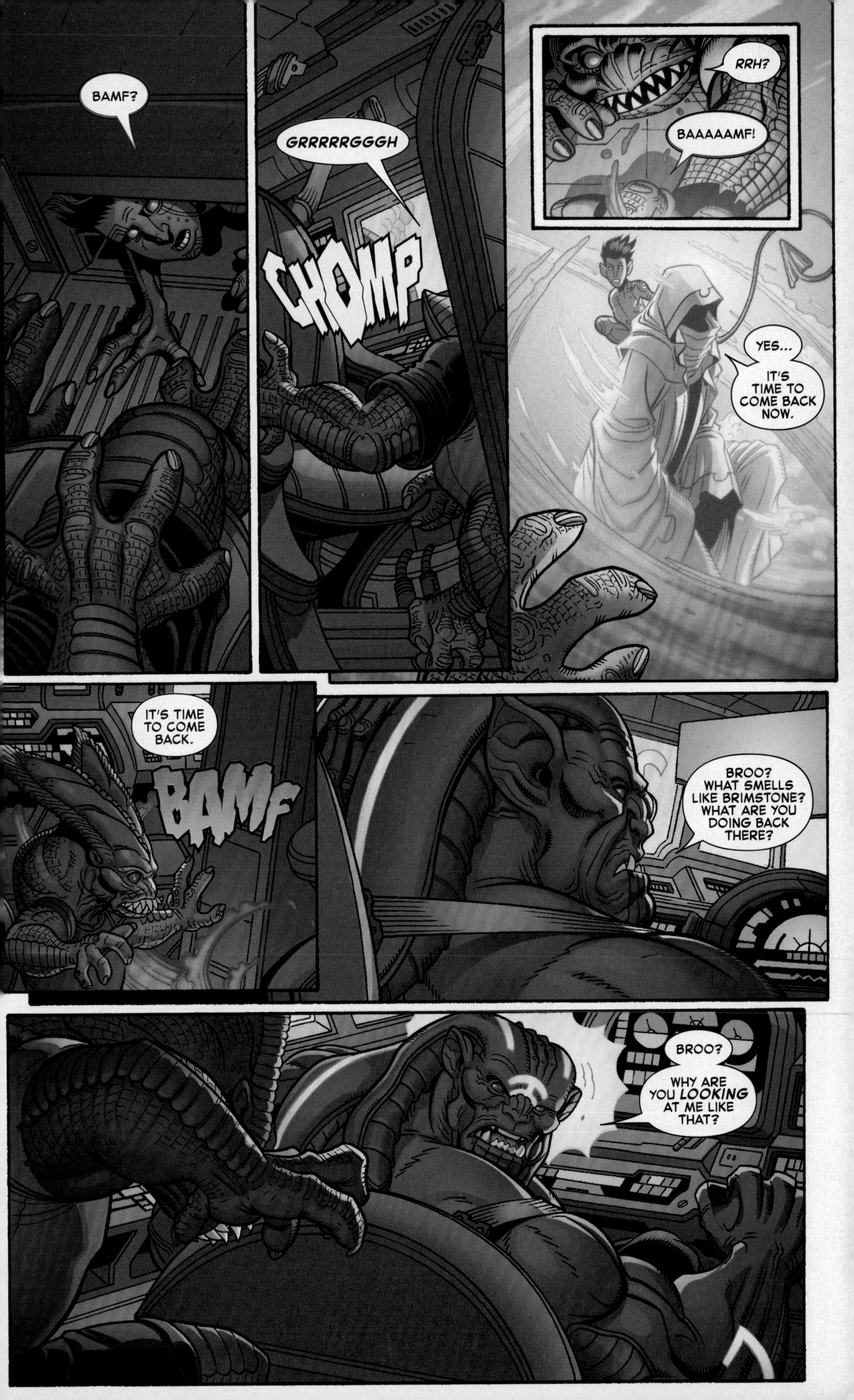
BAMF?
GRRRRRGGGH
CHOMP
RRH?
BAAAAAMF!
YES...
IT'S TIME TO COME BACK NOW.
IT'S TIME TO COME BACK.
BAMF
BROO? WHAT SMELLS LIKE BRIMSTONE? WHAT ARE YOU DOING BACK THERE?
BROO?
WHY ARE YOU *LOOKING* AT ME LIKE THAT?

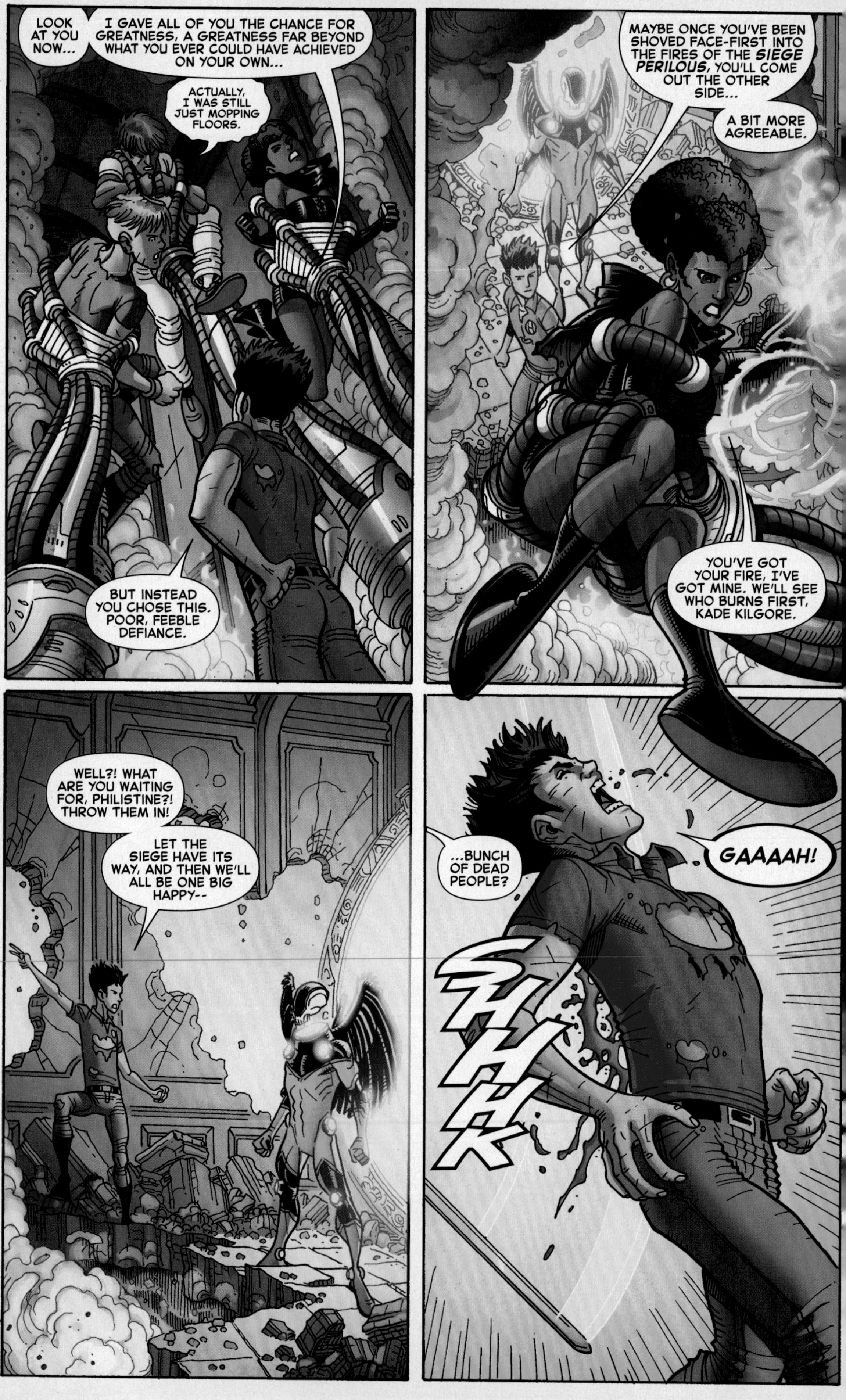
LOOK AT YOU NOW...
I GAVE ALL OF YOU THE CHANCE FOR GREATNESS, A GREATNESS FAR BEYOND WHAT YOU EVER COULD HAVE ACHIEVED ON YOUR OWN...
ACTUALLY, I WAS STILL JUST MOPPING FLOORS.
BUT INSTEAD YOU CHOSE THIS. POOR, FEEBLE DEFIANCE.
MAYBE ONCE YOU'VE BEEN SHOVED FACE-FIRST INTO THE FIRES OF THE SIEGE PERILOUS, YOU'LL COME OUT THE OTHER SIDE...
A BIT MORE AGREEABLE.
YOU'VE GOT YOUR FIRE, I'VE GOT MINE. WE'LL SEE WHO BURNS FIRST, KADE KILGORE.
WELL?! WHAT ARE YOU WAITING FOR, PHILISTINE?! THROW THEM IN!
LET THE SIEGE HAVE ITS WAY, AND THEN WE'LL ALL BE ONE BIG HAPPY--
...BUNCH OF DEAD PEOPLE?
GAAAAH!
SHHHK

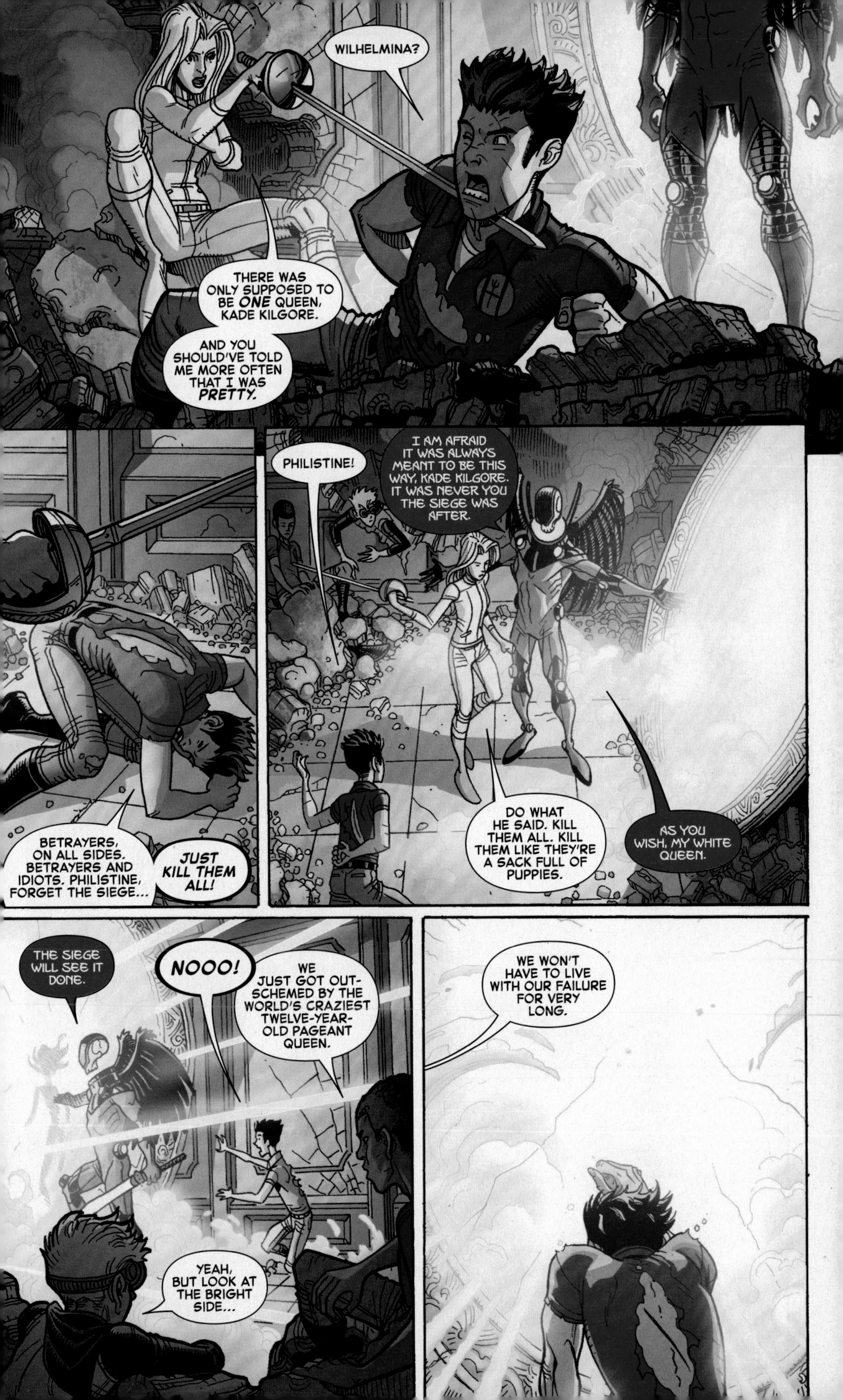
WILHELMINA?
THERE WAS ONLY SUPPOSED TO BE ONE QUEEN, KADE KILGORE.
AND YOU SHOULD'VE TOLD ME MORE OFTEN THAT I WAS PRETTY.
BETRAYERS, ON ALL SIDES. BETRAYERS AND IDIOTS. PHILISTINE, FORGET THE SIEGE...
JUST KILL THEM ALL!
PHILISTINE!
I AM AFRAID IT WAS ALWAYS MEANT TO BE THIS WAY, KADE KILGORE. IT WAS NEVER YOU THE SIEGE WAS AFTER.
DO WHAT HE SAID. KILL THEM ALL. KILL THEM LIKE THEY'RE A SACK FULL OF PUPPIES.
AS YOU WISH, MY WHITE QUEEN.
THE SIEGE WILL SEE IT DONE.
NOOO!
WE JUST GOT OUT-SCHEMED BY THE WORLD'S CRAZIEST TWELVE-YEAR-OLD PAGEANT QUEEN.
YEAH, BUT LOOK AT THE BRIGHT SIDE...
WE WON'T HAVE TO LIVE WITH OUR FAILURE FOR VERY LONG.

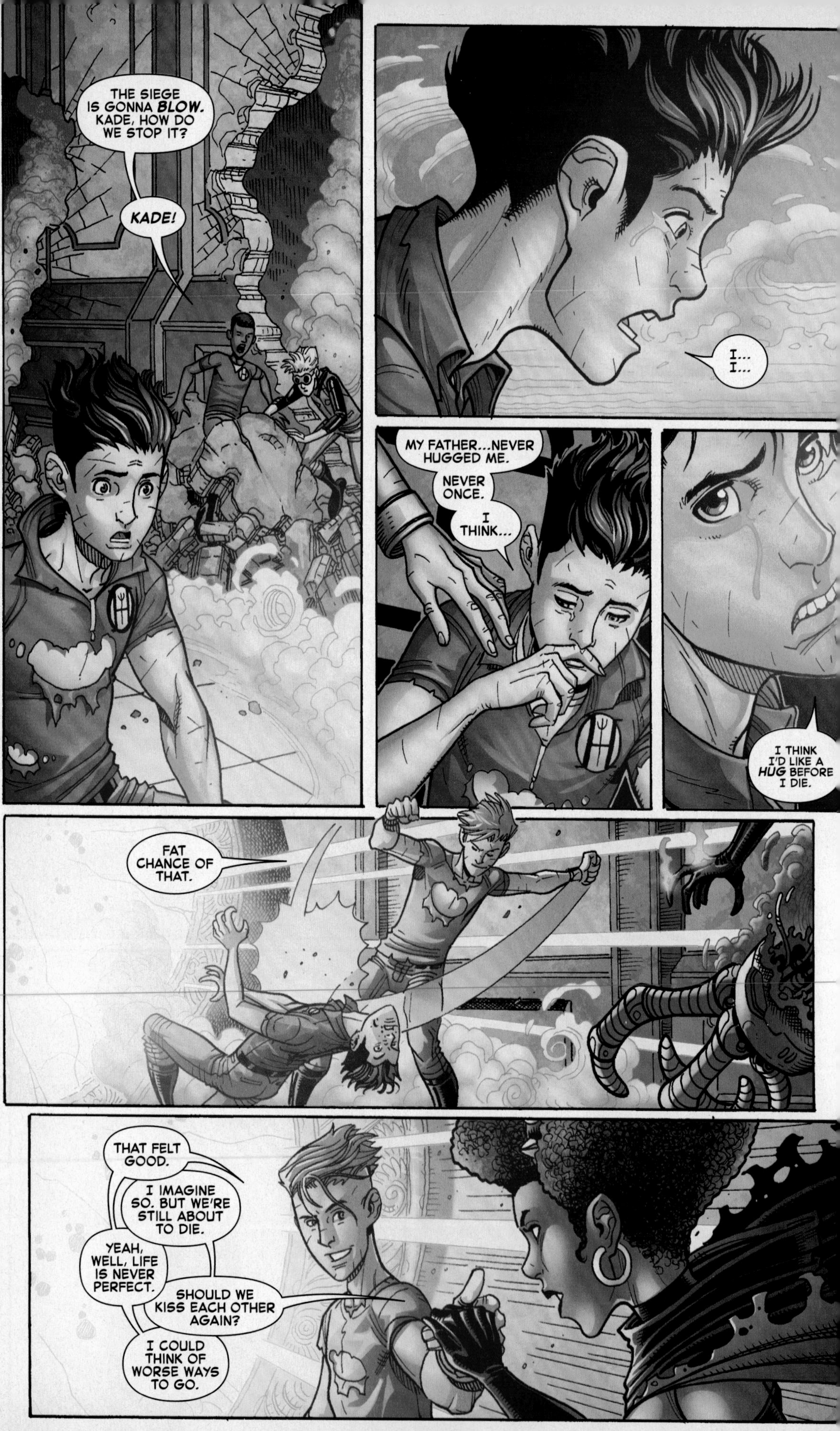
THE SIEGE IS GONNA BLOW. KADE, HOW DO WE STOP IT?
KADE!
I... I...
MY FATHER...NEVER HUGGED ME.
NEVER ONCE.
I THINK...
I THINK I'D LIKE A HUG BEFORE I DIE.
FAT CHANCE OF THAT.
THAT FELT GOOD.
I IMAGINE SO. BUT WE'RE STILL ABOUT TO DIE.
YEAH, WELL, LIFE IS NEVER PERFECT.
SHOULD WE KISS EACH OTHER AGAIN?
I COULD THINK OF WORSE WAYS TO GO.

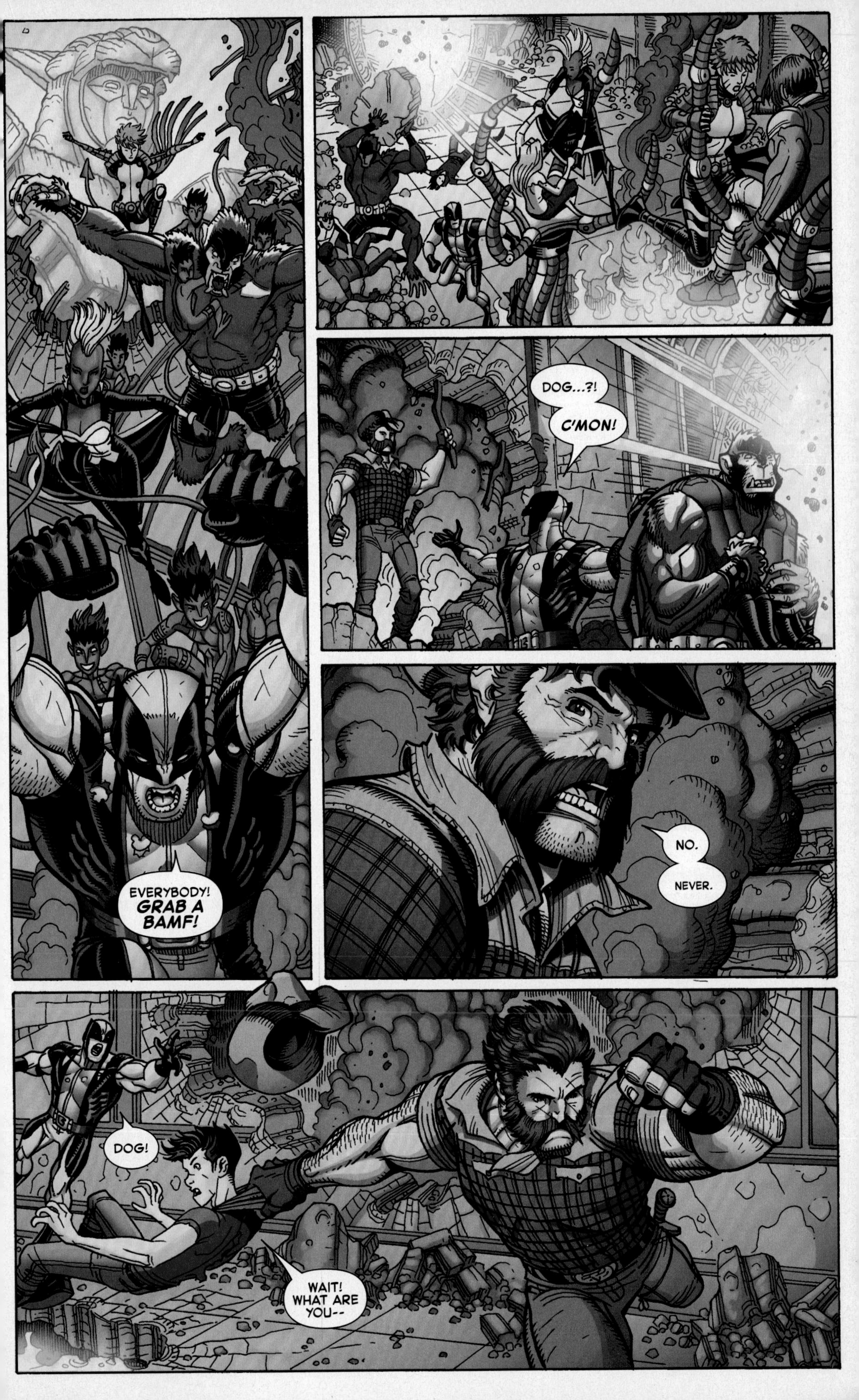
EVERYBODY! GRAB A BAMF!
DOG...?!
C'MON!
NO.
NEVER.
DOG!
WAIT! WHAT ARE YOU--

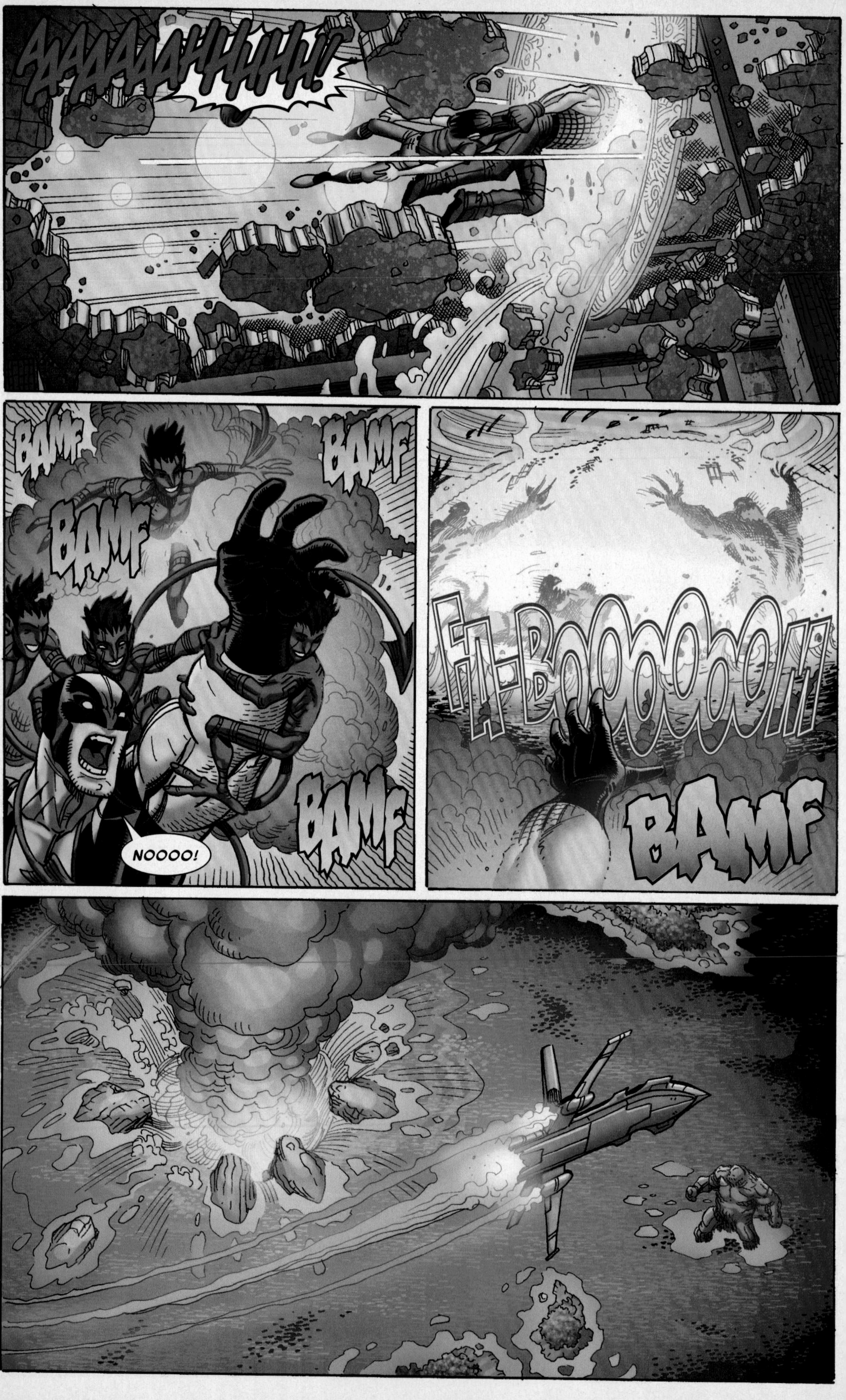
AAAAAAHHHHH!
BAMF
BAMF
BAMF
BAMF
NOOOO!
KA-BOOOOOOM
BAMF

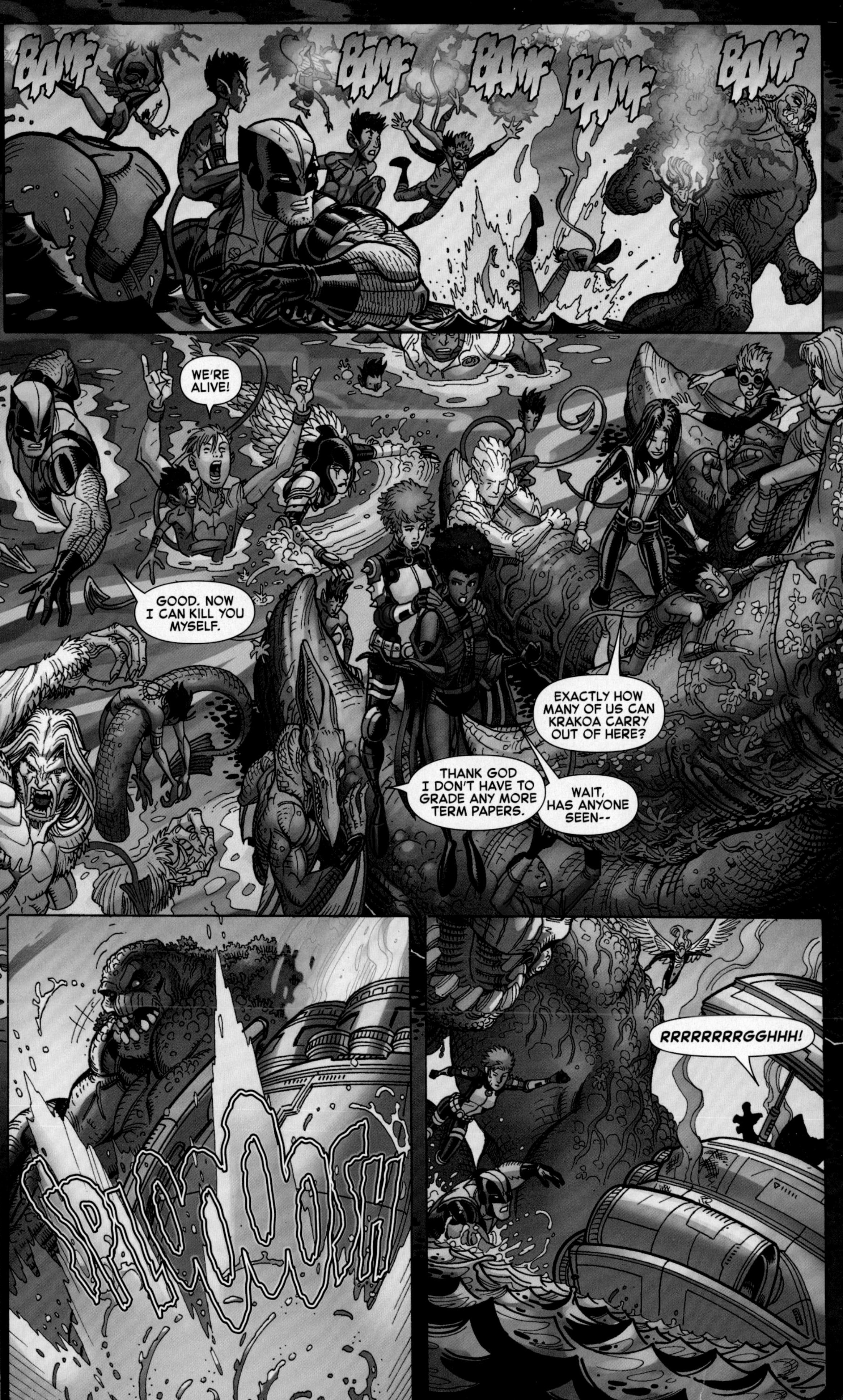
BAMF
BAMF
BAMF
BAMF
BAMF
WE'RE ALIVE!
GOOD. NOW I CAN KILL YOU MYSELF.
EXACTLY HOW MANY OF US CAN KRAKOA CARRY OUT OF HERE?
THANK GOD I DON'T HAVE TO GRADE ANY MORE TERM PAPERS.
WAIT, HAS ANYONE SEEN--
RRRRRRRRGGHHH!

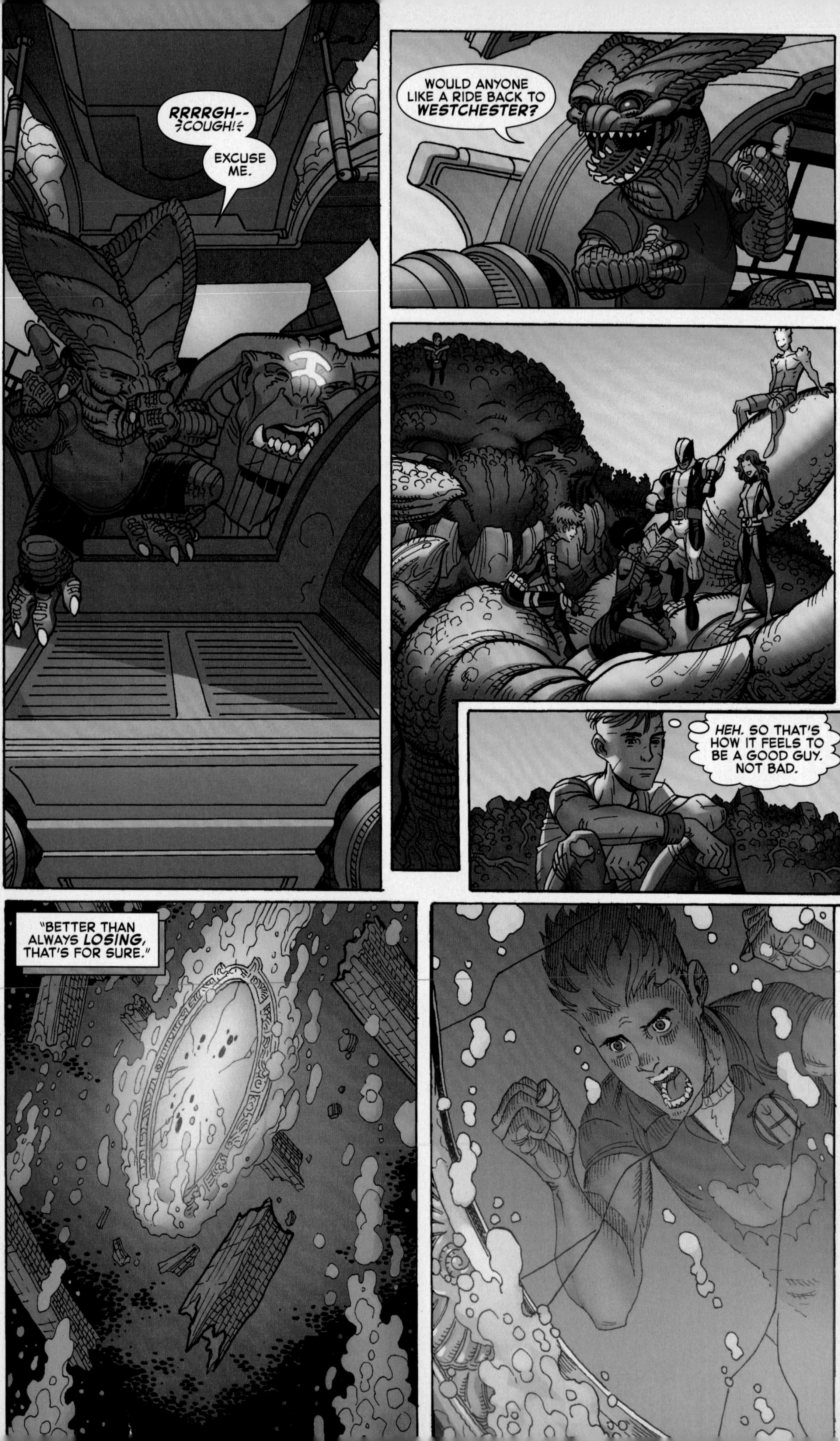
RRRRGH--
COUGH!
EXCUSE ME.
WOULD ANYONE LIKE A RIDE BACK TO WESTCHESTER?
HEH. SO THAT'S HOW IT FEELS TO BE A GOOD GUY. NOT BAD.
"BETTER THAN ALWAYS LOSING, THAT'S FOR SURE."

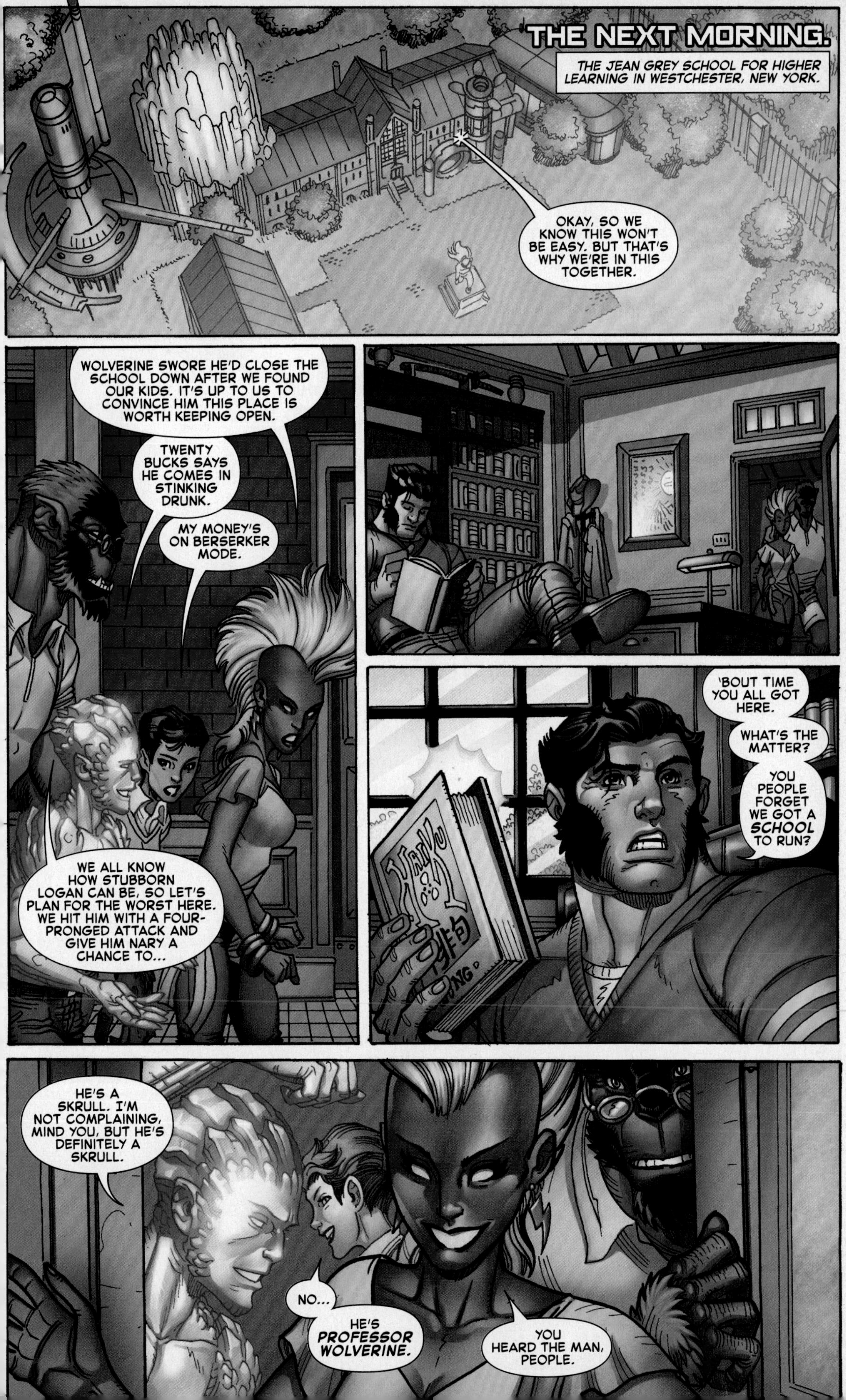
THE NEXT MORNING.
THE JEAN GREY SCHOOL FOR HIGHER LEARNING IN WESTCHESTER, NEW YORK.
OKAY, SO WE KNOW THIS WON'T BE EASY. BUT THAT'S WHY WE'RE IN THIS TOGETHER.
WOLVERINE SWORE HE'D CLOSE THE SCHOOL DOWN AFTER WE FOUND OUR KIDS. IT'S UP TO US TO CONVINCE HIM THIS PLACE IS WORTH KEEPING OPEN.
TWENTY BUCKS SAYS HE COMES IN STINKING DRUNK.
MY MONEY'S ON BERSERKER MODE.
WE ALL KNOW HOW STUBBORN LOGAN CAN BE, SO LET'S PLAN FOR THE WORST HERE. WE HIT HIM WITH A FOUR-PRONGED ATTACK AND GIVE HIM NARY A CHANCE TO...
'BOUT TIME YOU ALL GOT HERE.
WHAT'S THE MATTER?
YOU PEOPLE FORGET WE GOT A *SCHOOL* TO RUN?
HE'S A SKRULL. I'M NOT COMPLAINING, MIND YOU, BUT HE'S DEFINITELY A SKRULL.
NO...
HE'S ***PROFESSOR WOLVERINE.***
YOU HEARD THE MAN, PEOPLE.

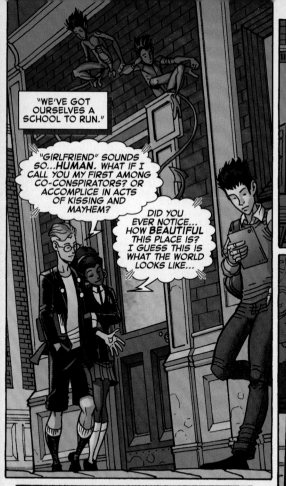

"WE'VE GOT OURSELVES A SCHOOL TO RUN."

"GIRLFRIEND" SOUNDS SO...HUMAN. WHAT IF I CALL YOU MY FIRST AMONG CO-CONSPIRATORS? OR ACCOMPLICE IN ACTS OF KISSING AND MAYHEM?

DID YOU EVER NOTICE... HOW BEAUTIFUL THIS PLACE IS? I GUESS THIS IS WHAT THE WORLD LOOKS LIKE...

"ONCE YOU TAKE AWAY ALL THE MONSTERS."

NOW THIS... THIS IS JUST CRUEL.

PLEASE, SEND US TO ANY JAIL YOU LIKE. ANYTHING BUT THIS.

ART CLASS 101, SAY HELLO TO OUR TWO NEWEST STUDENTS.

I REMEMBER FIGHTING FOR A VERY LONG TIME TO BE MYSELF AGAIN, BUT NEVER MAKING MUCH GROUND.

AND SUDDENLY, SOMEONE ELSE WAS THERE, GIVING ME THE PUSH I NEEDED, TELLING ME IT WAS TIME TO WAKE UP.

DID THIS... VISION OF YOURS HAPPEN TO COINCIDE WITH SOME SORT OF EXTRANEOUS EVENT?

YES. YES, IT DID, AS A MATTER OF FACT. STRANGELY ENOUGH, IT HAPPENED...

IT HAPPENED WHEN I BIT A BAMF.

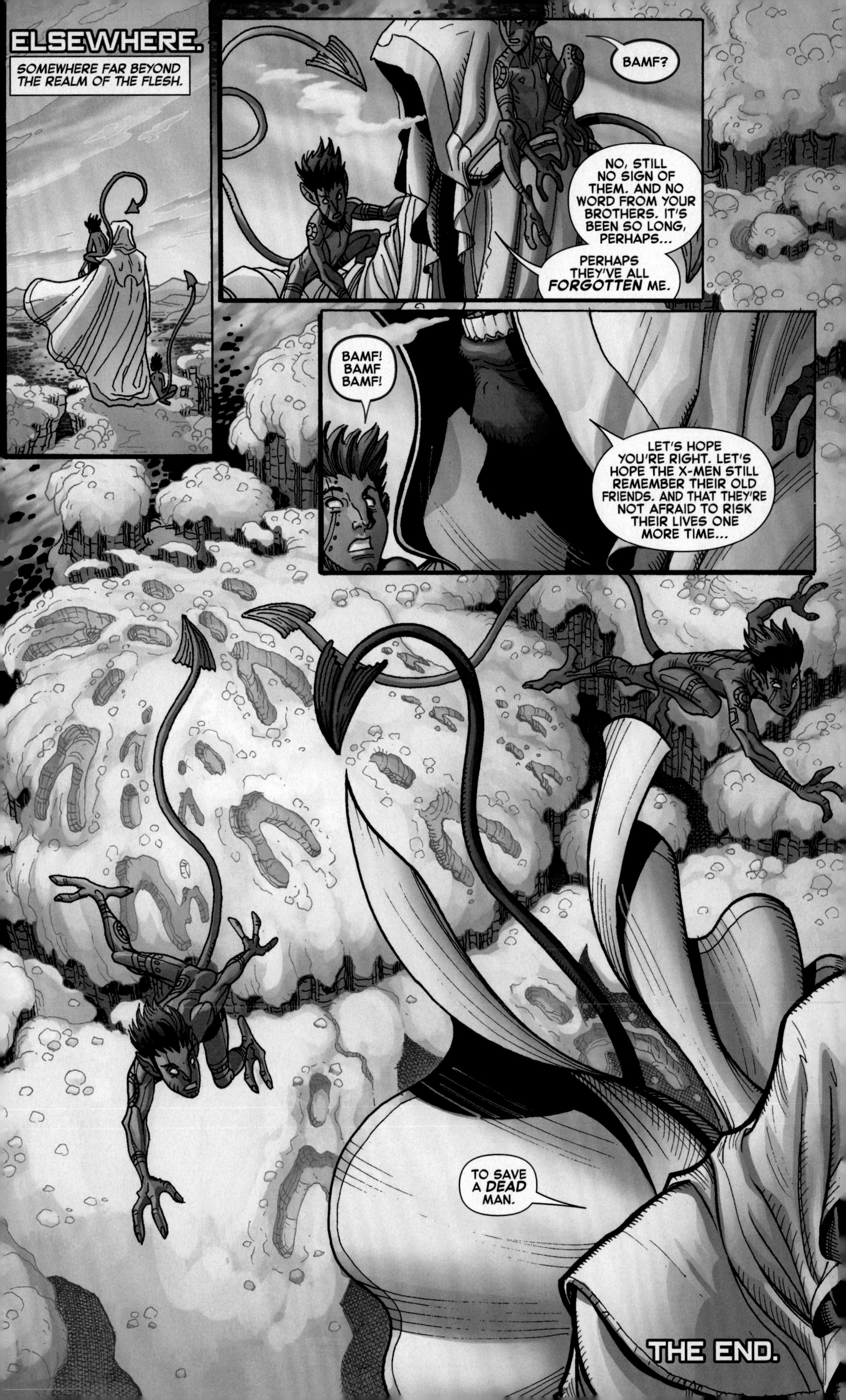

ELSEWHERE.
SOMEWHERE FAR BEYOND THE REALM OF THE FLESH.
BAMF?
NO, STILL NO SIGN OF THEM. AND NO WORD FROM YOUR BROTHERS. IT'S BEEN SO LONG, PERHAPS...
PERHAPS THEY'VE ALL FORGOTTEN ME.
BAMF! BAMF BAMF!
LET'S HOPE YOU'RE RIGHT. LET'S HOPE THE X-MEN STILL REMEMBER THEIR OLD FRIENDS. AND THAT THEY'RE NOT AFRAID TO RISK THEIR LIVES ONE MORE TIME...
TO SAVE A DEAD MAN.
THE END.

CHARACTER DESIGNS BY NICK BRADSHAW

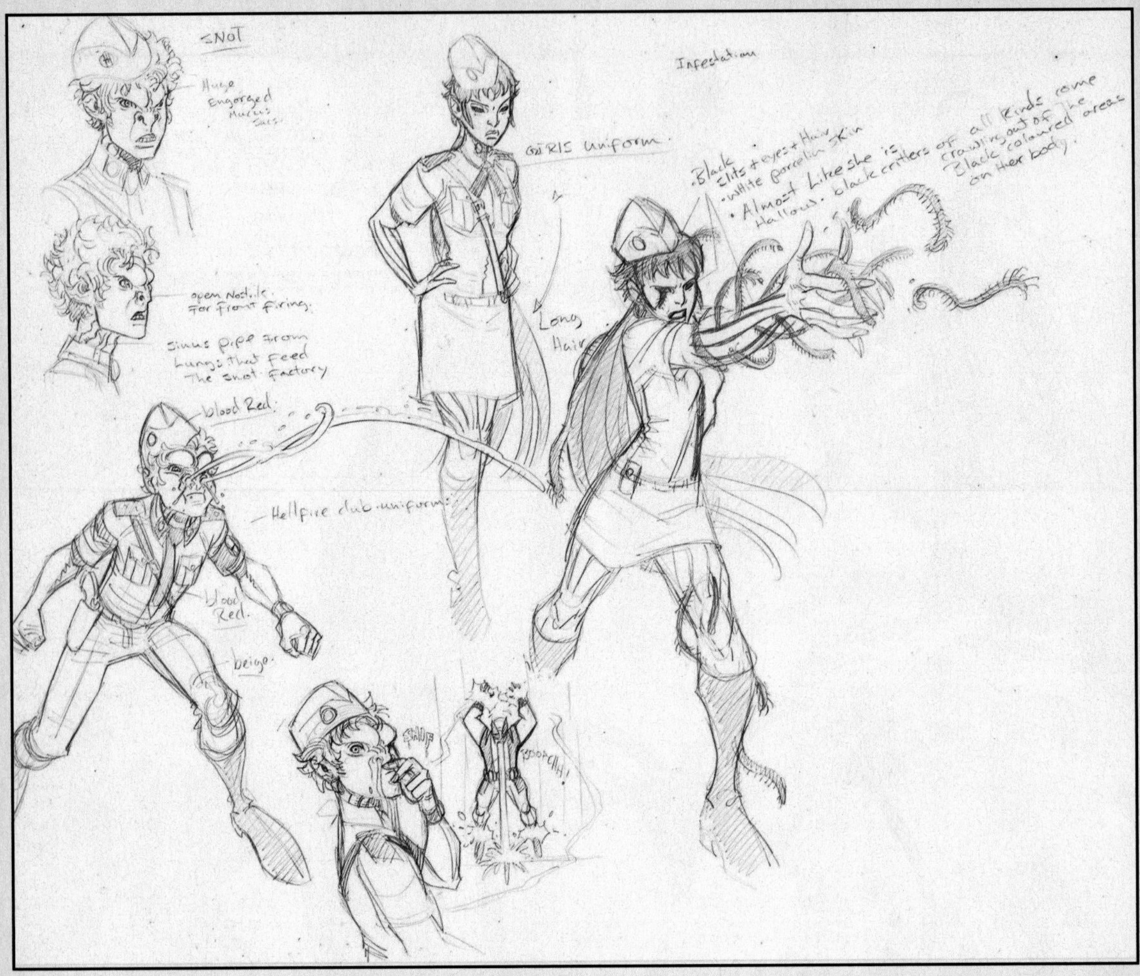
SNOT
Huge Engorged Mucus Sacs
open Nostrile For front firing.
Sinus pipe from Lungs that feed The snot factory
blood Red.
Hellfire club uniform.
blood Red.
beige.
GIRLS uniform.
Long Hair
Infestation
•Black Slits + eyes + Hair
•White porcelin Skin
• Almost Like she is Hallow. black critters of all Kinds come crawling out of the Black coloured areas on her body.

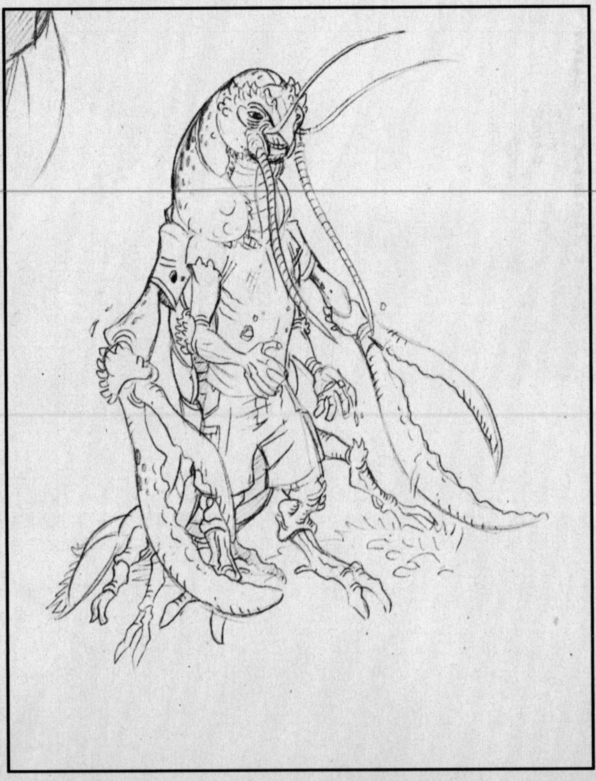